Whatever Happened to

Religious Education?

for David,

Penny Thompson

with much love,

Penny Thompson

The Lutterworth Press
Cambridge

The Lutterworth Press
P.O. Box 60
Cambridge
CB1 2NT

website: www.lutterworth.com
e-mail: publishing@lutterworth.com

British Library Cataloguing in Publication Data:
A catalogue record is available from the British Library

ISBN 0 7188 3039 3

Contents

Preface

2003 finds RE in England and Wales in a state of uncertainty. The Education Secretary has taken personal charge of the subject and declared himself keen for change. QCA, the Government body charged with curriculum development, has recommended a national framework for the subject. Representatives of the Churches have gone further and called for RE, like other subjects, to be determined nationally. Change to the 14-19 curriculum is upon us: marketed as a new way of 'doing education'. What place, if any, will be found for *religious* education? It is not that Charles Clarke (so far as one can tell) is against the subject, rather that it seems very difficult to define exactly what RE is. The Government values success but what, advisers may be asked, constitutes success in RE?

This book is about the nature and purpose of religious education. My argument is that a religion needs to be taught for what it is, for its own sake and for the inspiration that it (uniquely) offers. It must not be taught as an example of something else, a relic of interest only to antiquarians or a form of benign social manipulation. Christianity can be taught in a way that does not compromise intellectual freedom and without excluding contrasting perspectives on life. It needs to be taught in a way that exudes confidence, hope and imaginative possibilities. Only so will the faith be able to enchant the young. But a situation has arisen where teachers possessed of Christian faith feel unsure of their role and hesitant about a display of affection for the faith. My book tells the story of how this has happened and how the profession was led, erroneously in my view, to disavow notions of *teaching* the faith in the 60s and 70s. I show the weaknesses of current theory and set out the case for the committed and theologically sophisticated teaching of Christianity. A chapter on the law shows that this vision is entirely consonant with legal requirements.

My own story? I started as a teacher of RE in the mid 70s. I had a theology degree, an excitement for the faith and a desire to open up its treasures in the classroom. My colleagues in school shared this vision but I became aware that it was a vision under threat. I read articles, began to engage with the theoretical literature and then, five years on, pregnancy put a stop to such matters. Ten years later I returned to teaching and taught RE in comprehensive schools in Sefton between 1988 and 1998. I studied part-time for an M. Ed and began to write and publish articles. Increasingly unhappy with what it seemed I was expected to do and say in the classroom, and with my husband's support, I gave up my job to work on a book. Why was it that teachers like myself were expected to adopt the position of an agnostic? What was the point of having a teacher if her insights must be neutered in the classroom?

Could I, I wondered, make the case for the teaching of Christian faith from a committed point of view? It seemed an uphill task as I had come across no-one within the profession who was prepared to argue this. However I found support at the highest levels of academia. Professor Roger Trigg of Warwick, whose work I had read and admired, encouraged me to have a go. Professor Basil Mitchell, now retired from Oxford, showed great interest in my project. He walked me round the gardens of Blenheim Palace as we discussed RE and what had happened to it since he had first been involved as a member of a Commission set up by the Church of England in 1967 to make recommendations on the future of RE. He has acted as a mentor for the book, for which I extend my greatest thanks. Without his support and interest I would never have started. Martyn Relf is another supporter whose time and prayers I have valued more than I can say. I am grateful to the Bishop of St. Albans for kindly reading my book and contributing such a lively foreword. Edward Hulmes has shared his wisdom with me over many years. John Hull too has never failed to offer help, even though I am critical of his role in the development of religious education. William Kay, what can I say? He has always been there to encourage and inform me. I am grateful to the ex-bishop of London, Graham Leonard, who gave me three interviews as I struggled to grasp the idea that the law was indeed on my side. George Oliver and Richard Wilkins advised me over at least 15 years. Fred Naylor taught me a lot and I am grateful for his stalwart campaigning. David Harte helped me with the law, and made me feel that I had missed my vocation. To Ken Howkins and Mike Fearn I owe a particular debt. Both read through the manuscript at different stages and saved me from numerous errors. Marius Felderhof has read my work and inspired me. Jeff Astley is a giant and I am grateful for the gift of his magisterial work on Christian education. Trevor Cooling has suffered as much as anyone as I have tried to come to grips with my thinking on RE and I am grateful for his willingness to engage with my ideas. To John Sullivan at Hope, my special thanks. Thanks to our friends, Helen and Phil Hunter, to pupils and colleagues at Chesterfield, Range and Belvedere schools. I am grateful to Adrian Brink at Lutterworth Press. Others have contributed to this book and I thank them all.

My final thanks are for Andrew, my husband. He has always believed in me and not only supported me financially but offered advice (not always gratefully received). He has helped in countless ways and this book is dedicated to him.

Foreword
by the Bishop of St Albans

A book about religious education which is feisty, provocative and argued with passion is rare. This is such a book.

It takes on the giants of the religious education world and with audacity and verve challenges their influence and their power. That can be no bad thing, not because it is right to try to cut everyone down to size but because from time-to-time the accepted assumptions of any branch of education need to be rigorously re-examined.

There are some who might argue that the author tilts unfairly at some individuals and their causes, but then a quiet, balanced and moderate approach is unlikely, in a noisy world, to attract anyone's attention. This is a campaigning manifesto, a work of real courage which, no doubt, will be subject to some trenchant criticism. Nevertheless, the underlying issues which Penny Thompson seeks to address: the nature of truth, the nature of our society, the purposes of education, the significance of faith, the possibility of revelation, are those to which all of us need to give serious attention.

The gauntlet has been thrown down; it will be to the advantage of religious education, to children and to schools, if the challenge is accepted. A new and vigorous debate about religious education is long overdue – and this book by its sheer vivacity will make an original and important contribution to it.

Who will accept the challenge?

Chapter 1
Losing faith in RE

RE between 1961 and March 1963

In 1961 the Institute of Christian Education (ICE) published the first volume of *Learning for Living,*[1] with a new editor, the Quaker Harold Loukes. It was launched with a Christian manifesto:

> We shall try to set out the Christian judgement in terms that carry meaning to those growing up in modern society. We shall consider the Bible as a book about the human condition . . . we shall discuss ways whereby boys and girls can be awakened to this eternal and immediate dimension; and we hope that teachers will write from their own triumphs and disappointments about the kind of question that touches off the spark, and the kind of answer that keeps the flame alight . . . we who offer these pages are Christians. We believe that the Christian experience offers a true point of vantage for the view of the human condition.[2]

Loukes had published *Teenage Religion* in the same year, an account of the state of RE in secondary schools. Loukes reported some problems but was optimistic about the results and confident about the purpose of RE: 'the aim of scripture teaching is still, as it always was, to make a gift for a lifetime, so that men and women facing the problems of living and ageing should have beside them, open to their understanding, the infinite dimensions in which they stand'.[3] He wrote of many teachers welcoming the opportunity to bring children 'into contact with Christian values and providing a standard by which the current values of society can be judged'.[4] It was vital that 'the school leaver should have gained a measure of insight . . . a religious formula must become experimental, and must be seen to work, before he leaves'.[5] A passage that covers the sweep of biblical history ended like this: 'the love of God broke out through his death, swept out through his risen life into the lives of men, and spread through the world, triumphant again and again, wherever men were faithful'. The role of the journal was to engage in a 'conversation about one of the frontiers of Christian witness' in the attempt to interest, awaken and excite the young about 'what looks to them, in their tough-minded moods, impossibly complicated, unprovable and out of date'.[6]

The view of the Board of Education of the Church of England

A group headed by Graham Leonard set out a carefully argued position in relation to RE and worship in county schools in 1961. RE should be based on the Christian understanding of human nature in a way that allowed the young to raise questions and with due regard for the legal requirement for un-denominational instruction. The Bible should be taught as the record of the acts of God. Provision should be made for the development of particular attitudes in the young such as love and reverence for people and things. The teacher should show how 'as persons they are related to God and to the pattern of behaviour set forth in the Bible and in the life of the Church'.[7] Pupils should be helped to understand that work was the offering of talents in the service of God and the community. The Board was aware that the school community was not the same as the church community and that not all pupils were committed Christians. This fact, however, did not remove the need for some definite teaching. The document, reflecting worries about the permissiveness for which the 1960s were to become notorious, said: 'In an age when the "I leave it to you" attitude on the part of adults so often leaves the young bewildered, the need for specific, convinced, straight teaching, instruction and advice has only to be stated to be conceded.'[8] One of the serious weaknesses of the country was said to be 'the failure or unwillingness to be committed with its implications that no serious outlooks on life matter and that all truth is relative'.[9] The Board did not want such a weakness in the teaching of RE.

Views expressed in *Learning for Living*.

Within the pages of *Learning for Living* all seemed secure. The purpose of RE in schools was seen as close to, but not identical to, that of teachers in Sunday schools. Material designed for use in Sunday schools was sometimes recommended for day school teachers, although it is clear that publishers recognised a difference between the two situations. Conferences for teachers included worship and the worship leader was always advertised along with the main speakers. ICE organised many such conferences. It described itself as a 'professional association whose function is to help teachers and through them to present God's word to young people in schools'.[10] An Easter vacation course in 1962, organised by the ICE, was remarked upon for its fellowship, the quality of the worship and the sense of the need of the Holy Spirit in the classroom: 'we must increase our concern with the power which alone can make such education really effective'.[11]

The May 1962 editorial of the journal expressed concern about the difficulty of getting a hearing for Christian teaching but there was no doubt in Loukes' mind that this was what RE was about. In the same edition Colin Morris, a fellow of Pembroke College, Oxford, wrote an account of the

Christian doctrine of grace. A head of a grammar school understood RE as a challenge to the young to measure up to Christian ideals: 'The New Testament, in the hands of the right teacher . . . forces us to see and face the . . . basic questions about life. . . . It must be used . . . to help them see clearly their own moral natures, necessity of making moral choices and obligation to accept responsibility.'[12] This head wanted more opportunities for youngsters to give service and so to discover 'Christian joy'. A head of RE in a girls' school wrote that 'the primary lesson of Amos to our young people is that this is God's world'.[13]

What of the pupils? A report of teenage views in November 1961 said: 'the adolescent is asking to be introduced to the kind of thought which will help him to maturity and to insight into his own condition and that of the world at large. Many ask for a more adult treatment of religion and express satisfaction when this is received.'[14] The same survey spoke of a readiness to take religion seriously. Young people wanted to know 'what are the basic Christian doctrines and whether Christianity is the most communicative expression of the truth, over against other religions and various philosophical systems'.[15]

Loukes' survey of pupil attitudes in *Teenage Religion*

Loukes found that pupils in general were not against the subject, rather the way it was taught. They positively enjoyed discussion. Gaps in pupils' knowledge, boredom and resistance on the part of some pupils were problems highlighted in a similar survey carried out by teachers in Sheffield. Loukes responded: 'we should not find it disturbing or depressing. For when similar studies are made in other subjects the results are much the same. . . .'[16] He referred to studies of 14-year-olds' knowledge of grammar, which showed similar inadequacies. A year later Loukes related problems in RE to issues of presentation. He suggested that the Bible needed to be printed in smaller books and made to look attractive; perhaps portions could be read aloud like poetry: 'we skip and skim, select and summarise, bend the matter to our own ends. This is why we have forgotten as a generation, how to read poetry and it is why many cannot read the Bible. For the Bible is not to be mastered: it is to master us.'[17]

To preach or to teach?

At this point concern about preaching surfaced, a perennial worry of RE teachers. If one attempted to bring the faith to life in the classroom by encouraging commitment to ideals, by examining faith statements and the like, one could be accused of 'preaching', yet if one restricted teaching to the facts of scripture, one's teaching might be accused of lifelessness and failure to get to the heart of the matter. Teachers also felt unsure about directing pupils to Church teaching or practice for fear of falling foul of the legal restriction upon denominational teaching.[18] The Cornwall Agreed Syllabus talked of the professional concern of the teachers to avoid propaganda, while their inner conviction must drive teachers to do more than impart objective description. As Loukes and others felt, there were some things that had to be brought to life and that only a gifted and committed teacher could do this. And as a later editor, David Ayerst, was to say: 'it is no good asking the way to Paradise of a man who has only been as far as Kensal Rise'.[19]

In 1962 Loukes addressed the issue directly. He was concerned that although the teacher could not preach, there were surely some things that had to be insisted on and taught with passion, in particular the value of persons. He expressed it this way: 'A teacher after all is a person teaching; and though he may not teach in school what he preaches out of school, the person-teaching is the same as the person-preaching. A person cannot teach true science in school and false science out of school . . . the affirmation of humanity among the young, and the denial of humanity among adults. If no man is an island, then no man is two islands.'[20]

Hilliard's solution

However, some teachers felt unsure. F.H. Hilliard, Senior Lecturer in RE at the London Institute of Education, wrote a book in 1963 reassuring teachers that heartfelt, committed, exciting teaching of the Christian faith was what the whole project was about. He argued that RE had always been understood as the educational right of children. He showed how the concern to provide religious and moral education had been widely held and was not a response to the need of the churches. Parents wanted religious education for their children and many held that the Christian faith offered something of unique worth which should form part of the normal education of the nation's children, although the right to withdraw their child should always be given. Education was about passing on what is of worth: 'helping children to begin to enter for themselves into the best of the experiences which civilised men and women have learned to value.'[21] He argued that the school could not do this fully but schools could do something, sometimes a lot. Like Loukes, he argued that some things simply had to be taught vigorously, such as the freedom of the individual and aspects of behaviour. Freedom to choose meaningfully required knowledge of the facts and therefore pupils needed as full a knowledge as possible of Christian faith. This meant that the teacher should use the 'utmost imagination, insight, skill, and enthusiasm in order to present to children the importance and possibilities of religious faith and experience, in the hope that they may be aroused thereby to begin to explore them for themselves'.[22] The experience and knowledge of the teacher was vital: 'it and it alone will give to his teaching the sincerity and vitality which will enable the children to get a sense of the importance of religion'.[23] By the same token, teaching that lacked conviction and intellectual depth meant that children quickly lost interest. Openness to children's questions and willingness to discuss matters was part of the teacher's job.

The views of some other experts

Many leading figures in the RE world who subsequently rejected this vision of RE were at this time writing in its support.

One of these was the philosopher Paul Hirst who argued that there was such a thing as a religious form of knowledge which should be taught in schools on fully educational grounds. The religious form of knowledge, Hirst wrote, provided concepts and areas of experience which were *sui generis*, such as sin, life beyond death, explanations of why there is something rather than nothing etc. But they must be based on experience and work was needed on relating religious concepts to the experience of children. But teachers were up to the task: 'any number of teachers who are quite unaware of the logical issues involved manage to communicate successfully to their pupils the notion that God is not an object. Children usually come to understand matters of this kind in learning the proper use of religious language, within the context of their experience and not by being taught through logical considerations.'[24]

Another who wrote in favour was Ninian Smart. He permitted some comparisons between Christianity and other faiths and argued that the Christian could point to the fact that his faith contains both contemplation and worship of one God whereas other religions like Buddhism have only the former. [25] Edwin Cox measured success by how far pupils came closer to accepting the validity of Christian teaching. [26] Colin Alves said that lessons should challenge the prevailing permissiveness on an intellectual basis whilst the general organisation of school life should 'allow the grace of Christ to fulfil its positive work through our relationships'.[27]

The Turn begins

The Humanist challenge

In 1962 the journal reported challenges to RE from humanist organisations. Such challenges were not new but whereas previously humanist arguments had been firmly rejected, now it was to be a different story.[28] At first, however, there were calls to arms. Francis Venables, an ex-principal of Culham College (an Anglican teacher training college), wrote: 'there must be valid opposition to the contention of the militant humanist that no religion should be taught in schools.'[29] Sir Richard Acland, a passionate advocate of religious education who had written *We Teach Them Wrong,* went on the offensive against 'fundamentalist humanists'. Clearly perturbed, he warned that to engage in dialogue with humanists could be seen as a retreat on the part of Christians. After the AGM of the ICE that year a joint discussion was held in the evening with the Ethical Union (a humanist association) and agreement was reached on various matters. The following accusation by the Ethical Union was printed in *Learning for Living*: 'Christians are proud people, incapable of seeing other points of view and convinced that they have a monopoly of truth.'[30] It received no editorial rebuff.

Loukes gives up

This was in March 1963. Never again did Loukes argue that children should be taught the Christian view of reality as true. A year later he would resign from the post of editor. Why? In 1965 he published *New Ground in Christian Education,* following fresh research into pupil knowledge and attitudes. This book reveals a dramatic change in Loukes' view about RE: 'The argument so far must seem to many of my readers to be drifting in a somewhat depressing direction. If we cannot define our aims with any clarity; if we cannot circumscribe an area of ground to be covered, then how are we to move at all? Without an aim and without a syllabus, how are we to "teach"?'[31] Loukes began to express despair at what was going on in religious education. The aims of the recently republished 1949 Cambridgeshire Agreed Syllabus were said to be 'less appropriate to the serious discussion of educational aims than to the sermon directed at believers who have sung themselves into a coma'.[32] The language of faith was now perceived by Loukes as a barrier to faith, to be brought into the classroom only sparingly. But it could evacuate God altogether. Indeed where Loukes did write the word 'God', it was often placed between inverted commas.

Throughout *New Ground in Christian Education* Loukes showed great sympathy, even kinship with humanists, and it is not difficult to see a sort of conversion going on. In both *Teenage Religion* and *New Ground for Christian Education* Loukes suggested giving an overview of the Bible to pupils: the Exodus, the giving of the Law, the exile and the rebuilding of the life post-exile, the work of Jesus in reviving the true meaning of the Law, his death, resurrection and the life of the early church. In the earlier book God was mentioned four times, in the later book not at all. In the earlier book God was therefore involved in the story; in the later God is absent. Whereas in the first book, the Hebrews 'struggled back from exile, aware that the God of History demanded their complete allegiance',[33] in the later book, 'they returned full of fear, and designed elaborate rules to make sure they never again strayed from the path of utter rectitude'.[34] The story was told as an entirely human story in which the only reference to God is an 'it' created by the Hebrews out of their experiences.[35] The action of the God of love in the life of mankind confidently set out in *Teenage Religion* became, in the later book, the power of love to be found within the world of nature. Loukes was surely speaking of himself when he wrote: 'Modern men, and the children of modern men, can no longer hear in the Bible a direct "word of God" addressed to them in their condition; and the attempt to present it in those terms is doomed to failure. But the story of how primitive men struggled through their difficulties and came to a working understanding of life is, in our day more than ever before, a story of moment and power to move. In such terms, the Bible has still the power to set hearts afire.'[36]

The profession follows suit

From March 1963 onwards, the journal began to sound very uncertain about the basis of RE. By November 1964 it was clear that a major rethink of RE was under way when an article by the director of the British Humanist Association (BHA), Harry Blackham, was printed in *Learning for Living*. Blackham wrote: 'The readiness to think again is an opportunity to put religion in state schools on a sounder educational basis than it has ever had . . . a genuine educational approach that is not a Christian monopoly is becoming the better possibility which could conciliate non-Christians and gain the support of all genuine educators.'[37] This, the first occurrence in the journal of the use of the word 'educational' to imply that teaching which assumed the truth of Christianity went against the educational project was the statement of a humanist. Soon, mainstream opinion-formers in RE would take a similar line. Kathleen Bliss, General Secretary of the Board of Education of the Church of England between 1958 and 1966, wrote to Robert Beloe at Lambeth Palace on 14 July 1964 to express concern about a certain crumbling of support for RE in schools: 'There have been some Anglicans . . . who have weakened a good deal on Religious Instruction and worship in schools.' In September 1964 Bliss determined to write a background paper on attacks on religion in the county school.[38]

In January 1964, Don Hassall, a head of RE, felt it necessary to mount a passionate defence of RE based on Christian faith in the face of those who argued 'that the Christian minority has no right to advocate Christian standards during lessons in state schools'.[39] 1963 was the year that saw the foundations of RE severely shaken. 1963 was the year pinpointed by Callum Brown as the point when a profound change in thinking occurred in Britain. He writes: 'for a thousand years Christianity penetrated deeply into the lives of the people, enduring Reformation, Enlightenment and industrial revolution by adapting to each new social and cultural context that arose. Then, really quite suddenly in 1963, something very profound ruptured the character of the nation and its people sending organised Christianity on a downward spiral to the margins of social significance.'[40]

Problems raised

All of a sudden problems with RE surfaced and the talk was all of the need for change.

The Christian faith was in trouble

Bishop John Robinson's work, *Honest to God* was published in 1963. It appeared to question many of the traditional ideas about God and the Christian faith. The faith, Robinson argued, needed to be brought up to date. Talk of 'God' was no longer appropriate and must be replaced by concepts such as the 'ground of Being' and 'ultimate concern'. Its arguments were swallowed whole in the journal where Loukes wrote: 'how shall we talk now that we admit the old talk will not do?'[41] It might be better, he wrote, to do without the subject altogether and allow other lessons to take over what was needed in RE. Loukes' last volume as editor tackled prayer. He himself wrote that a time of cosy chat before sleep would be 'nearer to the root of prayer than meditation into the void'.[42] Ruth Robinson said that prayer must be given up. She wrote of a 'prayer shaped blank and no language to fill it out'. Anthony Brackenbury argued that RE was ripe for revolutionary change: 'we have to recognise that the world of nature is one, a natural world and not a natural world arbitrarily manipulated by a supernatural deity'.[43] An 'open letter' signed by university and college lecturers complained that Christian faith was being taught as if it 'possessed a universal validity which is now recognized not to be possible'.[44] Signatories included Harold Loukes, Edwin Cox, Richard Acland and Ronald Goldman. None were card-carrying humanists.

Eric Lord, a lecturer (later an HMI), asked teachers to face up to the changing place of the Bible in RE: 'Any claim of the Bible to objective relevance, as a record of events by which man's status and prospects have changed, we have set aside.'[45] J.W.D. Smith, a lecturer at Jordanhill College in Glasgow, said that Christian faith, undergoing radical reconstruction as it was, could no longer bear the weight of being the base of RE. Anthony Rawlinson, a head of RE, wrote an article called 'The Christless Classroom'. Rawlinson wanted to replace teaching about Christ with topics such as the family, money, work, leisure and friendship.

The Bible was not suitable for primary children

At the same time the research of Ronald Goldman was published. Goldman claimed that the Bible was too sophisticated for primary children and should be largely abandoned in primary schools. Parables and most miracles should not be taught at all before adolescence since children would take the miracles literally, unable to understand their 'symbolic' meaning. At this point Goldman wanted children to know and love God, but his books caused widespread alarm amongst teachers, particularly primary teachers whose main aim had been to teach children the Bible. In his editorial of May 1963, the edition that broke the Goldman story, Loukes wrote about 'blab', meaningless words conveyed to children through their RE lessons. A teacher who had learned to omit all reference to God and the Son of God, now had to omit the Bible too, at primary level at any rate. With prayer on the back burner as well, there did not seem to be much of a *religious* nature left to teach. Goldman, with his confessional stance, could have been presented as a proponent of Christian teaching, but Loukes and others interpreted his work as further evidence of the need for radical change in RE.

RE was failing

In 1965 *New Ground in Christian Education* reported the results of more survey work carried out by Loukes. It seems likely that this had taken place at the time when Loukes himself was becoming convinced that traditional methods were untenable and would not work.[46] Certainly *New Ground in Christian Education* includes devastating criticisms of traditional RE: 'we must . . . begin our thinking with the stark fact that the effort directed towards offering our pupils the Bible is misdirected, and is failing in its most elementary intention. Let them know the Bible, it was said. We tried, with a wealth of ingenuity and concern, to let them know it. And, at the end, they barely know the first thing about it.'[47] Loukes complained about 'compelling the children of non-Christians to be present at a Christian ceremony to which they do not attend or a lesson on Jonah to which they do not listen'.[48] Others followed his lead. Lord declared: 'I cherish no idea that if only we declaim the propositions of classical Protestantism in a louder voice the deaf will hear and the sleepers awake. We have moved on and there is no going back.'[49] One writer wrote about the 'statement that one hears from some Heads that children should not be taught about God because the conception is too difficult for them'.[50] David Sharp, a head of RE, wrote that lessons on God never got very far.[51] Sharp argued that pupils should be encouraged to find their own truth, or rather to 'feel for it' as the title of his article ('Feeling for Truth') implied. The 'open letter' argued that recent research confirmed that religious education was ineffective and was leading to the rejection of religion by the young.[52]

Society was secular

Some argued that society was now secular. RE could therefore no longer attempt to transmit Christianity as if it were true. It did not seem to worry its proponents that, taken at face value, this argument might tend towards the removal of any and all forms of religious teaching. Paul Ballard, a lecturer at Borough Road College, wrote: 'It must now be a matter of fact, whatever the hopes in 1944, that we have a secular society and that Christianity is maintained by permission.'[53] He argued against school worship, while recognising that the law was unlikely to change: 'as it is, it stands out like a sore thumb, a religious act in an irreligious setting, a faith act done in a world of disbelief. . . . For the state schools the only possible solution is to realize that the humanist is right and as a corporate function school worship must go.'[54] Smith argued that the transmission of Christian time-honoured beliefs and practices could no longer be appropriate: 'the tides of secular thought and life have swept away the familiar landmarks of moral standards and traditional belief'.[55] Catherine Fletcher, editor of the journal in 1967, wrote: 'we are no longer in a position to promulgate in school any particular religion or dogma.'[56] Glyn Davies, a lecturer in a college of education, was certain that there could be no justification for 'trying to foist it [Christian doctrine] on children whose parents do not accept these standards'.[57]

Religion was not a form of knowledge

Hirst changed his views on RE between 1963 and 1965. He argued that on philosophical grounds it was no longer possible to teach religion. Within maintained schools the curriculum should be concerned with teaching only what was known to be true. Only what was publicly justifiable, on publicly accepted grounds, could be taught as true: 'At the moment no such domain of agreed knowledge exists and there are no agreed principles of justification.'[58] Religion was not therefore a form of knowledge. Opinions or statements about what people believed were all that was possible: '1944 legislation in religious education is unjustifiable and . . . thorough open instruction about religious beliefs is all that we ought to have.'[59] By 1965 Hirst had come to doubt the possibility of defending Christianity on rational grounds: 'Clearly I wrote the paper [1963] from the Christian position I then held in defence of the claims to religious knowledge that I considered true and defensible on objective grounds. By 1965 and my paper in the *BJES*, I had become significantly less certain of religious claims to knowledge being justified in a way logically parallel to but unique and different in kind from, say scientific, mathematical or moral claims to knowledge. Having between the two papers read much more contemporary philosophy of religion I considered the issue of the truth of religious claims far less certain than I had previously thought.'[60] Christianity could no longer be rationally defended.

New Approaches to RE

New approaches were needed as a matter of urgency if RE were to continue. It did not take long for suggestions to come forward. Again, the critical date is 1963.

The 'open' approach to RE

A group of humanists and Christians met for two years before publishing a paper in 1965 called *Religious and Moral Education in County Schools* (RME). It was accepted that Christianity would continue to form a large part of the syllabus but there was no confident assertion that it should be taught positively and definitely. Rather the emphasis throughout was on openness and a variety of opinions being placed before the pupils. The suggestions for the age group 13-16 read:

> Wherever possible the course should draw on teachers with a variety of beliefs and standpoints working in an integrated team, and all alike should feel free to express their own beliefs, as personal beliefs. Where this is not possible, a teacher who deals with moral and religious views that are not his own must be extremely careful in his method of presentation, and scrupulous to avoid subtle indoctrination of his own standpoint.[61]

Secular agnosticism was to be deliberately brought to the attention of pupils by the teacher. The paper took for granted the fact that openness meant that no one view could be given priority in the teaching, but for pragmatic purposes most of the content would be Christian. Where a teacher possessed Christian convictions he or she must not allow such convictions to be given any more weight than views with which he or she disagreed. It was stated that parents and the public would need to change their expectations of RE.

The 'neo-confessional' approach

In 1966 Edwin Cox published *Changing Aims in Religious Education.*[62] Cox remained one of the most influential figures in RE up until his death in the early 1990s. His position was similar to that of RME but he expected a teacher to give weight to his or her own views. A positive attitude on the part of the teacher was necessary for pupils to make progress. This, combined with the fact that his suggestions for the syllabus were largely based on Christian faith, meant that his position would be labelled 'neo-confessional' in Schools Council Working Paper 36 (discussed in chapter 3). Cox said of the teacher: 'If he has deep convictions then they are part of the information he has to give, and he may reasonably tell his class that he believes that, if they think deeply, they will come to similar conclusions.' However: 'what he must not do is to say that 'his views are the only ones tenable by a thinking person.. . .'[63] The aim of RE was 'the giving to children of a religious view of life and then allowing them freely to make up their minds how that view shall express itself both in belief and practice'.[64] The crucial question was what Cox meant by 'a religious view of life'. Sometimes he meant the Christian view. He wrote of pupils aged 11-14: 'The aim at this stage then, is to help pupils to recognise spiritual experience and its expression in the Bible and to accord it respect.'[65] However Cox defined the religious view quite differently elsewhere in the same work. It meant:

· Man is part of creation and must respect it
· he must give consideration to his fellows equal to that he gives himself
· life has some overall purpose which has to be sought, even if it cannot be fully understood

·   apprehension of that purpose will give a moral code
·   beauty and the arts give access to that purpose.

Aware that such aims were rather vague, he said that these were the aims of education in general and that RE needed to have something distinctive to impart. This, he went on to say, was the posing of ultimate questions and the providing of information about the sorts of answers people have given and encouraging pupils to make up their minds. The distinctive aim of imparting 'a religious view of life' was, at this point, left to one side.

So there was ambivalence in Cox's writing. Sometimes he saw RE as the positive presentation of Christianity and at other times as the giving of information about a variety of viewpoints with no particular weight given to the Christian view.

Personal Search

'An Open Letter to LEAs' (mentioned earlier) was a manifesto for change in RE. It was written by those teaching RE in the university and college sector. They argued that openness meant abandoning teaching Christian faith as true. New, contemporary approaches to the Bible and religion were needed and they stressed the need to balance learning biblical knowledge with 'the broader dimension of children's needs'. By these needs were meant the making of critical choices, (a need which earlier 'old-fashioned' approaches did not necessarily neglect). At the same time the aim of RE was stated to be 'personal search rather than the imparting of a body of fact'. The next sentence pleaded for help from LEAs to support teachers in the 'occasional disputes and objections they may meet from those parents and churches who have not fully imbibed current theological ideas'.[66] Personal search could lead to a total lack of direction. One writer suggested that RE was 'a meeting point for boys and girls to listen to each other and learn from each other and be together'.[67] Paul Ballard wrote similarly that the school should be a market-place for ideas, although he maintained that the teacher was a Christian working at the frontier.[68] Robin Shepherd, an area secretary for the Christian Education Movement (CEM),[69] said that teachers too were to embark on a personal search. They must give up any convictions they possessed in favour of the 'wholly non-rational', the 'wholly other' element in experience: 'teachers and pupils [must] put aside all their preconceived notions, and enter into genuine search. The religions of the world and the practice of Christian churches stand open for study, like quarries of living rock, from which the honest person can draw the foundation stones upon which his own experience can build.'[70] A project which aimed for an 'unbiased examination of the concept of transcendence and the various ways in which men of different cultures have expressed understanding of the supernatural'[71] led to Donald Butler, a head of RE, including lessons on such topics as meditation, sacrifice of girls and

taboo.[72] David Sharp wrote about introducing a speaker on black magic and witchcraft. His approach was to adopt 'any relevant topic in an open-ended way'.[73]

Religionless RE

John Elliot, a research worker, warned that the teacher must not assume the truth of any Christian belief, neither sin nor the existence of God, nor anything of its moral teaching. The teacher must avoid any positive expression of belief since, Elliot considered, the positive expression of a teacher's belief would militate against free decision and would affect the 'marking out of the content of the lesson.'[74] Kenneth Birch suggested, in relation to John Elliot's scheme, that the teacher was best when invisible: 'We must at all times assume so great an attitude of neutrality as to be practically invisible'.[75] Jean Holm went further and argued that all forms of exclusively religious language must be excluded from the primary RE syllabus. No exposure to specifically Christian teaching could be given because the primary child, unable to exercise critical distance, would assume it to be true. And to do this was illegitimate: 'to assume the truth of the answers given by the Christian faith is legitimate within the Church and the Christian family, but it is not legitimate within the maintained school'.[76] So what could be taught according to Jean Holm? Christmas could be 'taught', but there must be no mention of the Incarnation. Easter could be 'celebrated', but there must be no mention of the Resurrection. The themes to be related to Easter were joy, praise, forgiveness and new life. Instead of teaching on salvation the classroom was to be made the place of creative relationships. The teacher must not say that God created the world, but he or she could say that man was dependent upon the world and responsible for it. Keith Wilkes suggested that following the logical positivists too closely had 'led her to propose the elimination of religion from the primary school'.[77]

RE as essentialism

The idea that all religions are expressions of a basic essence was put forward towards the end of the 1960s. The editor at this point was Catherine Fletcher, a Quaker. She considered that the best course for RE lay in broadening the scope of the subject to include many different expressions of the human psyche. She wrote that man must become aware of the destructive forces at work within himself in order to be able to let loose the creative force of love: 'it is a matter of tremendous significance that the insights of contemporary depth psychology are confirming the testimony of the teachers, prophets and mystics of the world's religions. For this testimony speaks of the reality of the Kingdom of God within, the Secret closer to a man than his jugular vein, the diamond centre, the pearl, the jewel that the dragons guard, the Buddha within, the Atman: symbols of the ineffable lying beyond the ego consciousness.'[78] In the same edition Martin Israel, a doctor, argued that the prejudices of the humanist and the religious sectarian should be transcended by a direct enquiry into the nature and reality of religious experience. The teacher would need an understanding of the truth enshrined in all religion. Such teaching might well, he thought, produce a generation of mature and enlightened adults and a renewal of the religious impulse which would transform the world.

By fastening onto the idea that all religions are at base the same and are a response to an aspect of human nature, the spiritual or religious, it became possible at one stroke to silence the humanists and those wanting to retain the status quo. The humanist was silenced because she seemed to exclude an important aspect of human experience and the Christian because he excluded the experience of other religions.

Conclusion

This chapter has told the story of how those in positions of influence within the RE profession lost faith in the task as traditionally conceived. A sudden and dramatic rupture occurred in the thinking of those responsible for leading the RE profession in 1963. They became convinced that the Christian faith could no longer be rationally defended and this caused them to see all sorts of problems with RE. Alternative approaches were put forward: diluted versions of the status quo, voyages of uncharted spiritual discovery or forms of essentialism that would not withstand critical enquiry. I shall show in the next chapter that it was possible to read the situation rather differently if one had not given up on the credibility of the faith and its importance in British society.

Chapter 2
Restating the place of
the Christian faith in RE

In this chapter I tell the story of those who, between 1963 and 1970, restated the task of RE as teaching the Christian faith. I begin by showing how the matters cited as problems necessitating change in RE were seen in quite a different light by those seeking to hold on to the traditional vision.

Christian faith could be defended

In response to the '*open letter*' which argued that the Christian faith no longer possessed validity, a contrary view was stated: 'Many [such] teachers (supported by a growing body of scholarly opinion) see no reason to abandon traditional Christian beliefs after they have scrutinized "recent theological thought".[1] John Goodall, a lecturer, said: 'I feel strongly that our young people need confronting with a Faith which is intellectually positive, exacting and coherent. . . . Every age sponsors, often as a result of intellectual crisis, a distinctive philosophical formulation of the truth in Christ. Its form in our own day may be now discerned, and it is for us to use.'[2] The task of the teacher was to 'show authoritatively that the Christian faith can stand on its own intellectual feet'.[3] David Hargreaves gave exemplars of how to teach the Trinity and the Ascension via analogies with a fourth dimension: 'It made both Christian and agnostic realise that . . . the Christian 'mysteries' are not escape clauses for theologians-in-a-corner but truths which challenge our hearts and heads in this age as much as that of the Apostles.'[4] By the mid-1960s, issues raised by John Robinson had been dealt with in the universities. Basil Mitchell had been writing defences of traditional Christian faith at Oxford for some time. These defences took full account of the work of Bonhoeffer and Tillich, whose writing found popular expression in *Honest to God*. There was in existence a body of theological thought,[5] some of which derived from the later Wittgenstein on language, that could have provided the counterattack to the positivism of John Robinson. For these theologians and philosophers the problems raised by *Honest to God* were old hat.

Goldman refuted

Peter Dawson, a head of RE, criticised Loukes for assuming that everyone agreed with Goldman's conclusions. Dawson referred to criticisms made by Hilliard[6] and by K.G. Howkins.[7] Hilliard argued that what was needed was an assessment of what children could learn as a result of good teaching, not what they happened to know without the benefit of lessons, which is what Goldman had investigated. Hilliard considered Goldman's research to be rough and ready. He recommended a longitudinal survey of what the same children knew at different stages of their education. Such research should take into account family background and the quality of teaching they had received. Howkins pointed out that Goldman had altered the Biblical account at some points, making the story appear more miraculous than it really was. Goldman considered that no-one of any maturity could accept the miraculous. Dawson commented: 'Goldman's research is significant only for those who share his attitude to the Bible and his view as to the purpose of religious education.'[8] Dawson warned: 'we must beware of a Gadarene rush away from everything we used to do into the as yet not very clear waters of the Sea of Goldman'.[9]

Successful RE

Dawson suggested that Loukes' results reported in *New Ground in Christian Education* demonstrated good biblical knowledge, not bad. Equally, the success of moral teaching reported by Loukes, said to have been effective in one third of lessons, could be a good record, given the nature of the topic. Dawson accepted that teaching of the Bible was sometimes irrelevant to the real purpose of the subject. What research had not shown, however, was that 'Bible teaching is always a lost effort'.[10] Loukes, Dawson judged, had overstated his case: 'in this respect it is typical of a good deal that is appearing in print from one side or another in the matter of religious education'.[11]

Almost every volume of the journal contained an account of successful RE: imaginative dancing of the Lord's Prayer, a ballad about Elisha, themes of guilt in *Macbeth*. Pupils in Kirkby developed Christian insights on family, community, service and aid; 15 and 16 year olds went out into the community on project work; primary pupils took charge of assemblies; the parable of the Lost Coin was approached through experience of loss; a lively lesson on immoral King David took place. Hilliard stressed that teachers were doing good work in RE and that 'far too little has been heard of their excellent work'.[12] He wrote of the many teachers who believed that 'judicious selection and imaginative presentation of traditional biblical and post-biblical teaching material can both gain children's interest and lay the necessary religious foundations for religious education in the *Christian* sense'.[13] Joan Truby, a primary teacher, wrote: 'How easily they are able to assimilate the most difficult conceptions and ideas if only we give them a chance. How competent children are!'[14] Christopher Campling, a school chaplain, said that the images of God in the Bible were not too difficult. He published a series of textbooks in 1964 and 1965 together with accompanying teachers' books to show how it could be done. These books sold well.

Society not secular

Philip May, a lecturer in education, pointed out that no arguments were given to support the view that society was newly secular. The claim was merely asserted: 'we are told that our society is "secular", "neutral", "multi-belief", that the 1944 Education Act's compulsory provisions automatically produce insincerity, and that (falsest of all) parents are indifferent about the religious education of their children.'[15] He himself argued against each of these assertions in the pages of the journal. He pointed out that society was 'officially Christian',[16] that Christianity was the religion of this country,[17] that 95% of parents supported the teaching of Christianity (he had carried out a major survey), that we were not pluralist in any meaningful sense (J.W.D. Smith himself had said that the proportion of non-Christian members of society was unlikely to rise above 5%), that RE was not about compulsion, and that his research had shown that parents were very interested in the religious education of their children. The Newsom Report, a government enquiry into the education of the average and below average child was published in 1963. This report had no hesitation in recommending that children still needed Christian teaching: 'they need to know what answer the Christian faith gives. This ought to be given in the most direct and plainest way possible . . . the schools of the land need immediately Christian teachers who . . . speak with informed conviction in a language the pupils can understand and who in terms of scholarship have kept on the Christian frontiers of today.'[18]

Hirst refuted

The theologian D.Z. Phillips chided Hirst for entering the debate on the side of 'keep religion out' and said that there must be public tests and controls in the matter of religion else it would have died out long ago. Phillips said that there had always been a measure of agreement about the meaning of religious terms; he gave the example that no Christian would believe someone claiming to have had a vision from God to kill all coloured people. Hirst seemed to be requiring an illusory gold standard whereby a public consensus on everything religious was required before RE could be taught in the classroom. To demand this sort of public agreement would be to rule out the possibility of teaching not only RE, but also history and literature: 'the mere fact of such disagreement does not lead to general scepticism about history and literature'.[19] Phillips' approach was to argue that religious truth cannot be verified 'objectively' in advance. This was partly because religious truth, in his view, had to be grasped intuitively. It is conveyed through story and the appeal to beauty and goodness. The only point in teaching religion at all is that there is felt to be something of worth to convey. He advised that children should be introduced to the stories and riches of Christian faith so that they could grasp for themselves what the faith had to offer. Hirst's method was a poor substitute, more suitably entitled Religious Facts or Religious Opinions than Religious Education. Bernard Curtis, a philosopher of education, argued that we do have tests to distinguish Christian beliefs, both to ascertain that such beliefs are religious and to ascertain how they differ from Buddhist beliefs and so on.[20] Furthermore, religious believers who claim that their religious beliefs are true, generally have grounds to which they appeal to justify their beliefs. Until Hirst stated wherein such tests fell short, there was no point in taking him seriously on the matter. Was Hirst saying that such canons of objectivity (in the case of Christianity for example) were faulty? If so, then this needed to be argued. Indeed, there needed to be discussion of the net result of the various claims about religious beliefs. Anything less was simply evasion of the real issues.

Hirst's position, Curtis argued, was based on the view that a teacher could avoid influencing a pupil in one way or another. It entailed the belief that it was possible to present what a Christian or a follower of another religion believed, without having any effect on how the child viewed the particular belief in question. The merit of such teaching was that it was thought not to develop the pupil in any particular direction but Curtis thought this was a grotesque mistake. To learn about love meant to learn that it was a good thing and to be disposed favourably to it. It was impossible to teach about a religion without giving some evaluation of it: 'either the teacher must show that he is not nudging children towards this answer or that to religious (and moral and political) questions, or he must accept some responsibility for "religiously educating" the children.'[21]

Criticism of new approaches

The 'open' approach
Members of the Schools Council stated: 'It is our view that the use of the word "open" in this context can be dangerous and misleading unless it is seen to be related to the basic assumptions from which we start our whole work as educators. It must not become an excuse for failure to define assumptions; this would lead to a theological indifferentism destructive of any valid concept of religious education.' If the Christian philosophy were not taken to be the base of the community life of the school, all that would be left would be 'exhortation or encouragement to social conformity'.[22]

A similar line was taken in a book following a conference, attended by

100 delegates, held at the Institute of Education in London in April 1965. The conference was called to counter moves by humanists and others which threatened to undermine the future of RE.[23] The book, entitled *Religious Education: 1944-1984* (RE 1944-1984), included the following passage written by Alexander Wedderspoon:

> Christian theology is not yet in such intellectual disarray that religious education need degenerate into mere hazy discussion, that 'exchange of mutual mystification' to which Professor Nineham refers. If by 'open-ended approach' is meant the critical, intelligent and informed presentation of biblical and doctrinal material by the teacher, followed by frank and open discussion by the class, then this is no more than trained and qualified teachers of religious education have been doing for years. If, on the other hand, it implies teachers abandoning what Christian scholars have taught for centuries in favour of embarking with their pupils on 'voyages of uninhibited spiritual discovery', then we must needs judge the enterprise to be ill-advised. One of the main characteristics of young people is still ignorance, and to assert that neither Christian theology nor Christian morality has any longer anything definite to teach them is to exhibit a dangerously mistaken humility.[24]

The idea of neutrality

M.V.C. Jeffreys, professor of education at Birmingham University, was strongly opposed to the idea of neutrality in education.[25] He wrote: 'religious education has been suffering from a loss of nerve. We take refuge in neutrality, in teaching about religion instead of teaching religion, in doubtful scruples about "indoctrination" because we are bewildered by the confusion of theological voices within the Churches and the new aggressive self-confidence of the secular humanists.'[26] He called the idea that the teacher who would lead his pupils to think for themselves must shelve his own religious opinions a dangerous heresy. It had got to the stage where a teacher could inform his pupils about religion but must not assault their minds even with reasoned conviction. The most likely result of this, Jeffreys argued, was not to stimulate the pupil into thinking but to suggest that religion was not worth feeling strongly about. He argued that the root fallacy was the assumption of an incompatibility between the encouragement of pupils' thinking and the positive expression of the teacher's beliefs. What was needed was to reject the indoctrination thesis for the nonsense that it was, and to recover confidence in two propositions. The first was that a teacher should present with sincerity and reasoned argument what he believed to be true, and the second was to respect the right and the duty of the pupils to do their own thinking. Any attempt at agnosticism and detachment would be impossible as well as undesirable. The pupil, he wrote, 'has a right to demand that his teacher be honest, that he be himself in the classroom and not an actor playing a part'.[27] Furthermore, Jeffreys argued, pupils had a right to ask what it was their teachers were nudging them towards.

Positive proposals

Before putting forward positive proposals it was necessary to reject the charge of indoctrination.

The rejection of the charge of indoctrination
RE 1944-1984 pointed out the offensiveness of such a charge which by implication rendered all religious educators prior to the mid-1960s unworthy of the name: 'It is, furthermore, gratuitously offensive to describe religious education in British schools as "brainwashing" or "indoctrination". This type of accusation is linguistically, psychologically and educationally false, enjoys extensive empirical disproof, and is used in a strangely emotional way by those professing to be rationalists.'[28] The same work talked about refusing to abandon children to the 'fatuities of secularism' and the 'bleak negations of "the humanist alternative"'.[29] Aware that the 1944 Act had not been followed up with sufficient enthusiasm, they expressed concern that RE must not become the 'half-hearted communication of half-comprehended truths by the half-trained to the half-interested'. Were this to happen, the report concluded, and were the subject to disappear, the fault would lie with the 'apathy, faithlessness, timidity, triviality and sheer incompetence of those for whom it was a professional responsibility'.[30]

The need for definite teaching
The idea that teaching could be merely teaching *about* a subject, as Hirst had called for, Jeffreys called nonsense and a nonsense that would not be allowed in any other subject. The job of the teacher was to present the truth as he sees it and his reasons for believing it, to create an atmosphere of honest and responsible thinking in which the right to an opinion must be earned by studying the subject, to insist that disagreement is legitimate and can be salutary but should not become personal hostility. If the teacher saw his task in this way then the idea of teaching about religion rather than teaching religion became irrelevant: 'Does it mean anything to say: Don't teach music; only teach *about* music. Don't teach science; teach *about* science. Or: this teacher is dangerous because he is too enthusiastic *about* the beauty of advanced mathematics; he should put aside his own personal opinions when he enters the classroom?'[31] What did it mean to teach a religion? Jeffreys' answer was that it meant that a teacher had to know it from the inside. No-one could understand religions without 'laying oneself

open to them, making oneself vulnerable to them. In the last resort, what the teacher conveys in his teaching is himself, with his convictions or lack of them'.[32] And he felt that to leave the young without guidance was to fail them at the point where they needed help the most.

Some lecturers' views

Keith Wilkes argued that what was needed was gradual and careful instruction in one tradition via its language, thought forms, history, concepts, rituals and ideas.[33] Only in this way could the central aim of RE be achieved, which was to deliver understanding of what it meant to be a religious believer. The ideal of critical openness, so beloved of those arguing for new 'open' approaches, could only be achieved by a thorough induction into one particular tradition of thought. Alan Dale, who had written paraphrases of both the New and Old Testaments to help children understand the Bible, argued that what was needed was a theology of Christian education, an understanding of the social world pupils inhabit and, above all, textbooks which would clearly explain the Christian faith, its history and what it had to say about where we were in the 20th century. He wrote: 'they [the teachers] do not want any "watering down". They want to go for the strategic Christian convictions – the growing points of the Christian vision. They want something that will appeal to the imagination of the young people. If these can see, in their critical years, what it is all about – so that they can say yes or no for the right reasons – they will be able to find their way in later years.'[34] In similar vein John Goodall wrote: 'We must get across to them the fundamental Christian claim. We must give to them some basic conceptual and logical tools. We must give strong guidance to their first essays at manipulating them. We do them no service by presenting them alternatives and inviting choices which they are not competent to make.'[35]

Some teachers' views

Furthermore, such teaching was appropriate for a variety of pupils. Don Hassall wrote: 'The believer has begun to work out the reason for his moral belief, and the agnostic and the atheist have been shown the Christian position and challenged to work out their own ideas. We have not left the pupils with a shapeless, useless idea. We have offered them a way of life which makes sense and tried to make them think their way through it in detail. . . . Our aim must be to put the Christian pattern clearly in front of him . . . to help him see what good sense Christian teaching makes.'[36] A remarkable account was published in 1968.[37] Its author was Mary Bray, headmistress of a secondary school for girls in Portsmouth where the average IQ of pupils was 86. It was not a church school but Miss Bray's declared aim was to create a Christian community based on Christian principles discussed with staff. RE lessons were taught in the best room in the school and great efforts were put into the effective teaching of the subject. She herself took charge of RE in the final year of schooling. She treated these lessons as adult lectures with invited speakers and small discussion groups. The aim of RE in the school was to confront each child with the basic truths of Christianity: God's nature, the life of Christ, the nature of man, life after death, the search for God in other lands, the Holy Spirit, the offering of life to God, moral and social pressures, the Church and the churches, some difficulties of faith, suffering and inequalities. Questions were invited, much was taught through dance and movement and one assembly was broadcast on television. Girls invited the elderly to a party so that they could learn in practice the lesson that it was 'more blessed to give than to receive'. One assembly a week was devoted to intercessory prayer for individuals and this occasion was often moving and even eagerly anticipated by the girls. Miss Bray found the girls to be spiritually very able, possessed of a hunger for the truth about life and what it was to be good. When you could achieve so much in a run-down secondary school, it was not surprising that Mary Bray urged the church to take responsibility for sending out Christian teachers into the state system.

Some evangelical views
In 1967 a monograph was published which distilled the views of evangelicals consulted over a period of two years by the education department of the British Council of Churches (BCC) as part of an enquiry into RE.[38] The view taken was that religious education was essentially the teaching and exploration of the Christian faith. Like music and art this involved an element of advocacy. The hope that faith might be evoked was expressed but it was not to be imposed or assumed to already exist amongst the pupils. A coherent picture of the Christian faith should be attempted, positive teaching given, the experience of God as Creator fostered, and the way Christian beliefs correspond to human experience of being in the world clearly shown. At the same time care had to be taken to select carefully what biblical and other Christian material was appropriate and to relate it to questions that were of concern to pupils. It was not necessary always to begin from the Bible but it must not be left out or given minimal importance. The penultimate sentence of the postscript to the monograph, said: 'we are not convinced that attempts to replace the historic faith by a mid-twentieth century mish-mash appeal strongly except to a vocal and persistent minority.'[39]

The Plowden Report
This seemed to be the feeling of the Plowden report, entitled *Children and their Primary Schools,* published in 1967. It was a Government sponsored investigation into primary education. It included a substantial

section on RE and worship, placed first in the list of curriculum subjects. The main report[40] recommended no change to the 1944 Education Act. Surveys had shown support for RE as envisaged under the Act and in current practice.[41] No serious difficulty was found with finding staff to teach the subject. The aim of RE was put like this: 'young children need a simple and positive introduction to religion. They should be taught to know and love God and to practise in the school community the virtues appropriate to their age and environment.'[42] The influence of Goldman is clear, here wielded to justify the positive teaching of Christian faith. A further statement made their positive view clear: 'Children should not be unnecessarily involved in religious controversy. They should not be confused by being taught to doubt before faith is established.'[43] Like *RE 1944-1984* they considered that the future of the subject lay with finding and training the right teachers.

Summary

By the end of the 1960s it seemed that the case for abandoning Christianity as the ground for religious education remained to be made in a convincing way. Alternative approaches lacked substance and strong arguments were advanced for continuing with the traditional way of teaching the subject. In 1970 the Church of England published the Durham Report, the result of a major enquiry into RE.

The Durham Report, *The Fourth R.*

The Durham Commission was set up by the Church of England Board of Education and the National Society in 1967. The foreword stated: 'the decision to establish the Commission arose from a widely felt need to examine the whole field of religious education at a time when hitherto accepted presuppositions were being questioned, the aims of religious education reconsidered, and methods of teaching transformed.'[44]

Composition of the Commission
On the Commission were notable academics from the fields of theology, philosophy, ethics and education. It was chaired by Ian Ramsey, Bishop of Durham, Nolloth Professor of the Philosophy of the Christian Religion at Oxford until 1966. His successor at Oxford, Basil Mitchell, sat on the commission and chaired the sub-committee on morals. There were five professors on the Commission; a further five sat as co-opted members on sub-groups, making a total of ten professorial contributors. Six professors alone contributed to the theology sub-group. Other members were serving teachers, church people and post-holders in universities and colleges of

education. They worked for three years before publishing. The report contains chapters on the history of RE, a review of contemporary theology and its roots, a theology of education, RE in county schools, moral education in county schools, collective worship, church schools, independent schools and a survey of RE in other countries. It has several appendices. There had been no such thorough investigation of RE in England and Wales before, neither has there been since.

Consultation

A public appeal was made by the chairman for comments from the general public. A questionnaire was sent out to 75 organisations thought to have an interest in RE. This included the secularist societies. Appendix A, containing 64 pages, indicated the views of a cross-section of the 75 organisations consulted. The Commission received 87 formal replies and 550 replies from individuals. These included replies from teachers' unions, educational administrators, chief education officers, County Council Associations, secular societies, parents' groups and of course the various churches. In large measure the replies stated that RE should be retained on its Christian base.

Conclusions

On the basis of such consultation and as a result of lengthy internal debate within the commission itself, the report made its recommendation about RE in county schools. The view taken was that RE should continue to be based on Christian faith for most pupils. It was argued that while there were perhaps many systems of belief or patterns of behaviour that could be presented to pupils, it was the Christian one that should form the basis of RE in this country:

> The aim of religious education should be to explore the place and significance of religion in human life and so to make a distinctive contribution to each pupil's search for a faith by which to live. To achieve this aim, the teacher will seek to introduce most pupils to that biblical, historical and theological knowledge which forms the cognitive basis of the Christian faith. This will be done with careful reference to the ages, interests, and degrees of comprehension of the pupils. The teacher will also seek to show his pupils the insights provided by Christian faith and experience into a wide range of personal, social and ethical problems.[45]

Essential for a grounding in one religion

The Commission argued that in order to begin to appreciate the force and attraction of religion (and there could be no education without such understanding) there was no alternative to studying one religion in some depth. The same argument held good for the possibility of pupils being able to make a meaningful choice. Since the study of a religion could not be divorced from the study of the culture in which it had arisen, it was impossible to study several religions AND hope to understand any one of them meaningfully. Teachers on the Commission[46] were of the opinion that you could not possibly teach other religions along with a proper treatment of Christianity:

> It would be educationally unrealistic to propose that all pupils in the schools of England and Wales should study the Bible and, as well, the Qur'an, the Bhagavadgita, the Upanisads, and the Buddhist scriptures. This would inevitably lead to extreme superficiality, even if there were enough teachers possessing the relevant qualifications.[47]

It was a simple fact that British society was closest to the Judaeo-Christian tradition and pupils would find it easiest to gain the requisite depth of understanding of Christianity than religions of the Middle and Far East.

These might be called the educational and cultural arguments. However the Commission argued for the place of Christianity on its own merits. Only the Christian doctrine of man, it was argued, gave adequate expression to the irreducible value of the individual human person. The Christian view of love and other beliefs about sin and Christian ideas of hope led to the following conclusion:

> The Christian contribution to modern education is an account of the individual and his potentialities which, as we have sought to argue, is more true to life than its alternatives, and offers society a more satisfactory basis from which its educational procedures can set out.[48]

Educational advantages of Christianity

Intrinsic to Christian theology is the call to reflect on, and interpret, the nature of the world. As knowledge of the world changes and develops so too does understanding of the Christian faith. While there are certain givens, these givens need to be returned to time and time again as knowledge progresses. Thus there is within the faith a certain capacity for self-criticism which is part and parcel of our understanding of education. The conclusion that Christian faith is particularly suited to our educational system is unsurprising since the faith largely created education as we know it. Christian faith, just like knowledge in other areas, is involved in a continuous process of interpretation, exploration and development of its own primary data. New insights are continually being generated from its treasury of faith.

The place of other religions

There was a place for the teaching of other religions at the top end of the secondary stage, and use was made of the 'inclusivist' position: the view that because the 'Logos', or word of God, is contained within every human being, God has not left himself without witness in any religion. There is therefore something of God in other religions which is to be welcomed and explored; but it is within Christian faith that the Logos is supremely revealed.

'Openness'
In relation to openness the position taken was similar to that of *RE 1944-1984*. It was argued that RE must be open in the sense of being open to criticism and debate with pupils. Such openness was entirely compatible with taking a definite line and defending it. The alternatives to taking the Christian position (both in RE and in moral education) were considered. The alternatives were either to take another definite position such as humanism, Marxism or another religion, or to take no position, perhaps by presenting a range of options without preferring any particular one. The report argued that no alternative model had appeared which could claim to better the Christian model in having been scientifically demonstrated or universally accepted. The possibility of taking no position was one that, particularly at the time, looked attractive. But the objection to it was that in matters relating to education it was impossible to maintain strict neutrality, even were it to be considered desirable. Inevitably, judgements would direct the enterprise, the more insidious for being unexamined. This being so, a judgement had to be made and it was the view of the Commission that a judgement in favour of the Christian view was the right one.

Indifferentism or essentialism the likely alternatives
In line with the view that neutrality would prove impossible as the starting point in RE, the Commission implied that if RE were not to proceed by taking the line that the Christian faith was true, either indifferentism or essentialism would result: 'The indifferentist view asserts that no prophet or religious teacher is necessarily of greater value than any other: the essentialist claims that there lies behind all religions an essential truth, to know which is the best and purest religious knowledge one can attain to.'[49]

Indoctrination
At the end of the report there was an appendix on indoctrination written by Basil Mitchell. All learning involves the introduction to an area of study which is held to reflect some truth and to be worthy of the attention of pupils and this is the same whether the topic is Mathematics or Religious Education. At first much must be taken on trust. When the pupil has grasped the basics, areas of greater complexity and uncertainty are introduced and the pupil learns to develop the capacity for creative work. At this point it may be that the boundaries of learning are extended and new paradigms perceived. Some basic assumptions are reviewed and modified. But this cannot happen without first taking such assumptions as read. What this means in RE is that some particular view must be taken and explored if progress is to be made from an *educational* point of view. However, this is not the same as indoctrination which takes place when

the intention is that pupils come to believe something without regard for evidence, or where pupils are induced to believe something through fear of the teacher or the consequences of not believing or when relevant evidence is withheld by the teacher. All were agreed that such methods were wrong and no-one seriously suggested that teachers of religious education were engaged in such methods, either then or before 1967.

Problems Ahead

But the omens were not good. The report was lengthy and measured. Its recommendations, summarised at the end of the report, did not contain a clear statement that RE should continue to be based on the Christian faith for most pupils. It referred readers to the chapter on RE in county schools, perhaps unwilling to take the risk of putting views in brief and being misunderstood. It was not long before a member of the Commission itself misrepresented its conclusions.

The Fourth R as explained by Colin Alves

The National Association of Schoolmasters (NAS) had issued a discussion paper, *Thoughts on a New Education Act* which suggested that any new act should rescind the compulsory RI and worship clauses. This proposal aroused such interest that the association held a day conference to discuss the matter. This conference took place in Birmingham on 30 December 1970 and was addressed by Colin Alves who had served on the Durham Commission. Referring to the Commission's view, he quoted the aim of RE: 'to explore the place and significance of religion in human life and so to make a distinctive contribution to each pupil's search for a faith by which to live'.[50] Leaving out the next sentence which made it clear that RE was to be based on the Christian faith for most pupils, he argued that the Commission believed that RE was to be about religion in general: 'In brief then religious education is to be understood as a process which helps pupils to understand the impact of belief and attitudes on human life and behaviour and so contributes towards each pupil's development of his own beliefs and attitudes.'[51] This was then contrasted with the 'earlier view' now said to be rejected by the Commission: 'the Durham Commission felt that this new concept of the subject, which it welcomed, was gradually superseding the older view which saw RE as a process of inducting children into a quite specific pattern of belief, of making them Christians or at least making them religious'.[52]

The view that RE should be based largely on Christianity was argued in three major chapters: Theology and Education (Ch. 2), Religious and Moral Education (Ch. 3) and Religious Education in the County School (Ch. 4). It was not possible to argue that they defined RE as the study of belief and attitudes in general. Indeed they clearly rejected this as the task of RE. Alves presented the conclusions of the Durham Report in a way entirely contrary to what they in fact recommended. Having sat on the Commission for three years, what he said would have carried weight with his hearers. Many would follow his lead and it is common, even today, to find experts quoting the phrase 'to explore the place and significance of religion in human life' without the following sentence next one which makes it clear that RE was to be based, for most pupils, on the Christian religion.[53]

It seems that Alves interpreted the *The Fourth R* in line with his own views about RE. He believed that while a school might advocate Christianity, this was not the task of the RE teacher.[54] In 1972 he stated: 'The RE teacher may well be quite legitimately helping his pupils in their search for faith, but on the question of which faith, the process must be an open-ended one.'[55] This was emphatically not the view of *The Fourth R*.

Conclusion

In this chapter I have set out the views of those who had serious misgivings about the sort of RE that was being suggested in certain quarters of the RE profession. It was said to lack discrimination, to require the teacher to become either a play-actor or invisible, to refuse the presentation of reasoned argument and to be unclear about basic assumptions. Any idea of passing on what was best in human experience or giving guidance to the young was to be abandoned in favour of uncharted exploration with blind guides to accompany them. Well-argued attempts to re-assert the traditional role of RE were put forward. Foremost of these was *The Fourth R*, the report of a Church of England commission. At a time of crisis the Church of England did what it surely exists to do: exert a mighty effort to undergird the role of Christian faith in society. It made a powerful case on educational grounds for RE, for most pupils, to be the introduction to Christian faith on the basis that it was true and worthy of their attention. But it was possible, by judicious omission, to misrepresent its case and it appeared that there were those who were willing to do so.

Chapter 3
The role of Ninian Smart

'It all begins with Ninian Smart.'[1]

In 1961, just as Harold Loukes was starting out as editor of *Learning for Living*, Ninian Smart was appointed to the H.G. Wood chair of theology at Birmingham University. He was 34 years old and had a background in classics and philosophy. In 1968 he was appointed to the newly created post of professor in religious studies at Lancaster. There he became renowned for his expertise and advocacy of religious studies. A visiting lectureship at Yale in 1955 had introduced Smart to a way of teaching religious studies in America known as 'neutralism'. He called it the 'secular idea' and was certain that this was where the future lay. He held this view as late as 1998 when he stated that one's own culture brings with it 'problems of built-in interpretations'.[2] A particular theoretical stance was to be avoided: 'if we build theories into our descriptive stance (say Marxian theory) we already cannot test the theory, for it has already infected the data'.[3] To gain accurate understanding of religions and cultures one needed to adopt what he called 'warm neutralism'[4] or 'methodological agnosticism'[5].

It is clear that he had an interest in changing RE. At a CEM conference in 1965 he had spoken of the neutral, secular attitude towards religion in the majority of universities. In relation to schools he said: 'the Christian view of man is applicable. But we need a reformulated concept of RE, seen within the context of contemporary educational thought and culture into which pupils are growing.'[6] In 1967 he set out his vision both for his work at the new university and RE in schools. He said 'we shall be especially concerned to work out the relation between Lancaster Religious Studies and the requirements of religious education in schools'.[7] He went on: 'Happily the Colleges of Education associated with Lancaster include divinity departments which may well help us in the University to look afresh at these needs.'[8]

It may have been Smart who coined the word 'confessional'. Speaking of the students at Lancaster, Smart wrote: 'it is to be expected that there will be many students taking Religious Studies who do so without professional or confessional interests in the subject; and this will be a chance for professional and confessional people (if I may so describe them) to work side by side with others who may look at religions rather differently.'[9] In 1969 the first conference of the Shap Working Party (SWP) was held at the Shap Wells Hotel in Cumbria at Easter. It was addressed by Smart who became its first chairman along with Hilliard. The conference was called by John Hinnells who taught at the adult education department at Newcastle University. The purpose of Shap was (and is) to promote the teaching of world religions in all stages of education.

This brief summary of the career of Ninian Smart up until 1970 shows that he was in a unique position to influence the course of RE. He was committed to finding a new approach to RE and able to offer considerable philosophical weight to his chosen stance. I now look at what he made of *The Fourth R*, whose philosophical pedigree was at least the equal of his own.

Smart's review of *The Fourth R*

Smart had little positive to say about the recommendations of the Commission.

- He objected to the suggestion that RI should become RE, preferring instead something like 'Religion'.
- He disapproved of the report's endorsement of school worship: 'RE cannot be candid till this religious assembly is cut out from non-denominational schools.'[10] He was scathing about the fact that the report found it necessary to 'talk about withdrawal by parents from this act (even for sixth formers: how alienating can you get!)'.[11]
- He disliked the fact that the report argued for retention of the conscience clauses: 'it must be bad education if there is a conscience clause. It must presume bias and unfairness.' In his view the conscience clause 'should be denounced daily by bishops, priests, evangelical laity and the ordinary man'.[12]
- He was against teachers in the dual system cooperating in RE:[13] 'this could be regarded as a sinister idea. Christians getting together to work the dual system are perpetuating the establishment.'[14]
- He criticised the Commission for laying undue weight on theology: 'it is possibly a defect in this report that it has not looked very critically at the nature of theology and its place in the intellectual firmament'.[15]
- The report had not given sufficient attention to defining religion. This meant that it was out of touch with the way the profession was going. He had 'grave doubts as to whether the theological assumptions in the report give sufficient definition; and even greater

doubts as to whether the definition would be acceptable across the teaching profession'.[16] His concern was to make sure that 'both in universities and in schools and elsewhere, the study of religion should, intellectually, stand on its own feet and not attract the criticism that it is determined by a particular theology or ideology. Thus it is important . . . that a genuinely clear idea be evolved of the nature of religion'.[17] The Durham Commission was not however the body to look to for such a task: 'to study objectives one must be critical and take into account both matters of logic and professional acceptability. In this respect a church report is bound to be problematic.'[18]

Smart clearly viewed *The Fourth R* as ineffectual and unlikely to cause many waves. In the second sentence he wrote: 'The report is a milestone for the Church of England, and people should note it seriously as they whizz past.'[19]

There is unfairness and caricature here. It was wrong to accuse the Commission of not engaging in a thorough exposition of 'religion'. They did in fact offer a standard definition, but their brief was to define religious education, not religion. The case they made, and made at some length, was for RE to be the teaching of the *Christian* religion. It is difficult to understand how he could accuse the Commission of not considering theology critically. A chapter was devoted to theology, both past and present, which even today could form a useful introduction to the topic for undergraduates. The view that RE could never be candid while religious assemblies took place in schools omitted whole swathes of argument in the report about the justification for worship in school. It ignored the strong support for worship which had been shown in a major survey by May and Johnston in 1967 and the findings of the wide consultation carried out by the Commission itself. Yet Smart gave no evidence to support his claim that the secular nature of society required the removal of worship in county schools.

It is difficult to take seriously the view that Christians co-operating within the dual system is dangerous and will promote the establishment, particularly since in the next sentence he talked about the days of 'Christians educating' never being better. To state that the report lacked logic and awareness of what was acceptable to the profession was an unwarranted slur on the Commission. In relation to a lack of logic, one can only protest that the report is a fine demonstration of careful and thorough argumentation. In relation to awareness of what would be acceptable within the profession, the Commission consulted widely over three years both within and outside the profession. The wide support claimed by Durham for its conclusions (and set out in full in an Appendix) was not mentioned in Smart's review.

Finally, and strangest of all, Smart nowhere set out the Durham Commission's most important recommendation: that RE should, on educational grounds, be an introduction to the Christian faith for most pupils. The main purpose of the Commission was to make recommendations for the future of RE at a time when the future of the subject was thought to be at stake and the RE world was in considerable uncertainty. Yet Smart did not note the fact that it was the considered conclusion of the report that Christianity should continue to form the basis of RE for most pupils in this country. In his concern to 'whizz by' the report he completely missed the central thrust of it.

How can this omission be explained? Either Smart chose to ignore it (but he did not ignore other aspects with which he disagreed) or the answer is simpler: he did not read the full report. The latter conclusion is suggested by the fact that his review is a list of comments on the recommendations set out at the end of the report, where, as I have already pointed out, the Commission did not state clearly what its view of RE was. Smart was at the time engaged in setting up the department at Lancaster and putting the final touches to his own work on RE, Schools Council Working Paper 36. It seems possible that, pushed for time, he read only the recommendations at the back of the report and did not fully grasp the ideas of the Commission.

In support of this view is the fact that Smart held that one's presuppositions 'infect the data'. A church report was 'bound to be problematic'. Believing this to be the case, he might have decided that the arguments of the Report necessarily contained bias for one point of view. Smart was himself an Episcopalian Christian but he could be disparaging of Christian scholarship. In 1988 he wrote that in his opinion 'a lot of theology is tertiary Sunday School'.[20] Indeed he viewed theology as a 'conceptual albatross round the neck of Religious Studies'.[21] Ninian Smart was not predisposed towards serious consideration of thinking that emanated from Christian sources.

Schools Council Working Paper 36[22]

In 1969 Ninian Smart secured the support of the Schools Council for a research and development project on RE in secondary schools.[23] The project got off the ground that year and in 1971 Schools Council Working Paper no. 36 (WP 36) was published as an interim report. Prior to this, Government funding for research in RE had been minimal. At this period it was largely CEM that provided advisers and professional expertise and syllabuses were determined locally, not by reference to any central state authority. It was therefore an imaginative and bold act on the part of Smart to approach the Schools Council. It also enabled him to act independently of any 'confessional' body, something he was keen to do for reasons of principle. I assume in what follows that as director, Smart was in full agreement with what was written. I therefore write as if Smart were the author.

The Project team consisted of Smart as director, one lecturer from a college of education, three teachers and a full-time secretary. It worked for 18 months before publishing. The team had carried out survey work in secondary schools and studied current literature in the field. Links with other Schools Council projects were made. Specialists in educational fields in Lancaster and abroad were consulted and over one hundred secondary teachers worked with the Project officers in the first stage. In addition a few lecturers, an RE adviser and others with specialist qualifications were co-opted, including representatives of other faiths. This meant that the project was entirely professionally based and did not consult outside the field of 'education'. In terms of length of time taken over the project, breadth of consultation, academic credentials and length, it was lightweight compared with the Durham Report. Indeed, it was made clear in the preface that the document was only a working paper: 'This is a working paper, not a report. Its intention is to raise questions for public discussion and to invite comments from those concerned with education, and particularly religious education, in schools.' Units of work existed but had not been trialled: 'by working in groups and sub-groups a large number of experimental "units of work" have been devised. These will be first tried out by their authors . . . and then, after revision, by a number of other teachers . . . it is therefore hoped to produce an analysis of what . . . is feasible as the content of religious education . . . for 11-16 year olds.'[24] However, a measure of confidence was felt amongst the Project members such that they could claim that increasingly the world of education was coming to a consensus about the future of RE, not just in England and Wales, but in 'almost every country of the western world'.[25]

Lack of an overview

WP 36's definition of religion in schools was close to that of Durham. Religion was held to be 'a distinctive way of interpreting experience, a mode of understanding; therefore anyone who grows up not seeing and feeling that there is such a thing as genuine religious belief is, to that extent, undeveloped and incomplete as a human being'.[26] Smart, following Phenix, agreed that a particular view had to be taken. He argued that RE could never be the study of mere facts separated from interpretation, even if such a thing were desirable. As in physics, facts only made sense when part of a theory.[27] This being so, the issue turned on which interpretation of the facts of religion was to be presented to children in the classroom. However, at this point Smart prevaricated: 'The main point is that . . . [it is] not the task of education to tell children which religious interpretation they should believe . . . [but rather that they should] enter with understanding and sympathy into a variety of perspectives.'[28] The teacher should adopt the position of 'procedural neutrality'[29] where he studiously avoids favouring his own interpretation of the matter under discussion. On the other hand Smart argued that critical evaluation of religious claims was necessary: 'It is not sufficient to parade alternatives before the eyes of the imagination and to leave it at that, as if there were no objective ways of judging their relative truth or adequacy. The special function of academic communities is to create schemes for the critical evaluation of interpretations originating in non-academic communities.'[30] But what schemes were to be made use of RE? Smart left this question hanging in the air.

The phenomenological approach

Smart presented a new way of helping children to enter into a variety of religious perspectives. This he called the 'phenomenological' or 'non-dogmatic' approach. A method of teaching was prescribed, based on the 'principle of intentionality'.[31] Attempts were to be made to understand what it feels like to be a religious believer, from the inside: 'to bring out the meanings and values present to the participants'.[32] He drew on the observation that young children were strong on imagination and had in large measure the capacity for self-transcendence. A Christian child could become a Jew for a day or an hour 'by witnessing a sacred festival or by acting out a part in an imagined ritual occasion. A Jewish child [in the primary school] can identify in imagination with the Muslim community, and understand inwardly, as a loyal player in the "game of faiths" what it means to go on pilgrimage.'[33] The paper argued that young children were ideally suited to this approach since their minds were not prejudiced or stuck in particular ways of thinking. They could make the necessary imaginative leap perhaps better than older children: 'Their imaginations have not yet been compromised by the demands of academic conventionality, and their thought processes have not yet been channelled into standard scholastic habits . . . they still have the capacity to envisage alternative possibilities . . . to construct imaginary worlds that are as real as those of everyday existence. Such a spirit is of the very essence in the life of objective rationality.'[34]

WP 36 set out the following aims:
- to promote awareness of religious issues
- to develop awareness of the contribution of religion to human culture
- to understand religious beliefs and practices
- to appreciate the challenge and consequences of religious belief
- to found such understanding on accurate information impartially assessed

Examples of possible objectives were set out by which such aims could be achieved, objectives which ranged widely and were notable for the number of times the letters 'e.g.' were used. The sense of imprecision was further underlined when the attempt was made to set out content in the light of the stated aims and possible objectives. Having hitherto insisted on the importance of relating objectives to aims before setting out content and method, the paper changed tack. It stated that the teacher should start from pupils' needs and interests, develop units of work based on these and then note the educational objectives they were likely to serve. A list of 'typical teaching units' was then given and the reader invited to match them up with objectives listed earlier. The teaching units covered a huge range of material from many different religions. For example:

·   *the mystery of suffering* in relation to Job, the Buddha, the Kerygma, Camus and Sartre
·   *enlightenment* in relation to angels in Luke, dreams in Matthew, Moses, Isaiah, Quaker 'inner light', Hinduism, Buddhism, Taoism, plus language, symbolism, doctrinal elements of Eastern religions
·   *personal relationships* in relation to groups and gangs, cultural and sub-cultural groupings, the ethical dimension of Christianity and other religious and non-religious groupings like Humanism.

The practical problem was that vast areas of study were indicated but no scheme given for sorting out which to choose within the limited time available to the teacher. The provisional nature of the scheme was indicated by the comment that how exactly it would all work out was 'currently being explored by a number of serving teachers who are assisting the present project'.[35] Left quite unanswered were questions about which religions to choose, how many and how much. It did not seem to matter.

A later chapter did offer some help: distinguish the observable aspects of a particular religion such as the rituals, customs, buildings, books etc. Next, study the teaching of the religion, the ideas and beliefs that underlie the observable aspects. After this, one could go on to discover what these external phenomena meant to the people involved in and committed to the religion – the 'experiential' or existential aspect. The idea was to achieve balance and breadth in order to avoid forming a one-sided picture of a particular religion. However, the same chapter went on to declare that religion *itself* was multi-dimensional: 'Smart emphasises that religion is multi-dimensional. It has, in fact, six major dimensions.'[36] Used in this way the six (later seven) dimensions functioned as a sort of inner logic which went to make up something called 'religion'. If *religion* itself could be said to be defined by these dimensions, if there was in effect an essence which could be identified in the religions, then coherence could be achieved. But WP 36 was ambivalent about this and did not make unambiguous use of such an 'essence'. Smart was never to outline what exactly the 'logic' of religion was. Indeed, as late as 1997, he acknowledged that we may not be able to properly isolate anything called 'religion' but must 'loosely adopt ordinary usage'.[37]

Supporting Arguments

It was stated that most RE teachers were moving towards this understanding of the subject: 'a great many teachers in secondary schools, dissatisfied with both the 'confessional' and the anti-dogmatic approaches, have been working their way, almost by instinct, to this – the educational approach'.[38] In fact this was the case not only in Britain, but also in all the countries of the West. Everywhere there was a 'remarkable consensus of opinion as to the answers.'[39]

Previous ways of teaching RE were stated to be inappropriate. One reason was the presence of a variety of beliefs within Britain: 'in a multi-cultural society there is no one religious (or anti-religious) position that can be taught in this way'.[40] Secondly, the majority of people in Britain no longer believed Christianity to be true. Thirdly, society was now secular and hence the education provided must also be secular. Fourthly, the 'confessionalist' aim conflicted at several points with the principles on which education was based. These points were said to be:

1. the modern RE teacher expected children to think, question and discuss as opposed to earlier times where children were expected to receive ideas passively
2. the modern teacher wished to include other forms of religious strivings
3. moral education was no longer synonymous with religious education

These three points were a direct quotation from a report submitted by the BHA to the British Council of Churches, an association which on any count represented a minority view. And they did not in any sense hit the target. No-one was suggesting that children should receive ideas passively, that other forms of religious strivings should be excluded altogether, nor that moral education equalled RE.

Relation to scholarly opinion

Chapter 3 was largely written by D.J. Bates, a college lecturer who went on to be a considerable force in the profession, and was a review of recent writing and research in RE. Bates cited three approaches.

The first was the 'neo-confessional', influenced by the work of Goldman and described as the open-ended approach to Christianity. This approach was stated to be the position adopted by Plowden, Newsom and all the recent agreed syllabuses. Writing of the latest agreed syllabuses Bates wrote: 'they are all Christian documents which assume that the fundamental objective of religious education is to inculcate Christianity.'[41] The approach was dismissed in one sentence: 'This neo-confessionalism, though undoubtedly sincere, cannot be the basis of religious education in maintained schools; it is just as open to objection from non-Christian teachers as the old confessionalism.'[42]

The second approach was that of Loukes and Acland. This took the view that all experience is implicitly religious and that religion could be understood as ordinary experience 'at depth'. It was said to fail as it lost touch with religion understood as including a transcendent reference.

The third approach was the explicit approach in which the favoured exponent was Ninian Smart, but also included were Cox and Smith. The approaches of both Cox and Smith were criticised because both fell into the 'neo-confessional' camp. Cox was stated to be in sympathy with Smart, but he differed in wanting to 'weight any syllabus more heavily with specifically Christian teaching'.[43] Smith was commended for arguing strongly in favour of an RE based on a neutral philosophical basis. However 'a concealed apology for Christianity runs through the book, despite the author's wish to avoid this'.[44] Of the three, it was only Smart that did not receive criticism.

This chapter confirms my view that, in 1971, the weight of informed opinion lay firmly behind the 'neo-confessional' approach to RE set out most fully in the Durham Report only a year earlier.

Criticisms

1. There is no 'logic of religion' and Smart was himself ambivalent about the matter. To the extent that he encouraged RE to be based on the six dimensions of 'religion' he was encouraging the pursuit of an illusion. Some at least of those involved in RE knew this. Raymond Holley, who taught at Borough Road College from 1969, attended a lecture given by Smart at an Easter philosophy conference in 1966. Here he heard for the first time of Smart's six dimensional concept of 'religion'. Holley and others present considered this view bizarre and philosophically quite unsound and he was disturbed to find, when appointed to Borough Road, that some of the staff there were firm followers of Smart's ideas.[45] Holley himself wrote an article pointing out that no-one had successfully been able to define the concepts that made up 'religion': 'The initial problem in determining the meaning of teaching religion is to know what substance to give to the notoriously difficult concept of religion.'[46] With no clear idea of the concepts of 'religion' there could be no education in 'it'.

2. WP 36 assumed that it was a straightforward matter to understand religions. At a time when some were concerned that the Bible was too difficult for children, it recommended that children should be

introduced to the Qur'an by adopting the device of stepping into the shoes of a Muslim. One could become a Muslim, or a Jew, for a day. Easy. Yet Smart himself acknowledged that to understand a religion involved study of many aspects which would take time and trouble. Smart trusted in the naïve and unproven view that children could enter, via the imagination, a thought world utterly alien to them. William Kay argues that Smart was asking young children to do something that was psychologically impossible for them.[47] Piaget showed that at the early stages of development, up to seven years old, children are simply not able to think outside of their own experience and imagine how others might see things differently from them. This means that they cannot engage in becoming a Jew unless they happen to be one. Children may act out a part, but in doing so will act out their own emotions and attribute them to the person they are playing. Kay questioned Smart on the subject at a conference some years ago and was told that he only meant that children should approach other religions sympathetically.[48]

3. Smart argued that those committed to one religion could not properly understand the religion of another because their convictions would 'infect the data'. The facts suggest otherwise. Some of the finest students of world religions have been committed to one particular religion. R.C. Zaehner, a Roman Catholic, was Spalding Professor of Eastern religions and Ethics at Oxford. Zaehner explained his method in this way: 'Another method which I have tried to follow . . . has been to study the non-Christian religions from the only point of view that can be central to me, that is, the point of view of Catholic Christianity, at least as I understand it. This was the method of the Jesuit missionaries of the 17th century. What they did, and what I have increasingly tried to do, was to study the main texts of the non-Christian religions in their historical development, to study them, so far as is possible, from the inside, and having studied them, to try to correlate them with aspects of Catholic Christianity which are of importance to me.'[49] Through the interplay of his own faith and his knowledge of eastern religions he was able to comment in a way that brings home the fact that great matters are at stake. He believed that the Indian religions in particular had something to teach Christians and that this 'something can help us to deepen our own religion and open up insights that were only dimly perceived before'.[50]

4. And what of the much vaunted necessity for the teacher to be neutral and for the syllabus to refrain from taking a stand on which religion was true? A sharp critic of this position was Edward Hulmes who argued that such a position owed much to liberal, secular and

agnostic attitudes and tended to be dismissive of all religious claims to truth.[51] He showed how RE had merely substituted one form of confessionalism for another. Indeed, given that Phenix was quoted in WP 36 to prove that all education must proceed via a particular theory which structures and gives meaning to the facts, it is surprising that the paper showed so little awareness of its own presuppositions.

5. Aims and objectives were vague. They did not give enough direction and one can see how they would lead to the voyages of unlimited spiritual discovery and flights of fancy that many at the time were so worried about. They may have served merely to give permission to those already launched on such experiments.

6. It was stated to be of great importance that children should learn to critically evaluate the religions they were studying. Yet no criteria were offered by Smart. Indeed in 1988 he wrote: 'To my mind the most important evaluative question of all is how we are to arrive at trans-religious criteria or trans-worldview criteria for selecting between or evaluating, religions or worldviews.'[52] The claim put forward in the paper to provide a critical, academic way of teaching religion and the religions was false.

7. It is untrue that most teachers were instinctively working their way towards his approach. Perhaps some were, and doubtless those who worked with him were won over to his side. Many teachers were happy to continue as they always had done until pressure was put on them to change. I give the evidence for this in the next chapter.

8. The word 'phenomenological' was used without proper definition. In fact WP 36 used it sparingly. It sounded suitably academic however and some would have known of the school of philosophy founded by the German philosopher Husserl which first used the term. Smart himself made little use of Husserl.

Conclusion

How convincing and how productive was the theory of RE offered by Ninian Smart? That he convinced many at the time is beyond doubt. Jeffreys saw in him a possible ally. Smart found a keen following in the members of Shap and soon the words 'phenomenological approach' were being intoned in syllabuses up and down the country. Smart was no mean intellectual to have on your side. To that extent it meant, however, that it was difficult to question him and indeed there were few criticisms made at the time.[53] What seems to have happened is that Smart's evidently academic approach was received with some relief amongst those who had already decided against traditional RE. 'Open' RE could not remain open for ever and Ninian Smart brought a degree of respectability to the idea of teaching religions (plural) such that it became acceptable to introduce 'real religion' into the classroom. This doubtless had a positive effect on the teaching of Christianity as well as other religions.

However, when one looks critically, and from a distance, at what was actually proposed in WP 36, a different picture emerges. It was launched on the promise of providing ways of evaluating the truth and worth of religion and the religions but failed to deliver any such criteria. Religion, it was stated, was to be the focus of study, not Christianity, and this argument appeared to broaden a subject now deemed hopelessly narrow. But religion proved so elusive a category as to have no depth at all. Without a solid base to the RE curriculum, a list of vague and curiously self-multiplying objectives was all that could be found to give direction to teachers. It is perhaps not surprising that teachers hit upon the six dimensions for the study of religions and misread them as a way of studying religion across the religions. Here lies essentialism with all its distorting of the great religions to fit each dimension. The only other way forward is a systematic study of each religion in turn. But which? How many? From what point of view? To answer these questions one must have a view as to which religions give the greatest access to the truth, which are of the greatest worth and which may safely be left to one side. But neutralism, even 'warm' neutralism, prohibits the taking of such a stance and indifference may be the end result.

The work of Ninian Smart was a direct challenge to the consensus expressed in the Durham Report and his clear rejection of it was to have far-reaching effects. Yet he never addressed its arguments directly. Indeed, he could even at times say that there was a place for the committed approach. And yet it may be that he was not entirely successful. In 1988 he could write: 'many teachers in the system still retain the assumption that religious education means inculcating Christianity of a sort'.[54]

Chapter 4
The RE Profession in the Early 1970s

Ninian Smart could not turn RE round on his own. A concerted effort over a period of time would be needed to take the profession with him, particularly since in 1970 the weight of opinion lay with the status quo. This chapter gives a picture of the situation across the profession at this time.

Three important figures within the RE profession abandoned the traditional view

John Hull

In March 1971 John Hull took over the editorship of *Learning for Living*. Hull set out a clear manifesto, one which contrasted sharply with Loukes' vision. Hull began by rejecting the idea that RE should continue to be the positive teaching of Christianity: 'It is becoming increasingly clear that in the county schools this subject can no longer be thought of as a process of nurture into the Christian faith nor can it proceed on exclusively Christian presuppositions nor may its content continue to be exclusively Christian.'[1] The only sort of RE acceptable to the state school was one given 'without favour and without discrimination' in relation to the traditions studied. On what assumption was RE now to proceed? The answer came in an awkward and laboured sentence: 'It must be a religious education based not an assumption that Christianity is true but on the belief in the importance of the study of the place of religions in the life of mankind.'[2]

Edwin Cox

The first article to appear under Hull was one by Edwin Cox, tautologically entitled 'Educational Religious Education'. Cox defined religion as 'man's attempts to find answers to his deepest problems' and he says, 'there is some justification for doing so'.[3] He argued that RE could no longer be based on Christianity because the faith was no longer credible. Christian faith emerged in the West, Cox argued, in response to certain questions which were no longer being asked today, since these questions have found a new and more satisfactory answer in science. He says: 'our age is one that has found the ideas that the church deals with not altogether relevant to the experiences of a scientific and technological age, and so has repudiated both those ideas and the authority of church leaders while still retaining religious sensitivity in changed form'.[4] Religion will not go away because 'our new problems make us approach religion from a new angle'.[5] Cox wanted pupils to take part in the project of developing new forms of religious awareness. There was serious business to be done to discover the new religion for the new age. And it was down to children to design their own religion. The teacher must not influence the thinking process of the pupil, but rather insist that 'a rational attitude to life includes making up one's mind on certain fundamental or ultimate questions of the nature of life and of human personality'.[6] Perhaps Cox had been stung by the accusations of 'neo-confessionalism' made in WP 36. Whatever the case, he lined up with the 'non-confessionalists' and those advocating personal search.

J.W.D. Smith

Smith too was soon to distance himself from any hint of confessionalism: 'If religious educators really wish to justify their task on educational grounds alone and this claim is now widely made – they must abandon Christian presuppositions. They may appeal to Tillich the philosopher but they should be aware of arguments derived from Tillich the Christian apologist.'[7] The problem for teachers of Christianity was that 'formal teaching is so discredited that subject matter is disappearing like the Cheshire cat. Little is left now but a rather nervous and apologetic grin.'[8] In 1975 he went further: 'Traditional Christian belief is dead, or dying, and cannot be revived in state schools.'[9] Smith wrote: 'traditional Christian themes, however skilfully interpreted, are not likely to satisfy intelligent and critical adolescent minds'.[10] A new edition of a book by Smith was reviewed by Andrew Bebb. In this spirited review, Bebb remarked on Smith's 'breathtaking criticisms of Christian teaching'.[11]

Hull, Cox and Smith, a powerful triumvirate, had openly declared that Christian assumptions could no longer form the basis of RE. The Durham Report did not receive a mention.

The Colleges of Education were divided

The colleges of education at this period were the major provider of teachers. The great majority of those who would go on to teach RE (which meant just about all primary teachers) were therefore prepared for the task in colleges of education. The attitude of the church colleges in the late 1960s may be ascertained by a study of their responses to a questionnaire sent out by the Durham Commission.[12] The majority argued for retaining the status quo. Salisbury College wanted the positive teaching of Christian doctrine and other ways of presenting the faith directly: 'It would seem very silly that the great stories of Hebrew times and of Christian traditions should become forbidden fruit while the myths and legends are freely offered, and very silly that the greatest interpretation of love should be dropped when love of all sorts is so much in the mouths and ears of the young.' John Sewell of Bede College, Durham, argued that Christianity must be taught on the basis that it is true. What was needed was a theology of education which authorised education on theological grounds rather than vice versa. Trinity College, Carmarthen, wanted provision for non Christian children to have some instruction in their own faith but stated: 'It is our firm belief that provision should be made in every school for children to be acquainted with *the* religious interpretation of life.' St Hild's College, Durham, said that any revision of the agreed syllabus system should 'secure that the content of the subject of Religious Knowledge is seen to be quite unequivocal in its concern for Christian belief, Christian worship and Christian living'.

Some, however, argued forcefully for change. Culham wanted a special place for Christianity, not so much for its own sake, but as an example of the 'differing kind of answers given by Man to the dilemma of existence' which would include a joyful explanation of the Eightfold Path. G.O. Robson at Keswick Hall College, wanted a firm line taken against any form of Christian monopoly: 'Religious Education should not be simply "Christian Education "in *any* circumstances. It should be "the study of religion".' B.K. Harding of St Martin's College, Lancaster, condemned the traditional approach in both content and method where it occurred in agreed syllabuses. He argued for the removal of the compulsory clauses and the conscience clauses of the 1944 Act which would be redundant under an open-ended approach to the subject. Bishop Otter College was equally forthright. In their view RE was a matter of introducing pupils to experiences which would lead to a right self-evaluation and to a valid perception on man and the universe. Enlightenment and understanding were what was needed, not conversion and discipleship: 'Other kinds of so-called RE should be abolished', a view held, with one or two dissentients only, by the whole staff.

Change could be rapid. At Saffron Walden in 1966 the course was entirely Biblical and Christian-based: 'detailed study of material suitable for children . . . in order to consider how to present it to, and interpret it for them, so that an interest in the Bible may be stimulated and sustained; in the Old Testament as the writings which Jesus was taught . . . and in the New Testament as arising out of, and giving meaning to the Old, and as containing the gospel of the Kingdom of God.'[13] By 1969 Saffron Walden was offering Biblical Studies, World Religions or Religion in Contemporary Secular Society. The purpose of RE was to 'study religion in some of its main aspects. Starting with an inquiry into the nature of religious experience, the attempt will be made to isolate the essential elements in this experience.'[14] Essentialism had triumphed.

Soon Margaret Thatcher would introduce major change in which many colleges were amalgamated or lost altogether. Church colleges did not escape the review and many suffered closure. Many colleges which supported the traditional view, Gypsy Hill, Salisbury and Bede Colleges for example, were closed, while some of the colleges who supported change, such as St. Martin's Lancaster and Bishop Otter, were retained. The loss of such church colleges may have meant the loss of a voice for traditional RE.

A case study – Borough Road College[15]

Under the energetic leadership of Howard Marratt, Borough Road College in West London began to attract students after his appointment in 1963. The ethos of the Divinity Department (later changed to Religious Studies) was said to be 'very open'. His 1966 prospectus stated that the department took no particular line in its teaching. He himself wanted to keep a special place for Christianity whilst introducing other religions and worldviews at the same time. But no priority was to be given to the Christian faith. According to Veronica Williams who was a student at Borough Road between 1969 and 1971, the great thing was to be on guard against 'indoctrination'. Marratt himself wrote in 1971: 'No longer doctrinaire in content, moralistic in tone and confessional in aim, religious education is rapidly discarding the narrowness of its past and is reaching a stage where it may take its place in the educational curriculum of the secular school set in the pluralist society.'[16]

The college soon gained a reputation for its teaching of non-Christian religions and became a centre of expertise along with James Graham College in Leeds where Owen Cole was teaching. At this point there were few resources for teaching world religions in schools. Marratt sent letters to embassies, religious groups, universities, missionary societies, etc., asking for information on all aspects of religions. They opened a resource centre which supplied teachers over the whole of the country with information sheets.

The National RE Centre

In 1971 Marratt wrote to the Department of Education and Science (DES) asking them to fund the Borough Road RE centre: 'For some time now the work of the Divinity Department has been expanding in such a way that it has attracted interest and correspondence that is now on an international scale. This has been especially stimulated by our acting as a centre for the study of world religions and HMIs refer a lot of people to us.' The DES gave its support in autumn 1973 so that a National RE Centre could be set up with the director's post funded by the DES. Its mission statement read:

The overall endeavour will seek actively to promote a more vigorous and healthy approach to Religious Education in the County school, while aiming to restore confidence and deepen the teachers' understanding of the nature of religious education.

The statement spoke of:

1. a 'new orientation required for a non-confessional, but basically educational, approach to Religious Education at primary and secondary level' and
2. a 'study of world religions in a multi-credal situation'

The National RE Centre with its collection of materials for use in teaching world religions had great influence. The centre ran courses, responded to queries and took under its wing much Shap work (for Shap see later). Its total teacher contact in the first year of operation was 975 with 450 replies to enquiries sent off.

The importance of Borough Road

Borough Road's success showed that RE could incorporate the teaching of world religions. During her time as a student Veronica Williams found that children in school who had previously been 'fed up' of lessons on Christianity would suddenly show interest when a new religion was introduced. Just as important it created a precedent for uncommitted students to enter the classroom without feeling that they had to teach anything as true. Borough Road did not have sufficient expertise on world religions amongst its staff and often invited visiting lecturers. Howard Marratt therefore came into contact with members of other faiths. Always politically aware, this experience led him to be instrumental in setting up the Religious Education Council in 1973 (REC), a group representing religious groupings of all varieties which was to act as a pressure group upon central Government. It is doubtful that any other college had quite the same influence on the Government as Borough Road had. Its importance was often to be felt through the pages of *Learning for Living*, where it was common to find articles written by its staff.

Treatment of those who questioned new approaches

A letter from the Rev. John Earwaker, a lecturer at the Sheffield City Institute of Education, was published in *Learning for Living* in March 1970. He asked what rational criteria advocates of the open approach had in mind to enable teachers to choose which religions or worldviews were to be taught: 'Are some forms of religion better than others? Which? Why? Or are we to say that anything is all right as long as it is "true for you"? This seems to me to be the first step in justifying *any* kind of RE in acceptable terms to anyone "of any religion or of none".'[17]

The next edition took the unusual step of printing several replies to his letter, four in all. Ninian Smart said that Earwaker's argument was 'not altogether clear and convincing', but did not go into detail and ignored the fact that Earwaker was not so much advancing an argument as asking questions. Smart did address one of his questions, however. He agreed that the question 'Are not some forms of religion better than others?' was legitimate. His answer was that we did not know. He turned this admission to good effect by arguing that there was a need to make more posts in religious studies available in British universities. Earwaker had not declared himself for or against the teaching of other religions in school. He had asked for discussion and a statement of rational criteria to enable decisions to be made about which religions to teach and what to say about them. Smart ignored this question. Instead Smart argued that traditional RE had alienated pupils so much that anything new had to be better: 'One can appreciate suspicions of comparative religion, but how much more heavily are these outweighed by the suspicions of lack of openness which alienate so many young people from traditional RE.'[18]

The other respondents also failed to address Earwaker's questions and assumed that he was defending the status quo. Earwaker, undaunted, replied. He wanted clarity over such matters as 'teaching about Christianity' and 'teaching Christianity' and had felt that the journal was failing to distinguish properly between the two. He wanted to open up debate on the fact that some teachers taught 'Christianity-*as-true* while teaching *about* other religions'.[19] He was concerned that just as students of literature were taught to make judgements about the relative merit of what they were studying so it should be in RE if several religions were to be studied by pupils. Unless this happened, one of two things would follow. One was that the question of truth and merit would be sidestepped and pupils would learn that there was no truth to be had other than what they themselves could make of the situation. Or, a type of syncretism would be taught, whereby areas held to be common to all religions were taught as true. Earwaker pointed out that if it was objectionable to teach Christianity as true, it was equally objectionable to teach Religion-as- true: 'on this view the RE teacher's role seems to be virtually that of the preacher of a world faith!'[20] Earwaker, an Oxford graduate, noted the lack of discrimination in RE and was concerned that RE needed to take note of philosophers of education, rather than ignore them as he suspected was happening. Speakers at conferences at the time similarly refused to take such basic questions seriously and accused those who raised them of misunderstanding at best. Earwaker felt he was being patronised. Considering those in charge to be impervious to rational debate, and frustrated at the way RE was being led, he took the decision to move out of RE into other areas of education.[21]

Kenneth Howkins was a lecturer at Balls Park College. Howkins experienced considerable opposition at the college. A Christian had put forward the money to send copies of his book which criticised Goldman to all the colleges of education, but when a copy reached Balls Park it was not put in the library. Jean Holm was head of department and wanted the college to be known as being at the forefront of education. She totally accepted Goldman. Later, after her departure to Homerton College, Howkins was told by her successor that the book was so badly written that if it had been written by one of the students, he would not have accepted it.[22] Howkins was also told that the book was 'banned in the college and banned in the library'. He told one of his colleagues about this who then leaked the information to the student magazine, and an enterprising student got to work. The next edition of the magazine asked students what a college should do if one of its lecturers published a work questioning the new way of teaching a subject in college:

> Was it a) discuss it? Answer: NO.
> Was it b) put it in the library and refer students to it? Answer: NO.
> Was it c) ban the book in the college and the library? Answer: Yes!
> Yes! Yes! Religious Studies Department, over to you.[23]

Howkins was an evangelical Christian and brought a critical mind to work on new approaches. Howkins' later book, *The Challenge of Religious Studies,* incurred the wrath of Howard Marratt. In a review Marratt accused Howkins of indoctrination, failure as a scholar and teacher, biased misrepresentation and casuistry. A letter from Howkins complaining that Marratt had not addressed the main argument of the book, let alone attempt to assess it, was printed in the next edition by John Hull.

Howkins stuck it out, continuing to point out uncomfortable truths to those who held what was becoming the orthodox view. It was not only those of an evangelical persuasion who felt uncomfortable. Keith Wilkes was an Anglican priest and a liberal churchman. He had contributed several times to *Learning for Living* arguing for Christianity to be taught positively. He experienced difficulties as Church people and clergy in particular felt excluded from schools, to be allowed in as exhibits only, preferably all robed up. Those, like himself, who did resist change and attempt to hold the line were made to feel unwelcome and out of place. He therefore made the decision to concentrate his energies on the church school sector.[24] Peter Dawson received abusive letters following his article criticising Goldman. Dawson and others were prepared to raise objections but it was difficult to stand out against what felt like a choreographed hostility.[25] Many simply gave up.

The vogue for the new in colleges
At Balls Park College lecturers were in the habit of taking on new approaches quite uncritically. This could confuse students. One student tried to teach a class of juniors about the afterlife in five different world

religions, all in one lesson. The class teacher (who told Howkins about this) asked the student what she was trying to do. She replied, in some distress, that the previous term Goldman had been all the rage, but now Goldman was out. She did not know what she was supposed to do. In Howkins' view lecturers liked to quote the latest expert, as it made them feel up to date. One of the problems was that lecturers in colleges were not always suitably qualified in theology and education. Jean Holm, for example, had never taught in a school, had experience in journalism and a degree in English. Lack of background in theology and/or education meant that some were not in the best position to be critical of the latest research. Howkins wrote: 'those who follow the cult of novelty must keep changing their ideas, as a novelty cannot remain as such for long'.[26]

Dismissive attitude towards conservative theology
In the view of Peter Dawson it was necessary to hold theologically liberal opinions to be influential in RE. At the time it was common to be dismissive of those holding a theologically conservative point of view. Evangelicals, according to Peter Cousins, were not taken seriously by college lecturers of a more liberal persuasion.[27] The Schools Council Working Paper 44 on primary schools failed to mention any conservative texts in their bibliography, a failure which Howkins took up with them. In view of the welcome given to the ideas of Goldman within the working paper, the failure to list Howkins' own critique of Goldman's work is academically indefensible. Howkins enquired as to why his name had appeared in a list of those contributing to RE in a questionnaire, yet not in the bibliography. He was told that only those books with which the members of the working party agreed were listed.

At Southlands Methodist College in South London, a vogue for liberal theology meant that those of a conservative persuasion were subject to attempts to undermine their faith. In the early 1960s a student was told that 'no intelligent person believed in the literal resurrection of Christ'. This student found herself battling against complacent lecturers who regurgitated half-baked German Old Testament scholarship and for whom Billy Graham, then in his prime, was anathema.[28] Evangelical students at this time found it hard to cope generally with the attacks made on their faith in some colleges; and for this reason the Theological Student's Fellowship (TSF) was set up as a means of supporting such students.

Some Colleges resisted new approaches

However, not all colleges were keen to change. John Hinnells[29] wrote of a degree of resistance from colleges and mentioned one in particular. He said that teachers tended to be more 'open' than the colleges: 'Few teachers at school or college have had the opportunity to study world religions properly. The colleges rarely offer the subject in any serious fashion and are sometimes behind the teachers in their openness. Few readers of ARE [Association for Religious Education] are, I suspect, as educationally backward as a state college in Manchester which still orientates its whole RE syllabus for specialists around the Old Testament (year 1) and the New Testament (year 2) and reflections on the Old and the New (year 3). Not a few of their 'output' come seeking help once they encounter the school situation.'[30]

In the same publication there were details of an in-service training course put on by the school of education at Bristol University together with the department of theology who had been providing theological 'updates' for teachers of religious education for several years. The teachers' concerns determined the content of the course which resulted in six themes. They were:

   The nature of religion and the nature of the Bible
   Celebration and worship
   Religious language
   Science, technology and religion
   Recent developments in the Church
   Ethics and society

The author, Sybil Hodge wrote: 'we deliberately avoided the 'Cook's Tour' approach and felt that study in depth of other faiths demands the cultural context and is catered for by the 'Shap Conference' soak-in course.'[31] This course addressed the questions that pupils asked from the point of view of Christian theology and attempted to answer them in creative ways that received a good response according to her article.

Shap Working Party

A conference was held in 1969 at the Shap Wells Hotel in Westmorland with the title 'Comparative Religion in Education'. At this conference it was decided to set up the Shap Working Party (SWP). Shap's concern was to broaden the curriculum of schools and colleges to include the study of religions other than (but not excluding) Christianity. At first its focus was on the study of comparative religion, sometimes known as CSR, but this was dropped in favour of world religions. Comparison implied a standard against which religions were to be compared and this in the past had been Christianity. The prime movers in Shap did not want to undergird this approach. Shap's original membership of 19 members included 3 university teachers of comparative religion, 7 lecturers in education and 9 school teachers. From the beginning Shap supporters had different motives for their involvement and this in turn meant that it was difficult to develop a philosophy that could undergird their work.

Shap, however, developed a reputation for the energetic promotion of world religions and indeed retains this today. Ninian Smart saw Shap as part of the campaign to change RE. He wrote an 'Epistle to the Shap Chaps'[32] in which he stated: 'the battles which Shap has fought for a wider view of Religious Education may have been victories but a string of victories does not constitute necessarily winning a war'. A Shap report in March 1972 was entitled 'Jobs for the Boys' and expressed the hope that a Shap person might be appointed to a vacancy at Coleraine University. A sense of oneness of purpose was helped by an anniversary dinner held in 1974 at which an Indian meal was enjoyed and members ritually signed a 'Shappati', which with a Shap map of regional groups, was consecrated and reserved for the tenth anniversary dinner.

Shap activities
Shap actively sought to promote their work by sending reports to journals and periodicals. It was hoped that a new periodical dealing with the comparative study of religion, being considered by Oriel Press, would provide a useful organ for publicising Shap. At first one conference per year was held, but this soon grew into five a year, at strategic points up and down the country, Shap, London, Manchester, Coleraine and Stirling. These conferences were intended to give teachers some basic knowledge of non-Christian religions. They held both annual and occasional conferences for teachers which averaged 4 or 5 a year and promoted extra-mural courses at universities. They worked on producing CSE and O level syllabuses for exam boards, set up sub-groups to work on appropriate syllabus development for different age groups, provided resources and publications, etc. Involvement of individual members also went on apace in work on the Schools Council, the General Studies Project, the Manchester Education Service and the Community Relations Council. Regional Shap support groups were set up around the country. In many of these activities they were following precedents set up by CEM, indeed many members of Shap had links with CEM. *Learning for Living* allocated a section to Shap in every edition which allowed them to publish details of courses and other information. Shap ran on a very small budget and had it not been for Borough Road, who undertook much of the administration work, it is unlikely that Shap could have functioned at all.

CEM
In 1970 CEM began to promote the teaching of world religions. It was common practice to introduce something of other religions at the top end of the school, often as a comparison with Christianity. Indeed Kenneth Howkins included teaching on other religions in the early 1960s. What

was different in 1970 was that CEM wanted to bring these religions into the teaching of RE at all stages and with no priority given to Christianity. In September of that year they brought out a series of working papers on the teaching of world religions produced by the CEM teachers' committee: world religions in the primary school, world religions at 13 plus and others. By 1971 the same committee had produced a professional code for an RE teacher. In January 1971 they began a primary mailing to match that already in existence for secondary schools. This was an important initiative in changing RE since it was in the primary school that non-confessional RE was felt to be the most problematic; young children being thought to need an unambiguous presentation rather than a series of options. May 1972 saw the fourth primary mailing and was entitled 'RE in a Multi-Faith Society'.[33] One contributor declared: 'A new approach to the teaching of world religions however, is one of the main elements of the new RE.'[34] Another maintained, speaking of Christianity and Islam: 'In no circumstances could it be the task of the school to adjudicate between them. In school, and in particular in the primary school, we are not concerned to make value judgements about religions.'[35]

ARE

ARE was set up in the late 1960s following an RE teachers' conference in April 1967. In November 1968 a constitution was adopted and an executive committee elected. ARE attracted evangelicals who were unhappy with the theological line taken by CEM. It was aligned with Christian faith and understood professionalism to mean non-alignment with any particular theological position within Christianity. Its bulletins spoke of the need for RE to give a positive Christian approach in the classroom. ARE sponsored a weekend course in 1969 to 'help those who are in contact with young people to find a positive Christian approach to the moral pressures exerted by society'.[36] An early leaflet declared the association to be professional and Christian in character. It went on, prophetically: 'By 1975 the climate of educational opinion concerning RE may be very different from that which obtains today. Now is the time to lay strategic foundations which, with God's guidance, will enable us to face the future with confidence.'[37]

However, Peter Lefroy Owen, the secretary whose energies matched those of Howard Marratt, soon insisted that the profession must not be aligned to any one faith. Kenneth Howkins saw Lefroy Owen evolve under his eyes. There was a degree of bad feeling at the time amongst members of the association over the matter. Lefroy Owen came to believe that ARE could promote the new professionalism in RE in a way that CEM could not, aligned as it was to Christian faith. So he took steps to deny that the association was in any way to be described as Christian. ARE was mentioned in a Shap publication as linked with Christian faith, whereupon Lefroy Owen

wrote to Shap: 'The ARE Bulletin is mentioned and given a warm write-up
. . . , but the effect is spoiled by the addition of the contentious words
"Christian basis" . . . put in the context of a professional subject teaching
association, the personal belief systems of its members are irrelevant, and
the assertion is thus open to misunderstanding and is potentially damaging
to the ARE.' [38] It was Lefroy Owen who insisted that the CEM could not be
a truly professional association because of the first word of its title
(Christian).[39] Nonetheless, ARE continued to attract many evangelical
Christians disaffected with the CEM. It acted as a rival to CEM, doing
exactly what CEM had always done, issuing bulletins and working papers
with articles and news of initiatives, much of a high quality. Another early
initiative was the recommendation to set up a National RE Research and
Development Centre.[40] One of the main aims of the association was the
setting up of teachers' groups up and down the country with the aim of
increasing their sense of ownership and control of the subject, an aim in
which they were largely unsuccessful.

The RE Council

The RE Council (REC) was set up in November 1973 after a year's
preparation. A small group was convened by Howard Marratt and included
Edwin Cox, Brian Gates, Rabbi Hugo Gryn, a Sikh teacher of Geography
from Leicester, and Stewart Sutherland. Meetings were often held in Gryn's
synagogue. It began with 35 organisations affiliated to the Council. The
aims of the REC were to promote mutual understanding between member
bodies, to work out together what the nature and practice of RE should be,
to provide a co-ordinated voice to those in authority in education and to
encourage research. Membership was confined to corporate bodies having
an interest in the teaching of RE. Two categories of membership were set
up, the 'confessional' representing church interests and religious bodies
and the 'professional' representing educational bodies. An executive
committee was elected annually, its structure being balanced between
'educational' and 'confessional' categories of membership. Edwin Cox was
the first chairman with Colin Alves and Peter Lefroy Owen acting as joint
honorary secretaries.

Thus the RE Council from the first enshrined the divide between the
professional and the confessional. This situation could be confusing. Was
the Catholic Education Council (or one could cite the Church of England
Board of Education) to be assigned to the former or the latter category for
example? The Council of Christians and Jews would seem to fit into the
latter category, but did this mean that they had no interest in education? In
practice what seems to have happened is that members sent one
representative to stand for them as a 'confessional' and one as a
'professional'. Clearly the divide was artificial and hard to sustain. The

significant point was, however, that a major new body in the RE world, which acted as a pressure group upon Government, was reinforcing the basic premise that an educational approach ruled out the confessional and vice versa.

Conclusion

Everything was in place for a major push forward. RE journals had come into line, along with major opinion-formers in the profession. Strong voices in some colleges were insisting on change, and where there was resistance it was belittled or ignored. A National RE centre with a major remit for world religions, along with the work of Shap, meant that resources were being gathered together for classroom use and the provision of training in the religions, now assumed to be a necessary part of the RE teacher's armoury. CEM had put its weight behind world religions and ARE had abandoned its early Christian stance. A body representing a wide variety of religious groupings had been brought into existence founded on the need for an 'educational' approach which, it was assumed, could flourish independently of any particular religion or point of view. The next chapter will tell the story of how teachers were persuaded to follow suit.

Chapter 5
Pushing the new Approaches

Most teachers in the 1970s were trained to teach Christianity with some comparative religion thrown in for older pupils. How could they be persuaded to change? A basic textbook was needed that would set out a theoretical and practical approach to the sort of RE now favoured. Michael Grimmitt, a lecturer at Westhill College in Birmingham, published just such a text in 1973.

What Can I do in RE?[1]
The title poignantly summed up the feeling of many teachers at the time whose confidence in what they were doing in RE had been undermined by the questionings of the 1960s and the plethora of new approaches of the 1970s. It was called 'a classic of the new RE' by one reviewer.[2] It was a huge success, being reprinted in 1976 and 1977, followed by a second edition in 1978 and a further reprint in 1982.

The book began with a clear exposition of what you could not do in RE. Grimmitt's answer was anything and everything that it had been customary to do in the past. RE required a total rethink. RE was producing children who knew little about Christian faith and who were, by and large, disinterested, even antagonistic. Nonetheless the faith would form a large part of the syllabus and indeed much of his practical section looks exactly the same as the sort of work that was going on in the 1960s.

So what was different? Grimmitt wanted children to be taught to see Religion (he generally wrote it with a capital letter) as 'a unique mode of thought and awareness' into which they needed to be initiated as part of their development as human beings. An approach which was educational, he argued, must initiate the young into what is considered to be worthwhile and which will contribute in specific ways to the forming of personality. It must offer a cognitive perspective which is a way of integrating knowledge into a whole and it must be done in ways that do not override pupil autonomy and involve the pupil willingly in the process of learning. This understanding of education was perfectly in line with the RE of the past. The difference lay in what it was that pupils were to be initiated into. For Grimmitt 'Religion' was non-controversial whereas Christianity, being a contested belief, was not. Christianity, he contended, was but one aspect of a larger form of knowledge (the Religious form of knowledge) and thus an RE based on Christianity would be partial.

But the concept 'Religion' was itself contested and it was not clear what the key concepts or structures of such a form of knowledge were: What were the core beliefs, values and attitudes into which pupils were to be initiated? In fact Grimmitt based his approach on Smart's six dimensions, working them into his own scheme together with selections from Goldman. At one point he acknowledged that his work was exploratory and unproven but reflected that it was better to risk failure with a new approach than continue with one that had failed. Phenomenology, Grimmitt argued, offered a way of teaching RE that allowed the expression of religious experience in the classroom. Ironically, for years Christian teachers of RE had avoided such a thing. Now Grimmitt encouraged teachers to fill their lessons with the forbidden fruit: 'RE, at least with primary school children, thus becomes a matter of immersing pupils in the spirit of a religion by letting them participate in and enjoy the excitement and drama of its stories and ritual . . . in order to give them a feeling of how man responds to his awareness of the divine.'[3] The examples given related closely to Christian experience. Forgiveness was emphasised, love, service and self-giving. The concepts of 'Religion' had a disconcerting tendency (given the rejection of the view that RE should *teach* Christianity) to exhibit Christian thinking.

Health warnings about 'confessional' resources

New classroom textbooks were urgently needed. Howard Marratt wrote: 'An outstanding weakness of many textbooks was their "defensive" attitude and their tendency to present Christianity as the 'superior faith' – whereas, in the main, teachers themselves were anxious to be objective and to show the value of each religion.'[4] In 1970 Colin Alves, book reviews editor of *Learning for Living*, began to vet all new books, materials and syllabuses for their 'confessional nature'.

Which books are 'confessional'?
Three years on, Alves was still having to contend with books that did not conform to new standards: 'not every educational publisher, or confessionalist publisher come to that, seems to be aware of the implications of the new situation . . . and as a result, *Learning for Living* is still being asked to review a whole range of books which are very difficult to fit into the new religious education scene. It is for this reason that I have decided to extend this edition of *Booknews* and look at virtually every book which has been sent recently for review.'[5]

This appears to have been a chastening experience for him. He began by admitting the difficulty of deciding which books were confessional and which were not. He was quite clear that the attempt to instil beliefs, whether Christian, religious or non-religious, rendered a text confessional. This meant that Alves wanted material to be presented in the form of an extract or what a person happened to believe. Taken to a logical conclusion, however, it ruled out a book that presented a sustained argument for anything, however balanced, or however many alternative views it considered. It allowed only those books to be commended that refrained from coming to a conclusion and made no attempt to persuade their readers. So Alves advised of a book by the American evangelical scholar, Os Guinness, that it should be for the personal use of a teacher only, as 'his purpose . . . is to show us the "bankruptcy of humanism" '.[6] The final book in this long review was a class text, said to be particularly unsuitable for classroom use because it provided Christian answers to 'Christian-type' questions, despite the fact that the questions were 'actual problems identified by the pupils themselves'.[7] Alves commented that 'the strictly non-confessionalist understanding of religious education has still not yet been grasped'. [8]

A commentary by R.K. Harrison was criticised because the author at times spoke 'as Professor Harrison, not simply as an interpreter of Jeremiah'.[9] The New Testament scholar A.M. Hunter was criticised for falling into personal comment on his material. Equally any attempt at Christian exegesis of the Old Testament was inadmissible. Derek Kidner 'interprets them [the Psalms] in the sense of imposing a Christian exegesis on the text'.[10] But the biblical scholar who refuses to interpret the Psalms in the light of Christian thought is not being neutral; he is refusing the validity of such an interpretation. He is either taking a Jewish stance or a reductionist approach that allows no room for progressive revelation.

Alves also rejected books that made an attempt to apply knowledge. So John Stott's commentary on 2 Timothy was said to be a careful, clear exposition of the text but must be rejected for class use because it went on to 'apply' the text to life today, rather than just 'elucidate' it. It might be thought that there was a theological agenda here and that what was being objected to was conservative theology. Certainly, Alves favoured the liberal historico-critical view of the Bible. However, Alves could find fault with more liberal approaches too. So a book about Taize, the work of the theologian John McQuarrie and the Roman Catholic writer Rosemary Haughton were all put under suspicion of confessionalism.

It was not just Christian confessionalism that worried Alves. He showed concern about Owen Cole's book *A Sikh Family in Britain*. It presented a very positive view of the religion. Was this not also going beyond the bounds of neutrality? And what was he to say about a pack produced by Help the Aged? He wanted to present it to children as a good and honourable cause to adopt, but worried that this would cross over the line of neutrality and suggest to children that certain actions were right and other actions wrong.

Other reviewers

Garth Read rejected *How People Worship* by A.E. Perry because it made judgements like 'with good reason', 'very aptly' and included an instructional piece on Christian prayer. He said that in this book educational aims had taken a back seat.[11] Later on Geoffrey Robson said that a Schools Council Publication, *The Man from Nazareth,* was hard to justify on educational grounds because Jesus was presented exclusively from a committed Christian standpoint. This book, with its 'blatant Christian assumptions' should not have seen the light of day in his opinion.[12] Robson warned that a series from Edward Arnold treated the question of myth in such a way that the pupil was told that the true meaning was to be found in the Bible even though the series contained stories from non-Christian faiths.[13] Rita Tyler noted Parrinder's evident sympathy for African traditional religion. She said that he 'does not write from the standpoint of an agnostic and sociologist'.[14] Sometimes books were criticised because they presented only Christian teaching. John Rankin disliked two books because they were too preoccupied with Christian things. A book by Joan Tooke was criticised because of its 'constant reversion to biblical themes'.[15] And was it fair to say of a book with the title *Jesus in our Age* that it directed 'too firmly towards a correct Christian answer'? [16] Michael Grimmitt criticised a book for interpreting the natural world theistically for young children but said that not to do so would be to assume a humanist view of the world. He recommended avoiding the topic of the natural world until children were old enough to handle different interpretations, but said he was 'open to correction' on the matter.[17]

The desire to be fair could lead to an inability to make any negative judgement at all. Roger Homan reviewed *Christian Deviation* by Horton Davies. He said: 'Professor Davies always makes the claim that he has tried to be fair to the religious movements he has examined, and in this edition there are signs not only that he has tried harder than ever but also that he is now succeeding. For instance, he no longer describes the Mormon Joseph Smith as "a leader with a powerful imagination" but as "a gifted leader": nor as "barely literate" but now, more kindly, as "relatively unlettered".'[18] Homan went on: 'like Horton Davies, Professor Hoekema is not content to be descriptive: both men feel it incumbent upon them to place the Christian groups they study along a right-wrong continuum and to attempt point-by-point refutations of their system of beliefs. However the dialectical approach appears to be tempered by the current fashion for ecumenism, and the result is heartening for those who look for objectivity.'[19] But Homan's 'objectivity' might well be termed lack of discrimination.

Ultimately the attempt to identify 'confessional' books was quietly given up. This left ordinary teachers in some confusion. They were still told, in serious tones, to avoid confessional texts, but it was very difficult to identify them.

Agreed Syllabuses

Ninian Smart's working party had studied the newer agreed syllabuses and found all to be essentially Christian documents. In January 1971 Donald Horder, a member of the WP 36 working group, criticised two supplements to agreed syllabuses where they assumed Christian commitment and praised them where they did not. Horder complained of 'biblical claustrophobia' and of 'the underlying assumption that RE equals scripture'.[20] In November 1973, John Hull, aware of the problem of confessional texts highlighted by Alves, and worried that teachers were engaging in a disguised form of Christian nurture, wrote: 'a basic change in the nature of the Agreed Syllabuses is called for. Previously, the agreeing parties agreed that what the syllabus taught was true. Now they can only agree that . . . it is worth teaching.'[21] It must have seemed an uphill task to get the syllabus conferences to change. Behind the scenes, moves were made (I give details in the next chapter) to bring about a change in the law and hand control to teachers' groups.

Examination syllabuses

John Elliot reviewed examination syllabuses. He surveyed six current CSE syllabuses and found that all six 'reflected a dominantly confessional approach to religious education'.[22] All were unsatisfactory because all assumed the truth of Christianity. He advised that the teacher must remain impartial as between different religions and viewpoints. CEM set up groups of teachers to study mode 1 CSE syllabuses. Elliot concluded that 'the majority either share the views I expressed or at least think they have to be taken seriously. This is some evidence for the belief that there is an increasingly substantial proportion of religious education teachers who are rejecting or questioning the confessional approach, and seeking aims which are justified "educationally".' [23] By contrast, in his opinion: 'the majority of CSE boards have hardly begun to accommodate and consider the debate.'[24] However, when Elliot attempted to pin down what was wrong with the existing syllabuses and what, by contrast, would put them right, it is difficult to see much difference. He wanted a syllabus which 'permits two radically different conceptions of a man's relationship to the universe to enter into a fruitful dialectic'.[25] To the extent that contemporary life was secular, by including questions which required the pupil to relate biblical teaching to life today, the syllabuses (labelled 'confessional') were doing what Elliot wanted them to do.

CEM wrote a paper for the benefit of CSE boards, which set out principles governing the choice of content for public exams:

· Knowledge of the plurality of belief and multi-cultural context of society

· Familiarity with a specific tradition, e.g. Christianity, Judaism, Islam
· The importance of Christianity in western culture

Hogbin commented: 'these presuppose the study of religion as an area of knowledge with its own criteria of judgement and theoretical understanding which provide its educational justification'.[26] This, of course, was the problem.

Publishing houses

It took time before publishing houses came on board. In 1977, Michael Grimmitt took the unusual step of prefacing his reviews with a lengthy rebuke for those publishing houses which were failing to keep up with trends in the profession. The Religious Education Press (REP) and Edward Arnold were said to be restricting curriculum development by producing old-fashioned books such as the Visual Old and New Testament series (Patston) and Horton's workcards on biblical topics. These were said to merely 'occupy' children.[27] Educational, rather than financial, considerations should predominate, he told them. However other publishers had changed their tune by this time and were offering books on world religions. REP was resisting current trends for the simple reason that they didn't agree with them. John Halsall, educational director at REP, stated: 'The REP philosophy is that any system of morality must be based on an act of faith of some kind, even if this is the secular creed enshrined in the United Nations Charter. Further, the best foundations for morality are to be found in the great creeds of the great world religions. Since we happen to be in the western world, the greatest emphasis should be placed on the Christian religion . . . religious education can provide appeals both to the reason and to the emotions – to the whole person.'[28]

TV programmes

Audio-visual material was always in demand for classroom teaching and so it was important that the new RE gained a hearing there too. Peter Lefroy Owen reported in 1972 that the BBC was slower than the IBA (forerunner of the ITV) to adopt the new ideas. He blamed the fact that religious programmes were passed to and from the schools and the religious broadcasting teams, and were presumed to have to be responsive to a Christian audience. Speaking of IBA's Believe it or not[29] series, Lefroy Owen said: 'It is probably one of the first attempts ever made to put out a series directly related to the principles of the "new RE" in the context of a public education system. The BBC have yet to take their first faltering steps in this field (how unadventurous can you be – BBC?).'[30] However, by the summer of 1977, just as the publishers were coming into line, so were the producers of educational television programmes. Desmond Brennan stated that Ninian Smart had been acting as adviser of a series on world religions which was scheduled for 13 programmes.[31]

Teachers reluctant to take on new approaches

Grimmitt wrote that the major difficulty to be faced was the teachers. He wrote: 'the need for openness and breadth of vision that the phenomenological approach demands requires an adjustment in attitude on the part of many teachers. The change in emphasis and content away from Christianity towards Religion is likely to be seen by many teachers as unnecessary and undesirable. The acceptance of World Religions an *integral part* of RE *at all stages* is likely to take time and be the cause of disputes and disagreement among school staffs.'[32]

The Schools Council Primary RE Project published their recommendations in 1972, following a survey of 213 primary schools. The report found that a few teachers regarded it as their duty to 'instil Christian beliefs into the children in their charge'.[33] Others effectively communicated this aim in practice: 'Other teachers, by using religious words without explaining them, telling Bible stories uncritically, and engaging children in specifically Christian worship, are suggesting to children that they ought to adopt a particular point of view and accept one body of belief rather than another.'[34] The 'Goldman' effect was wearing off and teachers were reverting to previous methods of teaching the Bible.

Peter Jarvis, a lecturer at Dudley College, surveyed the aims of primary teachers in the county area of Warley. He found teachers reverting to teaching the Bible in the old ways, despite all they had been taught at college. The overall picture was of a traditional, Christian and biblically based RE lesson. Outside speakers were all Christian functionaries and the 'confessional' religious broadcasts were widely used.[35] Shap reported that teachers were still resistant to change and that attendance at in-service training on world religions was poor: 'we must beware of thinking that the movement towards "Shap ideals" is well under way. It is not. We are not by any means out of the wood yet. At university, college and school level, many (most?) are still unwilling, unsure, ignorant, badly equipped, or "faint but pursuing."'[36] Jack Hogbin stated that 'the reception of Working Paper 36 by teachers of RE has disappointed many who hoped for a broadening of the approach to the study of religion in schools'.[37] He said that where this was the case it was generally because of commitment to Christianity. In the same edition Grimmitt spoke of the 'persistent interest on the part of many teachers in using biblical material.'[38] Teachers in at least one authority, Lincoln, showed open resistance: 'as has happened in Lincoln, there may be misgivings, particularly amongst teachers who are deeply committed personally, about the omission of biblical content.'[39] In 1974 a panel of teachers working in seven comprehensive schools in Hartlepool published a list of aims in RE similar to those of the Durham Report. They referred to opinion polls which showed that the bulk of the population claimed allegiance to Christianity, conformed to social customs of Christian background and were guided by Christian principles.[40] However it seemed that in London it was different. Kenneth Hyde, chief inspector at the Inner London Education Authority (ILEA), wrote: 'There seems to be a growing consensus among teachers that religious education involves a comprehensive study of religion.'[41]

Efforts to bring RE teachers into line

In-service training

One answer was to increase in-service training. An REC document, 'What Future for the Agreed Syllabus?'[42] argued for extensive in-service training so that existing teachers could adapt their methods to the new concept of the subject. Glyn Davies said: 'One reason that the evangelistic minority is allowed to exercise so much influence is that many teachers feel themselves ill-equipped to cope with the new RE, however dissatisfied they may feel with the old.'[43] What was needed in his view was 'widespread training and retraining of teachers capable of introducing children to the full riches of world religion as a universal phenomenon'.[44] He expected conflict, to which the right sort of training was the answer: 'A great increase in in-service training is surely an urgent priority in the ideological conflict which will determine the future of RE.'[45] To the idea that Christian teachers had 'something to teach about God' Davies had this to say: 'I do not believe that this confessionalist approach should be tolerated in a state educational system.'[46]

J.G. Harris, a lecturer at Caerleon College, argued that the necessary changes were so profound and so important that consideration should be given to making such training compulsory for RE teachers. He wrote: 'it is not outside the bounds of possibility that such attendance–especially in a time of rapid change-should be considered as a statutory requirement as well as a right'.[47] The spectre of compulsion now haunted the teacher of religion. Harris instructed teachers to adopt a less didactic role and to become more adept at the role of counsellor and advisor than that of teacher. He wrote: 'The teacher is much less the person who knows all the answers and much more the counsellor, adviser and stimulator to those who carry out their own exploration into the religious dimension and devise their own approaches (albeit under winsome guidance).'[48]

But what exactly was RE changing to? Harris wrote:

If we are to see an increase in such courses . . . a well defined structure needs to be developed providing a proper incentive for teachers and schools. Clearly the content of the courses will be a major consideration, with some attention to the need to keep teachers up to date with developments both in religion (a hybrid term in this context) and in educational theory and practice. The case for greater professionalism in the teaching of religion will, in many instances, call for a new style approach. This must arise out of the needs of the classroom and of teachers, meeting in consortia, who see the need for this and press for further specialist help to achieve it. They will embody more of an experimental workshop pattern than a formal lecture group, for progress will come through the attempt to work out improved professional methods and approaches.[49]

It seemed that the new RE was still at draft stage in 1973.

A major survey of RE teaching in 245 secondary schools in Lancashire was carried out in the early 1970s. The adviser for Lancashire, Ian Birnie, called a conference in November 1972 to discuss the situation. The survey had found that nine out of ten syllabuses were biblical and traditional. Birnie seemed keen to change this: one of the two main areas for in-service training was related to the weak commitment to world religions found amongst the Lancashire teachers. Robin Shepherd, a CEM regional secretary, described the typical teacher as a moderate Christian chap who cared about his pupils and had had a strong exposure to church in his youth. Shepherd said that it seemed inappropriate to ask of these folk whether they were professional or confessional.[50] They just got on with teaching what they knew and discussing it with pupils. However, the new RS was fast being erected into a creed and the 'moderate churchmanship of Lancashire is retreating before it'.[51] Colin Alves, was depressed but reflected that change could come quickly. He urged that those involved should press forward hard 'in the hope that the moment of breakthrough may now be near'.[52]

The role of *Learning for Living*

The journal sometimes spoke directly to teachers in a voice of authority. Alves issued a reminder to those RE teachers 'who still present Christianity in the belief that it is true and in the hope that it will convince' that they had 'a professional obligation to alter their approach'.[53] Hull wrote of the 'crisis of conscience of the Christian religious educator'. He needed convincing theologically that it is right to jump into the Ark with the 'clean and the unclean beasts'.[54] Persuading Christian teachers to remain at the helm would be a 'major pastoral problem'.[55] He could lose patience however. In 1977 he wrote about hostile Christians who pressed for the old way of teaching RE, wanted Christian nurture and rejected new approaches. Such ill-informed teachers, he advised, should read the CEM statement that showed how modern RE was justified from a Christian point of view.[56]

Justifying the 'new RE' to Christian teachers

Here I set out arguments made at the time to persuade Christian teachers that it was right to teach the 'new RE'.

The View of Colin Alves

Alves published a book in 1972 called *The Christian in Education.*[57] It was addressed to the Christian RE teacher. It is a masterly book, written to clarify the situation and give help to Christians worried about introducing other religions in the classroom. He started from the position that, in matters to do with religion, one may not claim to be in possession of the truth since it is beyond rational grasp. Teaching anything as true, whether it be Christian faith, secularism or any other point of view, was not admissible. He wrote: 'The secularist just as much as the fundamentalist needs to keep his exclusivist beliefs firmly in check if his RE teaching is to be truly open-ended.'[58]

This, he said, left the teacher of RE with one of two choices: take a relativist stance or set aside (in the sense of bracket out) his or her own beliefs: 'A Christian of any other persuasion (than that of relativism) has to take the specific step of deliberately setting on one side his own beliefs about the comparative value of other religions before he can start to teach from a properly open basis.'[59] This would not be possible for the Christian who believed that God had revealed the truth to mankind. Such a teacher will 'feel impelled to teach the truth to his pupils. He will of course want to use the most effective means to this end and these may well include methods which appear to be "open" methods, such as discussion or comparative study of beliefs, but these will be employed solely to make his own pupils more receptive to "the truth" when it emerges, and he will not count his teaching as successful unless ultimately all his pupils come to see the truth as he sees it.'[60]

For Alves, it was permissible to set the truth of Christian doctrines to one side, since his view was that God does not reveal *knowledge*, so much as a *relationship* (my italics) with Himself. The Christian could be sure that God had acted in history but the record of God's acts (the Bible) was imperfect and no absolute reliance could be placed on it. Christianity offered 'vehicles of vision' but not 'the truth'. The Christian therefore, like all others, was engaged in an exploration. God was continually making himself known to human beings in diverse ways and what mattered was that pupils were encouraged to search and be open to new insights. A teacher would be successful if pupils 'come to recognise that they too have embarked on a continuing exploration, a deepening of insights, and have not already attempted to settle behind fixed walls (either of belief or unbelief) such as would prevent any future movement or development of awareness.'[61] This seemed to give permission to launch pupils off, once again, on uncharted voyages of spiritual discovery. Christianity must take its place alongside other 'revelations', revelations which too must accept their place as 'vehicles of vision' only. But the claim that God makes Himself known via diverse revelations is itself a claim to know the truth. Alves, perhaps, would not count his teaching successful unless pupils came to see the truth as he saw it. Yet those Christians who believed that the Christian revelation was unique were required to set such a belief to one side, and refrain from pressing it.

The View of John Hull

The issue did not go away. John Hull argued that, as part of education generally, RE rested upon the virtues of rationality, sensitivity and integrity. RE required commitment to these educational virtues and openness to unconstrained exploration. These two virtues were then said to be characteristic of Christian faith. The image of the pilgrim people in the Bible was a type of the atmosphere in the RE classroom: 'The attitude of openness, trust and hope, symbolized by the Biblical image of pilgrimage, is characteristically but not exclusively Christian.'[62] Christian theology was always on the move, open to new insights and the need to be self-critical: 'the self critical theological enterprise of the Church (surely one of the glories of Christianity) and the idea of a critical, open education flow from the same complex of Christian ideas'.[63] Christianity would therefore welcome an RE that was open to exploring other religions. So the CEM statement said: 'It is proper, therefore, for the Christian Education Movement to continue to promote religious education including an open, critical exploration of, for example, world religions, religion and life in both history and contemporary society, and to do so not in spite of its Christian position but because of it.'[64]

Few would want to argue with the view that Christian theology requires openness to criticism and to lay its tradition open to new insights as history moves on and presents new challenges. But this is not the same as entirely open-ended exploration. In Christian thinking openness to the new does not mean abandoning the tradition but rather allowing the tradition to look again at what it believes in the light of new insights and knowledge. In other words, openness in Christian faith is a particular kind of openness which must always be related to the holding of a tradition. The openness that Hull had in mind was quite a different thing. It seemed to require openness without commitment to a particular tradition and it is not clear that the Christian who held to the truth of his tradition would be able to engage in this. It will be noted that the commitment Hull accepted in relation to RE was to the academic virtues of rationality, sensitivity and integrity. Such virtues were compatible with a commitment to Christianity but were not a substitute for it. It seemed to require teachers to sit lightly to their commitment to Christian truth. And it was this issue that some Christians were having difficulty with.

A Groundplan for the Study of Religion (1977)[65]

What was also needed was a coherent alternative to the positive teaching of Christianity. *A Groundplan for the Study of Religion* was intended to meet that particular need. Some of the best minds of the RE profession worked for three years before publishing. Colin Alves spoke in the preface of the lengthy discussions which took place at every meeting and of labouring together over the report. The working party of 14 included inspectors of RE, heads of RE, headteachers, teachers in colleges and universities, the director of the National Society's RE centre together with his Roman Catholic counterpart. Ninian Smart and Paul Hirst were members, as were John Hull, John Elliot and Edwin Cox. A phalanx indeed.

The working party attempted to set out areas of central importance in the study of religion: the essential concepts or knowledge necessary to an understanding of religion, together with criteria for evaluating its claims. What they produced was in fact limited; they acknowledged that their work was both tentative and only a groundplan. Indeed, considerable emphasis was put on what *Groundplan* did not offer. It was not a syllabus, it did not consider the important area of how to relate religious knowledge to the experience of pupils. It did not offer a taxonomy of religious objectives or even attempt to map the content of a curriculum. Rather it outlined 'categories of possible curriculum objectives'.[66] It claimed only to map the sort of areas that needed to be covered if proper study of an educational nature was to take place.

While the publication contained 57 pages the groundplan itself covered a mere three pages. It was divided up into sections: knowledge, understanding and evaluation. Knowledge covered the context of the tradition being studied, the main persons and events of the tradition, different modes of expression, major beliefs and practices, myths, ethical demands, rituals and primary documents. Understanding included ideas about the natural world in the tradition being studied, the nature of man, ultimate reality, emotions connected with being a follower, ritual acts, mission and witness, devotional practices, etc. Evaluation of the tradition being studied included knowledge of differing interpretations of the tradition, the use of different criteria to judge the tradition, and a personal evaluation.

Despite its title and its own stated aims, *Groundplan* concerned the study of religious traditions rather than 'religion'. The teacher was to use it as a check to make sure that all relevant aspects of a tradition had been considered. No attempt was made to set out particular attitudes to be developed other than those necessary to begin the study. The teacher might not inculcate any attitudes at all, since this would be to evangelise or predispose pupils to one religion rather than another. Neither did they set out particular skills unique to religious studies. This area was said to be underdeveloped: 'Little work has been done on the possibility of identifying the skills (if there are any) that are common to *all* forms of religious understanding, the skills characteristic of what Philip Phenix has called "the synoptic realm of meaning".' [67]

Groundplan offered a checklist of areas of study to be undertaken when examining individual religions. No doubt this was useful. What the *Groundplan* did not offer was a map of the concepts, skills and attitudes relevant to a form of knowledge called religion. Indeed nothing was said about religion at all. Exactly what cognitive perspective was to be gained by such study was not addressed. Clearly it might be expected that pupils would know a great deal about religions by the end of schooling. But which religions and why? And what meaning were pupils to assign to the word 'religion'?

Conclusion

A clear agenda to end the Christian hegemony in RE was vigorously promoted by certain members of the RE profession. Concerted efforts were made by key individuals and organisations to influence publishers, TV, the exam boards and teachers. Henceforth any attempt to teach the Christian faith as true would be firmly rejected. This meant that an element of imposition was felt, and not just by those who believed that the change was for the worse. Robin Shepherd, commenting on the 1975 Birmingham agreed syllabus, seemed to make a plea for the old days when 'we ourselves tasted our food and selected our durables with solemn joy . . . [now] we must read words about the goods to know if they be good for us'.[68] D.E. Bennett, who worked for CEM between 1962 and 1968, stated that there was great freedom at that time to explore and develop different forms of RE.[69] This changed in the early 1970s when a party line began to appear and multi-culturalism seemed to be imposed on everyone.[70]

The approach taken by reviewers amounted to censorship of any text or resource that betrayed a committed viewpoint. Their eye was on Christian commitment but because this could not be stated, it was commitment itself that was attacked. This bleak outlook was given up when it was realised that it ruled out just about every book of worth. Attempts were made to reassure Christians of the value of the 'new RE' but they were not convincing. It might have been possible to mount an argument that there was some truth in some religions, perhaps following a Logos theology, but this was difficult when commitment and belief were prohibited.

Efforts were made to mount a coherent alternative, but *Groundplan* proved to be a disappointment. Nonetheless they pressed on. In addition to persuading teachers of the need to change, it was necessary to do something about the agreed syllabuses which determined what teachers could do in the classroom.

Chapter 6
Taking Control of RE
from the Churches

Syllabus conferences were (and are) part of the tradition of RE in England and Wales. This chapter sets out this tradition of RE and explores efforts to remove control of the subject from the churches and the syllabus conferences.

RE before 1870

Before 1870 free education for English and Welsh children was largely provided by the National Society, an Anglican Society, and the non-conformist British and Foreign Schools Society. Religious education and daily worship were part of the remit of these schools. By 1870, despite Government grants, it was clear that the churches could not provide for the increasing numbers of children. The 1870 Forster Act provided for school boards (precursors of the local education authorities) to build and maintain schools. The tradition of religion in education was continued, but not without difficulty. Denominational rivalry was eased by the Cowper Temple clause, enabling a compromise to be agreed: board schools could begin each day with worship and teach religious education, but nothing distinctive of a particular denomination was taught. The years after 1870 were dogged by controversy, however; RE was sometimes reduced to the mere reading of the Bible for fear of contentious interpretation.

To overcome this problem the first syllabus conference was set up in 1923,[1] when teachers and representatives of the Churches came together in West Riding with the blessing of the local board, to agree a syllabus for the schools in their area. This meant that principles, aims and methods could be established for the subject in a thorough manner. It also set a precedent of local determination of RE by agreement, which continues today.

The 1944 Education Act

The 1944 Act built on and strengthened previous practice. It made it compulsory for local education authorities (LEAs) to set up an Agreed Syllabus Conference (ASC). The ASC was made up of four committees, each committee having one vote. All committees had to agree a syllabus for it to be adopted. Committee A was made up of representatives of the non-Anglican churches, Committee B the Church of England, Committee C the teachers' representatives and Committee D the LEA. RE and a daily act of collective worship were made compulsory. In Wales there were three committees, the Church in Wales being included with the other churches. As had been the case since 1870, parents could withdraw their children from either classroom instruction or worship or both, and teachers could also withdraw from worship and/or giving instruction. LEAs were given the option of setting up a committee, called the Standing Advisory Council on Religious Education (SACRE). The SACRE was a body whose role was to oversee the implementation of the syllabus and give advice on RE and collective worship.[2]

The Act and the clauses on RE were the result of a three-year consultation, often referred to as a settlement or partnership between the Government of the day and the churches. It established the 'dual system', whereby the state undertook to support both church and county schools in differing proportions. The religious question was of particular significance since many schools at the time were still owned and run by the churches. Many of these schools were in poor condition and could not maintain either their buildings or sufficient staff and so they welcomed state finance, although they were at the same time worried that the schools would lose their religious purpose under control of the state. Butler's solution was to allow for the churches to have representation on governing bodies of county schools and to guarantee that the religious needs of children would be met by making RE and worship compulsory. The provisions of the Cowper Temple clause of 1870 were taken over and applied to the new situation where many of the church schools, particularly the non-conformist schools, had now joined the state system.

The Act did not specify that RE should be Christian. It was felt that a court would have difficulty making a judgement on a theological definition if a challenge were made to the effect that a syllabus was not of a Christian nature. Furthermore, it was thought that syllabus conferences, with strong representation of the churches, would use their veto to make sure that syllabuses were based on the teaching of Christianity. However there were schools where there were significant numbers of Jewish children. The word 'religious' was sufficiently flexible to allow for Jewish children to have a syllabus agreed that was suitable for them.[3] Syllabuses agreed between the years 1944 and 1971 show that this is how the law was understood for the years immediately following the passing of the Act. Syllabuses were essentially introduction to the Christian faith, with some treatment of other religions at the upper end of the school.

Churches should give up control of RE

In an editorial in the summer of 1973 John Hull commented on the major emphasis that had been placed on world religions in RE since 1970. Insufficient attention had been given to the 'subtle change in the relationship between the religions and religious education. The religions have always been thought of as the sponsors of RE. The religions have controlled the content of religious education. They have done this either through having their own schools or (as in the case of the Church of England and other Christian denominations) through their control of the Agreed Syllabuses granted by the 1944 Education Act'.[4] The change in relationship would be hard for the religions to swallow but swallow they must: 'It is not pleasant to discover that religious educators, the very ones who might be expected to be the front line troops, are no longer willing to identify themselves first of all with the interests of the religious institution or to place as their number one priority the spreading of religious faith. When for centuries you have had power to bind and loose it is very humiliating to be told that you are only a very interesting object of study.'[5]

Hull declared that it would be a 'serious injustice' not to treat the religions as in principle alike: 'the monopoly of Christianity is thus broken and from this break flow all the questions about the place of Christianity in religious education today'.[6] He castigated religions and ideologies for always wanting to take control of education to promote their own particular point of view. All religions, not just Christianity, were cast in the role of control merchants needing to be tamed. A similar argument occurred in a chapter of a book published by the National Foundation for Educational Research: 'the effect of removing religious education from its traditional context within Christian nurture is that there is now in principle no closer relation between Christianity and religious education than there is between Islam and religious education.'[7]

Others sought to drive a wedge between the churches and RE. Lefroy Owen wrote to the editor of the Times Educational Supplement (TES), complaining about the way the TES handled RE: 'Forgive me for illustrating my point from the last inset of 9 April 1971: page 39 includes the title, in large bold letters, "Religious Education" yet the article in the front page is called "Can the Church survive?" The fact is that the educational aspects of a curriculum subject called "RE" are quite unrelated to the survival or otherwise of the established church, or any minority religion for that matter.'[8] McClure's response to ARE was to say that their view was a minority one and that 'most educationists still hang on to the approach that RE is the Church's fifth column into the maintained system'.[9] Lefroy Owen invited his readers to write in: 'If you think Stuart McClure seems to have as yet an insufficient understanding of the present position, or if you feel the TES has any responsibility in helping to give cognisance to the unashamedly educational viewpoint, why not drop him a line and tell him what you think?'[10]

Furthermore, church representatives would not have sufficient knowledge to prescribe what should be taught. This view was expressed in 1971 by John Sutcliffe, Secretary for Christian Education for the Congregational Church in England and Wales: 'the more religious education develops into an exploration of world religions and cultural attitudes the less church people will be competent to collaborate on Agreed Syllabus

Committees were these . . . still thought desirable'.[11]

ARE submitted a statement to the meeting set up to look into the creation of a national RE council (REC). Lefroy Owen told the churches to refrain altogether from making statements on RE; any representations that they made would not, the statement said, help the cause of RE. RE must stand apart from confessional bodies and be seen by all concerned not to be promoting the cause of any one religion, but rather to be promoting 'educational' concerns: 'RE in this country has a long history of ecclesiastical domination to live down and the new approaches to the subject can best be helped by confessional bodies avoiding any representations which are implicitly or explicitly "on behalf of RE".' [12] The Church of England, Lefroy Owen recommended, should not be represented on the full RE Council, but rather be granted associate membership only. The Free Churches should hover even lower down the scale, somewhere between associate and observer status.

Agreed syllabuses should be given up

In his third volume as editor, Hull recommended abandoning agreed syllabus procedures and replacing them with teams of teachers who could take advice from the churches and other bodies. Others made the same case. Jean Holm said: 'There can be no place in the future for Agreed Syllabuses as prescribed in the 1944 Act.'[13] Alan Loosemore, adviser to West Riding, concurred. He traced the history of the agreed syllabus in the West Riding and suggested that the next step would be the abolition of the procedure. Owen Cole called for a new Act that would end the partnership between the church and school: 'the old partnership between church and school is at an end and the open study of religion (which must include alternatives to religious approaches to life) is seen to be incompatible with a compulsory act of worship in state schools'.[14] Worship, agreed syllabuses and the withdrawal clauses must go, and the only remaining area for legislation concerning religion in education should be that concerning denominational schools.

A different argument was put forward by Allan Wainwright. He argued that the agreed syllabus system needed to go because it allowed teachers to continue with the old approach. The prescription needed to rein teachers in was unlikely to be written into an agreed syllabus; it was too controversial and would not find agreement by committee. He said: 'to spell out a particular approach to RE which specifically rejects the aims and approaches which many people hold to be the essence of the task is a very different matter. One questions whether the present Agreed Syllabus Conferences are the appropriate bodies. The mere fact that in Schedule 5 of the Act the representatives of the Churches come first on the list is an indication of the way they will be considered. And even if the Church representatives are themselves convinced that to propose a non-Church approach is the right thing, they have to remember that an agreed syllabus is a public document, and that it will do no good for the sort of storm to break over such a document as – in my view – is inevitable.'[15] Clearly, the plan to give more control to teachers did not extend to giving control to teachers with the wrong ideas.

ARE too wanted the law changed to give teachers control of the syllabus. ARE recommended the setting up of National Guidelines which could then, if desired, be taken up by local groups of teachers who would implement them as appropriate for local conditions. The LEA would have the right to convene conferences of teachers to do this. ARE suggested a draft wording for a new Act. Reorganisation of local government was taking place and there was the prospect of numerous new syllabus conferences being set up to agree new syllabuses. To pre-empt this, ARE suggested that a circular be sent to all authorities in advance of the new Act, instructing them to set up meetings of teachers to work on guidelines that the RE Council would be asked to write. The ARE paper shows that they, like Wainwright, anticipated opposition and were prepared to act despite it: 'Faced with the prospect of the statutory conferences being convened as a result of local government reorganisation, we decided that amendments should be made sooner rather than later. Amendments are a calculated risk now, in the light of present opinion in Parliament and the nation; but such opinion is quite unpredictable even five years ahead.'[16]

What Future for the Agreed Syllabus?

In 1975 the move to abolish syllabus conferences and the links with the churches found expression in a discussion document published in glossy format by REC called *What Future for the Agreed Syllabus*? In fact one of the first tasks REC set itself was to consider the future of the agreed syllabus system. A working party, set up in November 1974, stated that RE had changed and new structures for its delivery were needed. A new 'public definition of the subject' was needed, together with guidance to teachers in selecting material and methods. This was, of course, what syllabus conferences did. The document revealed concern about the teaching profession who had not been trained to teach the 'new' subject. Therefore, they could not be entrusted with the task of writing syllabuses and so the working party advised that a legally constituted body be set up to work on compulsory national guidelines. Groups of local teachers would then work out ways of implementing such guidelines locally. The national conference proposed by the working party was to be entirely independent of the faith communities. Such bodies should have the opportunity to submit suggestions but 'the drafting body should be under no obligation to, or subject to the veto of, any sectional interest'.[17]

At this point the representatives of the churches and religious groups on the REC proved decisive. At the November meeting of the full REC it became clear that members had serious reservations about the recommendations. The Council did not adopt the working party report and no clear policy on the matter could be relayed to the Government. Instead Edwin Cox was charged with writing a further paper, published as a further contribution to the debate, not as a policy document. Edwin Cox forwarded a copy to Shirley Williams, the Secretary of State for Education. In February 1978 Williams wrote: 'Thank you also for forwarding a copy of your report on the future of the agreed syllabus. I note that it has been published as a further contribution to the continuing re-examination of religious education and hope that it will help to promote wide and informed discussion.'[18] She took no action.

Moves to set up a National Advisory Group

Another early initiative of the REC was to instruct Howard Marratt, Jack Hogbin and James Thompson to look into the question of the supply and training of RE teachers. Surveys were sent out to the 33 LEAs that had RE advisers, to colleges of education and to the teachers' professional organisations. The report recommended more initial training of teachers, more in-service training, more effort to attract recruits, better RE provision in schools, more RE advisers and a national framework for the subject.[19] In-service training was a priority, linked with the need for a new understanding of the subject. REC recognised that many teachers had been trained to do a very different job from that now seen as necessary. But surveys showed that in-service attendance was poor. Head teachers did not turn up, even when the topic was worship, for which they had a direct responsibility. Only 20% of RE teachers invited ever attended.

The final paragraph contained a surprise. A plea for a national advisory group to oversee RE was made: 'The respondents were of the implicit and sometimes explicit opinion that a national impetus to the situation is necessary. Such an impetus would need the support and involvement of HMIs, who would need to be brought together at national level with representatives from LEAs, colleges and teachers. Such a group would have the necessary professional status for its guidelines to carry weight in local situations.'[20] Guidelines were to be drawn up without reference to churches or religious groups. It seems that the poor response to training in new approaches led the working party to argue that nationally imposed guidelines were needed to secure compliance. But existing arrangements could cope with an increase in in-service training, more teachers and better resources. Shirley Williams was not impressed. On 29 June 1976 she wrote back: 'In the circumstances I think it would be open to misunderstanding to consider the establishment of a national religious education advisory group. Under the Education Act 1944 it is for each local education authority to adopt an agreed syllabus which has been recommended by local representatives to reflect local needs and interests. The Government have no present plans to change the law in this respect as I again made clear in answer to a Parliamentary Question on 13 January.'

Attempts to change the law were beginning to look fruitless. However, an attempt to get round the agreed syllabus occurred in Bradford during this period.

The Bradford Supplement

Agreeing a syllabus could be a long business, and conferences were unpredictable. Owen Cole was part of an initiative in West Riding to set up a working party to advise on a new direction for RE in Bradford schools, where increasing numbers of families from non-Christian faiths had been settling throughout the 1960s. This working party produced what became known as the Bradford Supplement, issued as a supplement to the existing 1966 agreed syllabus some time between 1972 and 1974. The supplement, entitled *Guide to Religious Education in a Multi-Faith Community*, stated that RE was concerned with 'the objective study of the phenomena and beliefs of religion and with a personal search for meaning'.[21] It is clear that the opportunity afforded by the cultural situation offered hope of making progress with the new concept of RE: 'The supplement is produced in the belief that to base religious education solely on Christianity does justice neither to the local scene nor to the reality of religious experience. . . . The situation is a demanding one for the teacher since new and far-reaching responses are required if the opportunities existing in Bradford are to be seized; a reconsideration of attitudes as well as the acquiring of a new body of knowledge may well be involved.'[22] Teachers were encouraged to adopt the approaches outlined in Working Papers 36 and 44 and to make use of CEM's Primary scheme. The supplement consisted largely of information about five religions with some short theoretical sections. It adopted the view that no criteria exist upon which objective judgements can be made as to the truth of a religion, arguing that such judgements are a matter for personal choice.[23] It was assumed that the teacher would no longer engage in apologetics in the classroom and that a change of stance on the part of the Christian teacher would be necessary. The responsibility for beliefs and attitudes lay largely with the home: 'even in matters of personal hygiene, school can only co-operate with the home. So with religion, what the parent does not provide he cannot expect the school to give.'[24] This rather undermined the reason for having schools at all. It also underestimated the effect of being taught that there is no way of coming to an objective decision in the matter of religion.

The supplement had no legal force. To the extent that it was offered without the agreement of a legally constituted conference, it verged on being illegal. Although it instructed teachers to use material in the supplement in conjunction with the agreed syllabus, no attempt was made to relate the new material to the agreed syllabus at any point. Rather than point the reader to the sections in the agreed syllabus for material on Christianity, it had its own sections on Christianity. It was hinted that some of the material in the agreed syllabus on the Old Testament would have to go, as also would some church history. The reader receives the strong impression that the supplement was intended to be a replacement.

Although written for Bradford schools, the working party considered its work to have implications for a wider area and to be suitable for all children. It produced a statement of policy that was widely distributed: it was sent to every LEA in the country and to the Secretary of State for Education, for example. Bearing a close resemblance to the recommendations of the REC's document, the statement recommended that control of RE should be in the hands of teachers, working with representatives from the religions: 'Guidance to schools may be given in a voluntary handbook of suggestions or through a local advisory panel, but whatever the source, the agreement as to the matter to be taught and the method by which it should be taught would (in contrast to the provisions of the 1944 Act) be between teachers and representatives of the major world religions and other stances for living.'[25]

The Bradford Supplement and the statement which followed it, were examples of a group actively promoting a shift in RE, while bypassing the agreed syllabus system. But it could not be guaranteed that other authorities would allow an *ad hoc* group to have such influence. Still, it set a precedent. What nobody could have known was that a properly constituted syllabus conference was soon to be convened, which, in view of the Government's reluctance to change the law, would set a much more important precedent.

The Birmingham agreed syllabus of 1975[26]
In the late 1960s Birmingham City Council was making provision for the increasing numbers of Asian families that had settled in the city. The education committee asked the Birmingham SACRE to consider a new syllabus of religious education that would take into account the presence of immigrant communities adhering to non-Christian faiths. The SACRE was addressed by Geoffrey Parrinder of London University, an expert in non-Christian religions. Following this meeting, an Agreed Syllabus Conference was set up. John Hull was involved early on as was John Hick, a professor of theology at Birmingham University. These two powerful

figures in the university, keen to see change in RE, found themselves on Committee A, the other churches' committee. It was particularly ironic that John Hull, vigorously arguing that the churches should cede control of RE, should find himself in a key role in his capacity as a churchman, not an educationist. One representative each from the Muslim, Jewish, Sikh and Hindu communities was appointed to membership of Committee A. A sub-group was appointed to work out the principles upon which the syllabus would be based. John Hick was largely responsible for the work of this sub-group, and at a meeting of the full conference, with Alderman Easey in the Chair, a paper outlining principles and a framework for the syllabus was enthusiastically accepted. Working parties were set up to work on material for different age groups, with one having an overall co-ordinating role. On the insistence of John Hick, Harry Stopes-Roe, the campaigning member of the British Humanist Association (BHA), was co-opted on to both the working party for the sixth form and onto the important co-ordinating working party. He was not however a member of the conference itself.[27] On the teachers' committee was Peter Lefroy Owen. Some of the most powerful voices for change to the basis of RE found themselves sitting on the conference. In addition Edwin Cox and Ninian Smart delivered lectures to the conference.

Further consultation was not thought necessary. The Rev. Charles Buckmaster was a member of Committee B, but did not discuss the syllabus with his colleagues at St Peter's College in Saltley, so that they only knew about it after the draft was made public. In the aftermath of controversy, Knight visited the Bishop of Birmingham to discuss the syllabus; it seems that the syllabus was news to the Bishop also. It is significant that to Knight, their proposals did not seem particularly controversial.

The Birmingham ASC were, however, aware of the pioneer status of their work, and felt that what they were doing might well prove to be as influential in its day as the Cambridgeshire syllabus was after the 1944 Education Act. Limiting consultation to the professionals in RE was a sign of the times, and fitted in with the new mood that wanted to disassociate school RE from any notion of being an 'arm of the church'.

The Syllabus

The syllabus, finally agreed and adopted by the Education Committee in 1975, was a slim document with an introduction and set of topics to be covered at different ages.[28] RE was an 'educationally valid component of the school curriculum', devoted to a 'critical understanding of the religious and moral dimensions of human experience and away from attempting to foster the claims of particular religious standpoints'. Pupils were to be assisted in a search for personal meaning by informing them in a 'descriptive, critical and experiential manner about what religion is'.[29]

Between ages three and eight a selection was to be made from each of five topics: festivals of five religions (more from the Christian religion than the other religions put together), rituals and customs, stories from world religions, the world of nature and relationships in five religions. For eight to twelve year olds there were five areas: ideals for everyday living, festivals and customs in the five religions, sacred places in five religions, sacred literature (including the Bible, the Gita, the Upanishads, the Ramayana, the Qur'an and the Granth) and ways of living which involved stories from world religions of founders and exemplars of faith. Particular reference was to be made to Jesus, Peter, Paul, Rama, Sita, Krishna, Muhammed, the prophets, Abraham and Moses, the Rabbis, Nanak and Gobind Singh. From twelve to sixteen pupils were to engage in systematic study of religion by taking one major and three minor courses, one of which must be Christianity. One of the minor courses offered was a non-religious stance for living. Also included were problems such as identity, morality, relationships, the aged, race and community issues, war, famine, etc. Study in the sixth form included Buddhism, philosophy of religion, the arts and religion, mysticism, great leaders motivated by both religious and anti-religious feelings.

A thematic approach to religion was to be taken at primary level, followed by a systematic approach at secondary level. Selection was left largely up to the teacher since it was felt that every situation was different.

The Handbook to the syllabus

The Handbook to the syllabus covered a great deal of ground. It is one of the most thorough and teacher-friendly handbooks ever produced. It was packed with resources, bibliographies, ideas for lessons and essays on topics such as worship. All this befitted a publication that was breaking new ground.

The Handbook did not envisage schools as explicitly religious communities: it wrote of a 'growing realisation that county schools cannot be regarded in any sense as religious communities'.[30] It followed John Hull in proscribing much of what had been done in collective worship prior to the early 1970s for example.[31] Yet throughout the Handbook there was reference to introducing children to the 'heart of religion'. At nursery/ reception level, teachers were to provide a secure environment where children felt loved and safe. By doing this teachers would be playing a 'vital part in preparation for a deeper understanding of life', since 'dependence and trust lie at the heart of religion'.[32] Experience of the religious life was to be a present reality too: 'Religious Education in a very broad sense is taking place through every activity, every encounter, every relationship . . . it is through underlying assumptions of school life that religious education is going on.' Teachers were to create an environment in which many of the values fundamental to religions could be appreciated and felt emotionally. Values included the view that life is meaningful, that human life is about living freely and responsibly, that care for others is an absolute value, along with moral values such as honesty, courage and persever-ance. A sense of wonder was to be developed. Pupils should grasp the 'wholeness' of things, and should develop into people who were thoughtful and tolerant adults first, and Muslims, Christians, Jews second. A particular theistic view was said to be a presupposition of the theology of themes: 'The thematic method presupposes that however else God may speak, he speaks to men through their apprehension of the physical universe and of the moral, personal and specifically human aspects of their own lives.'[33]

Pupils were to engage in community service, to develop particular moral qualities, to develop positive attitudes of caring towards the aged, the sick and the community in general. Pupils should choose responsibly and learn to avoid 'blind commitment' by arriving at their own value and belief system after thinking at depth about the various options. The adoption of a coherent way of life was to be approached via a study of as many of the options as was possible, given time constraints. The inclusion of humanism, even communism (later to come under fire from the public) must be seen in the light of the perceived need to make pupils aware of the widest possible range of views so that they could make an informed choice. What beliefs and values were adopted did not seem to matter.

Reaction to the syllabus

It came as a bitter surprise to the conference that the education committee rejected the syllabus outright. Legal opinion was taken. Counsel stated that the four page syllabus did not give adequate information as to the nature of the syllabus, and that non-religious stances for living could only be presented in contrast to religions. More detail was put into the syllabus, and the following sentence was added by Hick and Knight in relation to non-religious stances for living: 'such contextual studies contribute towards a critical appreciation of the distinctive features of religious faith'. By this means the units of work on communism and humanism were saved and the syllabus adopted. A public outcry ensued. Objections centred largely, but not solely, on the fact that communism and humanism formed part of the syllabus. A debate was held in the Cathedral, the Bishop summoned Knight, and letters were written to the papers. But it survived.

Conclusion

For a syllabus which claimed not to promote any one set of beliefs, Birmingham 1975 was remarkably prescriptive. It insisted that pupils become personal idealists (a point taken up in the next chapter). At the same time pupils were taught that there was a 'heart of religion' which emitted a recognisably Christian beat. The Birmingham syllabus bears the imprint of John Hick's philosophy, a pluralist paradigm of religion where all religions are seen as attempts to conceive the 'Real' and none may claim to have a greater grasp on the truth than any other. This was the religion that was to form the common basis of the school. Yet it is by no means clear that everyone endorsed such a religion, nor that the public, parents and Parliament had given its blessing to such a view.

What Birmingham showed was that the agreed syllabus system could be used to bring about the sort of RE that the profession wanted. Legal objections to the syllabus were advanced, but not sustained. After Birmingham, concerns about changing the agreed syllabus system were not so evident. While the law might require non-religious stances for living to be presented in contrast to Christianity rather than in their own right, such a slant could be disguised by wording in the syllabus to allow teachers to exercise their discretion. The profession learned that it could turn the law to its advantage.

However, there was a world outside, and that world was beginning to take notice of what was happening in RE.

Chapter 7
A Fightback in the 1970s

The publication of the Birmingham syllabus brought the issue of what was happening to RE out into the open and provoked powerful criticisms.

Agnosticism, scepticism and personal idealism

Bishop John Taylor's analysis of the Birmingham syllabus was encapsulated in the title of an article 'Initiation into Agnosticism'.[1] The syllabus, he argued, relativised all religious and non-religious faiths and was based on scepticism. The effect was to convey to the young a 'distinct bias against confidence in the historical basis of Christian faith'.[2] However, the same sceptical and fiercely self-critical attitude did not appear to be applied to other faiths which were treated with reverence. He was unhappy about the description of former methods of RE. They offered 'a tendentious and distorted account of the aims and methods of religious education they are seeking to replace'.[3] Lesslie Newbigin, just returned from missionary work in India, made a similar diagnosis. Talk of indoctrination merely served to disguise the fact that agnosticism had replaced the positive teaching of Christianity as the basis for RE. The Birmingham syllabus had in effect adopted scepticism, based on a positivist view of reality which itself had helped to undermine Christian faith. Taken to logical extremes this would produce nihilism to which fanaticism would be one inevitable reaction.[4] The theologian, John McIntyre, warned that the descriptive presentation of religions 'gives an immediate advantage to the non-religious, the agnostic position. In fact, one standard attack on religions is to show their variety and to add that it is a matter of indifference which you choose.'[5] Daniel Hardy, also a theologian, described the Birmingham syllabus as an exercise in personal idealism, which he located somewhere between agnosticism and scepticism.[6] Individual religions might form the subject matter of the syllabus but they were there as tools to be used in the process of finding meaning. The pupil was to be his own designer, his own Bahai inventor. The Birmingham syllabus said to children that the world is as each pupil designs it. Hardy sensed that the presentation of a variety of viewpoints without any attempt by the teacher to discriminate between them would convey the view to pupils that what is common to the religions is what really matters.

What is religion?

Difficulties with the concept of religion were often pointed out. John Greer, a lecturer in Northern Ireland, noted that contributors to a new book on RE, including Smart and Marratt, had a serious problem with defining the word.[7] Smart was not unaware of the difficulty and spoke only of 'formal features' which allowed Maoism, for example, to be categorised as a religion along with Christianity. In Greer's view, the writers failed to engage with what a 'form of religious knowledge might look like'.[8] The philosopher John Wilson said that much new RE failed because it had no clear idea of what religion was and therefore what would count as success in learning about it. Having given up on teaching Christianity, a vacuum had been created which the profession did not know how to fill. As a result, teachers rushed from one idea to another: 'we mess about, filling in the time.'[9] He too criticised Smart for being vague and while claiming to treat of religion as a *sui generis* category, in relation to which one could chart progress, in fact spoke most often of the religions.

Incoherence and lack of rigour

A head teacher, Derek Webster, wrote of a crisis in RE, describing the present situation as one which 'tends to dismiss confessional religious education (or neo-confessional) without any proper analysis of what it is or how it relates to the concept of authority, commitment and indoctrination'.[10] The RE profession, he charged, had no taxonomy of its own, lacked precise operational aims and ways of evaluation, and was weak on research. The sociologist David Martin had made a study of approved RE texts. He considered that they 'face no issue seriously. . . they are vehicles for airing nice sentiments . . . in the higher ability ranges it is appalling that classes in RE absorb this febrile opinionation while classes in Mathematics are absorbing topology and in English are reading Donne'.[11] Geraint Jones expressed the view that a certain loss of touch with the real situation was becoming apparent. Throughout his long career in RE, Jones had been aware of the inadequacies felt by many RE teachers. Jones commented: 'Where in the name of all that is sane, can we expect to find teachers of religion capable of studying at such depth and within such a compass as what is clearly necessary if the suggestions of some theme or project or syllabus makers are to be given effect?'[12]

Poor education

H.B. Atkins, a head of RE, noted that presenting religions and other belief systems to children as equally plausible amounted to a demand that schools should give up educating: 'Educationalists are assumed to have no capacity in the discernment of any order of priorities in the responses of man to God and the world nor in the selection of that which is *worth* communicating to their charges. . . . We submit that no responsible educationalist can give his or her consent to such a view or to any such proposals.'[13] Truly child-centred religious education, he argued, involved the teacher conveying definite religious convictions to children which children could accept or reject: 'for the child the teacher is expected to hold convictions that are attested by significant historical events and give rise to a worldview of life that has stood the test of time. On educational grounds he or she (rightly) expects no less.'[14] David Martin concurred. The idea that 'you can't decide for other people' was in effect to abdicate the scene and to leave a vacuum for others to fill. It succeeded by asking questions such as 'Which standards? Why these particular standards? Are there not many standards to choose from? Who are you to choose?' The answer was not to cave in to such questions but to reiterate that a choice must be made: 'if we do not like the risk of establishing an order which stands for the good and true and beautiful as we see it, then others will do it for us'.[15] He believed that this approach could be an excuse for sloth: 'sloth is a deadly sin and the father of lies knows how to feed it'.[16] One function of education is undoubtedly to develop children's ability to discern and discriminate between good and bad, true and false. But criteria have first to be supplied to do this. Newbigin wrote: 'a pupil will develop the proper critical faculties in the field, by a process which must begin with the uncritical acceptance of models which are part of the culture and experience into which the pupil is growing up'.[17] D.G. Attfield argued that to get to the level where real criticism was possible required significant knowledge and a sympathetic guide who was able to present material as at least 'possibly true'.[18] But the trouble was that the new RE seemed to proscribe this.

Evasion of truth claims and the destruction of faith

McIntyre wrote that the final emasculation of the faiths which the descriptive method attempted was the denial to them of truth claims.[19] Geraint Jones wrote: 'I fear very much that what is now being proposed could become a behaviourist, logical positivist, existential wasteland where, because so much is offered and so many contrasts – and indeed – contradictions are left unexplained or unanswered, there must be a real danger that everybody's religion will become nobody's. The repeated, much-emphasised objection to any "confessional" teaching of religion would . . . in itself prove my point.'[20] Edward Norman went further.[21] Such teaching threatened to destroy any faith that pupils might have: 'One of the great evils of the "open" approach to religious education is that it will actively result in the positive destruction of a lot of the children's religious faith, by throwing the authority of the school behind the relativistic attitudes to the basic criteria by which moral and religious values are determined.'[22]

The attack upon culture

W.H.J. Earl, HMI, wrote: 'I am concerned about the inadequacies and loss of nerve which seem to infect RE in many schools. . . . We shall serve our pupils very ill indeed if we fail to give them as clear an understanding as possible of the religion which has been the most potent inspiration and critic of the civilisation which they have inherited.'[23] McIntyre wrote of the subtle challenge to the truth of Christianity. Because the Christian faith was at the root of culture, the move to descriptive forms of religious education was also challenging the roots of the dominant culture: 'for the sake of the subordinate cultures and the other faiths which sustain them, we have to ensure the continuance of the dominant culture and the values, ideas, concepts and beliefs which are its inspiration. To neutralise, subjectivise or to treat indifferently with those of other cultures, the values of the dominant culture is to place the whole system at risk. There are ways of questioning and radically examining the concepts of the culture without reducing them to an indifferent level with those drawn from other faiths. We dare not, therefore, opt out of our responsibility of ensuring that the values and beliefs which have been the source of the culture which we inherited are passed on to the next generation. We must be one of the few generations in history which has failed to feel sufficiently strongly about our own values, moral standards and religious convictions to secure their transmission to the next generation. A widespread support for descriptive religious education coupled with failure to construct an effective system of moral education has come to ensure a minimal adoption by the next generation of the values, beliefs, attitudes which our fathers and mentors passed on to us.'[24]

What did the critics propose?

In various ways, the critics proposed the teaching of Christian faith.

B. Pierce-Jones wanted the teaching of hard concepts such as miracle, self-sacrifice, communion with God, prophetic messages. He understood the problem of finding teachers capable of this level of teaching. He suggested that each school have a specialist RE teacher freed to travel all the classes in order to give pupils the 'maximum experience of religion that is consistent with professionalism and with the requirements of Parliament and the parents'.[25]

David Martin saw RE as the passing on of a tradition rich in resources, introducing the young to ever increasing complexity and richness. Through such a transmission experience is both understood and corporately realised. Such teaching feeds a sense of place, of knowing who you are and why you are. He wrote of the 'repository of religious language' and in this he included the Authorised Version of the Bible and the Book of Common Prayer. If RE rejected the way of disciplined learning of particular traditions, it would risk losing all touch with rationality.[26] In relation to the English and European tradition there was a rich vein to tap. Martin wrote of 'such preachers as Bach, Michelangelo, Dante and John Donne, the builders of churches and cathedrals, the framers of liturgies and translators of the Bible'.[27] He rejected the idea that the great classics of secular and religious poetry could only be taught in the sixth form. This was a capitulation to low standards. For Martin RE was 'a habituation to poetry and a shared language'.[28]

John Bradford, concerned about the direction in which RE was going, wrote a series of letters to the press. He suggested that RE should no longer be compulsory, but where it was taught it should be 'an intelligent if not progressive but essentially supportive treatment . . . of Europe's mainstream religion – Christianity'. The answer was not to introduce relativism, a recipe for spiritual anarchy. He hoped that the teaching profession itself would issue the much-needed corrective. Ignorance of world religions was best dealt with in other subjects alongside study of the cultures of other societies, perhaps in social studies or geography. Exposing pupils to a variety of belief systems without a special brief for any would lead to a profound sense of isolation and alienation from religion *in toto*. What was needed was a study of the threat of secularisation which 'erodes not only spiritual but human values. It would seem that the best way of answering this might be by building up our distinctive national Christian culture-rather than by trying to live it down.'[29] Of more relevance to pupils than world religions was the fact of growing links with Europe which offered rich possibilities of study of the common Christian heritage found there.

Basil Mitchell[30] argued that what was needed was to make the young aware of the intellectual and spiritual inexhaustibility of Christianity in a way that enabled them to understand and engage in the process of subjecting that tradition to criticism. Mitchell argued that there must be a tradition that focuses the learning. All creative and original thinkers have first absorbed the best work that has already been done. Every genius is heir to a tradition, against which he or she rebels. It is of vital importance that the young be exposed to a particular tradition. Without such an introduction there could be no possibility of critical or creative thought at all. In turn it is through criticism that a tradition renews itself, expressing new and creative insights. It was necessary to make the tension between tradition and criticism fruitful. The teaching must begin with certain givens, basic

Christian beliefs for example, but these givens must be subjected to searching criticism and exploration. This was because the dynamic nature of human life is such that the tradition will always need to be reinterpreted in the light of current knowledge and the current context. So both faith and criticism are needed.

What lay behind it all?

David Martin argued that change was conceived and brought about by an alienated sector of the intelligentsia who inhabited the institutes of education. The cause was a reaction against authority and the common identity which explained the tendency for some to dislike being identified with the status quo. Such intellectuals could not believe that such things as national traditions still mattered to the populace at large. These intellectuals therefore undertook to 'enlighten' the 'People' so as to persuade them to reject all coercive symbols of external identity. This led them to propose a lurch into individualism which would, in his view, bring about severe impoverishment. Religion, in this view, must have nothing to do with coercion to conformity and its outward symbols: 'Insofar as religion can be admitted at all it must convey pure inwardness.' Roy Porter had come under pressure to teach Marxism in Christian educational courses at Southampton University in the 1960s. Porter too felt that the institutes of education and their influence upon the teacher training colleges was a major factor. During this period education became a faculty on its own; and this led to a certain isolationism. This was not unwelcome to educationalists who may have felt the need to assert their own identity; but it meant that they operated independently of the academic scrutiny of their peers.[31] John Bradford noted that the new approach was gaining the status of an a priori assumption. In his view 'a phenomenologically-oriented caucus of RE professionals has surreptitiously "taken over" and become a Super power of RE curriculum innovation'.[32] He was particularly scathing about the report of the REC,[33] which recommended the scrapping of SACREs and the wholesale adoption of a Religious Studies approach 'as if all discussion on the subject was now beyond anyone but a professional elite'.[34]

Edward Norman noted that in the early 1960s, to the delight of intellectual humanists who had been campaigning for years to remove the compulsory religious instruction clauses from the law, church leaders began to work on their behalf. It began, in his view, with a book published in 1963 criticising Christian teaching for being a propaganda experience.[35] Then 'the spores multiplied and began to germinate all over the place'[36] such that now 'almost the whole of the educational establishment appears to regard the "new RE" as self-evidently right'.[37] The 'open approach' in RE was merely a device by which the approved attitudes of the alienated intelligentsia were able to propagate their views. Having decided that a new 'open' approach was needed, many of the theorists of the new approach 'fall upon the existence of immigrant communities as practical evidence of their contentions with barely concealed pleasure'.[38] The much heralded reluctance of the young to accept inherited values was the product of their teachers' reluctance to teach them. One head teacher had been so shocked by Norman's advocacy for traditional Christian teaching that she could not envisage herself discussing the matter with him. Yet for most parents, Norman argued, it was Christian truth that was the basis of the moral order they would most want their children to learn at school: 'the future therefore should not lie with the opinionated minority who clamour for a secularisation of the nation's educational system. . . . There are no inexorable pressures making it impossible to continue teaching Christianity in schools – only a powerful lobby from a small section of society addicted to highly unstable fashions of thinking.'[39]

The likely outcome

These critics gave warnings which have proved remarkably prophetic. Norman warned of 'a great moral chaos' in the decades ahead if the 'whole absurdity is allowed to go on that long'. Humanism would be the winner and the destruction of children's faith the result.

He thought perhaps the best thing was for RE to disappear from schools but felt the religious education industry in the universities and colleges of education would lean on their powerful sense of moralising to maintain its existence. Bradford warned that the adoption of curriculum neutrality in RE would lead to greater calls for church and other faith schools. It would have the effect of increasing national secularisation and reducing the sense of there being a Church of the nation. The abandonment of any sense of what is true in religion (implicitly conveyed by studying a wide range of belief-systems without a special brief for any) would lead to increasing irrationalism in the population as a whole and the adoption of irrational and harmful beliefs such as the occult.

ARE mounts some resistance

Between 1976 and 1977 ARE began to regret the part they had played in promoting the new RE. The Rev. Raymond Abba had been chairman and joint editor of the Bulletin since its early days. His view had been that RE must adapt to the new climate that prevailed and that Christian teachers must present religions and non-religions as equally viable alternatives to the Christian faith, in the hope that the Holy Spirit would speak to pupils: 'it is the Holy Spirit who elicits the response. When Jesus is presented in the company of Gautama, Confucius and Mohammed he needs no commendation of ours.'[40] He was, however, never altogether happy with this position and his last two editorials reflected a somewhat agonised questioning concerning the direction he had helped RE to take. In Bulletin 21, (1976) he began his editorial with these words: 'many of us who have endeavoured to keep abreast with recent thought in this sphere [RE] have tended to accept some aspects of the new movements too uncritically'. In his final editorial before leaving for a new job in Australia he wrote of the need to 'look to the religious foundations of our society and realise the need for ensuring that the religious heritage, upon which both our culture and common life are based, is handed on to future generations'. He went back to the 1944 Act to argue exactly the case for RE that was argued then: 'The purpose of the legislation . . . was not merely to provide for the giving of factual information about religion in general, or even Christianity in particular; its aim was to give expression to "the desire to revive the spiritual and personal values in society and in our national tradition".' Abba went on to argue that the great mistake of the 1970s and one which he himself had made, had been to accept an antithesis between the 'confessional' and the 'educational': 'The antithesis is false: it is based on the assumption that an educational approach must be purely descriptive and "objective". This is bad educational philosophy: there is no such thing as "objective" history, to say nothing of music, poetry and art. . . . Education is concerned, inter alia, with the exploration and transmission of our cultural heritage. In this Christianity has in fact played the dominant role: shaping our music, literature and art; moulding our democratic institutions; providing the spiritual and personal values in our society; giving both an understanding of human existence and a faith by which to live. It is with this vital aspect of our cultural heritage as a whole that the religious clauses of the 1944 Act are concerned: the statutory obligation for religious education to be provided in every state school is intended to safeguard its transmission, through both instruction and worship, to the coming generation: unless this is done, RE is not doing its job.' This looks like a confession and a sincere admission that ARE had got it wrong. And with that he went to Melbourne.

Peter Lefroy Owen was having second thoughts too. He suggested that 'social "mishmash", world religions and the phenomenological approach had had their say'.[41] He wrote of rumblings from different sources which he welcomed, all asking questions as to what had happened to the teaching of Christianity in RE. He then listed sources of help and suggested what to do, although much of his article was a request to the Government to put money into surveying the provision of RE rather than doing something about what was being taught. On October 23, 1976 ARE held a day conference, notable for the concern expressed by many to bring back the teaching of Christianity and to resist the new approaches. Edwin Cox spoke about REC's recent publication *What future for the Agreed Syllabus?* Cox must have been surprised by the barrage of criticisms he received. Partly as a result of this, the ARE penned a response to the REC document which was significantly different from their earlier submission: 'The ARE executive committee has noted the evidence from the House of Commons debate on March 19, 1976 and from the national press and other sources of a growing desire within the nation for RE in state schools to be primarily concerned with the transmission of the Christian faith and ethic, which is the clear intention of the 1944 Education Act. At their recent Annual Day Conference, ARE members expressed a deep concern that the Working Party report, although embodying some sound educational principles and ideals, was vitiated by its complete silence regarding the centrality of the Christian tradition, in marked contrast to its expressed willingness to include other life-stances.'[42] Their response was in fact highly critical of the proposals of the REC and represented a significant opposition amongst an association that a few years earlier could have been expected to endorse such a document.

The Nottinghamshire Agreed Syllabus

Nottinghamshire published its agreed syllabus, entitled *Quest,* in 1977. It was published soon after the groundbreaking Birmingham syllabus and is notable for the way it heralded a return to Christian teaching. The main body of the syllabus reflected an almost total concentration upon Christian material, even at sixth-form level. This fact justifies the comment in the preface made by the Roman Catholic Bishop of Nottingham: 'In these modern times, with the many difficulties facing our young people, one is concerned with the lack of definite Christian teaching in so many schools. The Religious Adviser for Nottinghamshire and his team have made a mammoth effort to remedy this. . . . I hope that . . . the pupils taught will become better children of God, and better citizens of the State.' A lengthy section (25 pages) on the history of the Christianity in England and Nottingham was included at the front of the syllabus while a shorter section (11 pages) on world religions brought up the rear. Yet some at least of the conference expected world religions to feature prominently since it was said in the introduction to the section of the syllabus for twelve to eighteen year olds that 'Time should not be devoted to world religions in the fourth and fifth years as in the older syllabi, but the subject should be continuously considered at every stage of the child's curriculum.'[43] But there was nothing in the detailed syllabus on religions other than Christianity prior to the sixth form.

Quest therefore reflected a degree of compromise. The choice of title was very much a slogan of the 'open approach'. The introductory sections[44] accepted the conclusions of Goldman and WP 36 and insisted that 'honest doubt' was at all times preferable to 'biased belief'. The opening statement recommended that the syllabus was better understood as a list of suggestions than a syllabus to be followed progressively one page at a time. This looks like an apology for the syllabus. And what did it mean to say that once teachers had absorbed this syllabus they might 'wish to experiment with some of the RE material produced by the Schools Council'?[45] The later Loukes was quoted at some length and a set of aims offered (said to be neither all-encompassing nor absolute) which lacked internal coherence and some of which gave little direction. How, for example, could the fact that the personality of the teacher has an effect on the child be conceived as an aim for RE?

Jack Priestley disliked it and was worried that it represented a swing back to the old days, a 'backward step, a return to the past which is no longer there, an essentially reactionary approach'.[46] He found the style and tone to be 'professionally disagreeable'.[47] The adviser for Nottinghamshire, David Bennett, sensed that his professional colleagues were not too pleased with him.[48]

However, the syllabus-makers at Nottinghamshire had put their effort where it mattered most and made sure that the syllabus itself insisted on proper Christian teaching at all stages. The syllabus was found entirely acceptable to teachers in Nottinghamshire and was sold widely all over the country. All that was needed was for other conferences to stand firm in this way and the situation might have been retrieved. The Rev.R.S.C. Baily, a member of the editorial working party, stated that he and others on the conference were dismayed when Hampshire and other conferences later produced thin syllabuses which contained no proper academic study of anything.[49] Their view had been that a proper study of one religion was needed and in this they followed *The Fourth R*. Clearly the Nottinghamshire conference included Anglicans and others ready to insist on their view. But once again, the omens for the future were not good. The introductory sections seemed to apologise for the syllabus. The Christian emphasis had been maintained but was justified by appeals to the opposition. Still, Nottingham had set an example which was in clear contrast to the approach taken by Birmingham.

Conclusion

Powerful criticisms of change in RE were voiced at the time which received little in the way of rejoinder.

However, the difficulty of reiterating the traditional view may be seen in Lesslie Newbigin's article where he wrote that it was difficult to see what could replace the approach of the Birmingham syllabus. Furthermore,

Martin was a professor of sociology in London, Mitchell was professor of philosophy at Oxford, McIntyre was professor of divinity at Edinburgh, Newbigin was a missiologist and Bradford found himself out of a job when his college was closed down. None were directly involved in the RE profession or on syllabus conferences where they might have been able to exert influence. All were voicing their concerns as individuals and as outsiders. They were not organised, as Porter himself admitted, and their protests were not co-ordinated, unlike the opposition, which as previous chapters have shown, was clearly focussed on bringing about change. Still, they had raised important questions and the country seemed to be taking notice.

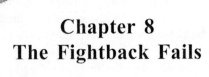

Chapter 8
The Fightback Fails

The Order for Christian Unity

The Order for Christian Unity (OCU), an ecumenical Christian charity, had received many letters and enquiries expressing concern about RE. They instigated a survey of head teacher opinion in 1973. Every secondary head teacher (about 9000) in England and Wales was sent a questionnaire. The response rate was low, 25%. 97% of responses were in favour of Christian Education being maintained and improved. A few replies proposed moral education instead. A large majority 'showed relief that a Christian organisation was prepared to recommend specifically Christian education'.[1] Results of the survey were sent to all MPs, and meetings were held on two occasions with Secretaries of State for Education. In 1975 a letter was sent to all Directors of Education in England and Wales, appealing to them to ensure that Christian Education was maintained in RE. In November 1976 OCU organised a day conference at Church House in London to debate the future of RE and the place of Christianity within it. The conference adopted a ten point target (addressed to the churches and Government) with an addendum: 'The Conference would wish to see secured for the future a specifically Christian content of Religious Education in our State Schools.'

A Question in the House of Commons

A few months earlier a four-hour debate on RE had been held in the Commons. Michael Alison had tabled a motion 'that this House recognises the need to maintain and improve the opportunities for religious education and an act of worship in schools'. He opened up the debate: 'It will not do, in my view, to interpret "religious education" as education about religion – that is, to give information about, let us say, Christianity and other religions – in a detached, analytical fashion, as if they were objects capable of some kind of biological dissection. It must go further than that.'[2] He wanted RE to be based on Christianity 'up to the point of commitment'. He talked about a school with 50% immigrant children taught on the basis of the Bible with hymns and readings and only one child had been withdrawn.

Only 5% of replies to a survey had claimed to belong to other religions or none. He pressed for Government money to support RE. David Weitzman spoke of 'deterioration in the religious and moral instruction of our children in recent times'.[2] Rhodes Boyson commented that the decline in the teaching of the Christian religion found no support in the country as a whole. He wondered what had happened in Birmingham where children between three and eight years old were to learn the festivals of five religions: 'One wonders at the decline of religious inspection and leadership that has tolerated such syllabuses.'[4] The result would be that children would lose a sense of which religion they belonged to. He wanted RE to be given by committed Christians and to give a proper sense of direction. W. van Straubenzee put the changes in RE down to the fact that humanists were disproportionately represented amongst teachers whereas in the population as a whole there was a strong degree of attachment to Christian belief and practice. Alan Clark viewed the BHA's pamphlet[5] as an outright attack on society since it attempted to undermine the beliefs of that society. He said: 'Christianity is concerned with the soul and redemption – if they have no belief at all, if even their ancient and traditional beliefs are removed and the vacuum filled simply with a lot of illogical and conflicting claptrap having the guise of giving breadth of philosophic understanding, the disillusion which will follow is something for which I am certain we shall all pay a heavy price.'[6]

Patrick Mayhew said that there were many evils, but Christianity was not one of them: 'Let us acknowledge that Christianity is the true source of what is best in our history and what is best in our distinctive way of life today. If that is its source, let us acknowledge how decadent we should be if we did not lead our children to it at their schools.'[7] Norman St John Stevas, on behalf of the Opposition, spoke of the *trahison des clercs* 'destroying values of religion and civility which form the basis of our society'[8]. He quoted the Chief Rabbi who had argued in *The Times* in January that there could be no brotherhood of man without the fatherhood of God.

Margaret Jackson, on behalf of the Government, put another point of view. She said that there were many different views on the topic of RE and that in many areas RE teachers had welcomed the new approaches. Teaching should be objective and involve sympathetic and informed enquiry instead of pre-judging conclusions. Michael Marshall rebuffed this attitude by declaring that in the House there was near unanimity about the need to reclaim the Christian foundation of Religious Education: 'we should speak out firmly. . . . The lead that we should give is to reaffirm the need to preserve and protect the kind of Christian faith that is shared by the majority of our people.'[9]

The motion, a mild one, was carried. But it gave notice that some at least in the Commons were aware of what was going on and did not like it.

A Question in the House of Lords

On 16 February 1977 Lord Longford rose to ask: 'What steps is the Government taking to provide an adequate supply of qualified teachers of religious education?' Baroness Elles spoke about the demise of the teaching of Christianity in county schools. She used the word 'mish-mash' to describe the new way of teaching RE. She said that teachers were now afraid to talk of Christianity and the Bible in the classroom. How, she asked, had this situation come about? There had not been a press campaign, no pressure from parents, nor had the law been changed. The new RE represented a denial of the truth of Christianity itself. Furthermore the presence of religious believers of other faiths was sometimes used dishonestly as 'another subversive way of trying to denigrate Christianity and stop it being taught'.[10] In her opinion the problem lay in the colleges of education where there had been widespread condemnation of confessional teaching.

Lord Macleod quoted a poem by an RE teacher, Mrs Sandeman, which highlighted the problem. The poem was called 'I only teach RE' and included the following verses:

Oh no, I'm not a Christian, a Moslem or a Jew,
Involvement would unsettle my objective point of view,
And when I take my lesson I don't moralise or preach:
In religious education basic facts are all I teach.

I give notes on each religion, however small or odd,
The dates of every prophet and the names of every god.
And when the facts have all run out I turn to other creeds;
Trotsky, Marx and Lenin fill my syllabus' needs.

I do not teach morality or charity or hope,
Such abstracts as the love of God are not within my scope.
Their spiritual development does not depend on me,
No! Let them get their faith elsewhere, I only teach RE.[11]

As in the Commons, there was strong support for the Christian basis to RE. A Jewish peer, Lord Janner, argued that the common Judaeo-Christian heritage was vital for society in order to lift the perspective of children beyond selfishness and materialism. Children should be taught their own religion. Baroness Masham said she had found her faith at school through a Christian teacher; she spoke of her work as a Borstal visitor and wanted RE to give standards, vision, hope and purpose to children who were adrift. Lord Vaizey called a multi-faith approach intellectually and morally threadbare. Lord Donaldson, for the Government, stressed the Christian content of RE. In a debate lasting four hours much had been done to raise the profile and importance of RE and he pledged that the Government would do all it could to meet the concerns of the House.

Debate in the House of Lords on 18 May 1977

Three months later, Lord Blake, the eminent historian, attempted to get a more specific commitment from the Government. He put a motion before the House concerning the lack of a Christian element in RE. This debate attracted 36 speakers and lasted eight hours. Lord Blake said that teachers and parents were perturbed about the nature and adequacy of the Christian element in RE in state schools. During the last twenty years Christian teaching had been crowded out by the teaching of other faiths or eliminated because RE periods had ceased to have any religious content. He wanted the Department of Education and Science (DES) to send out a circular stressing that the spirit, if not the letter, of the 1944 Education Act required the centrality of Christianity and the teaching of the Bible. On educational grounds the young needed access to their western cultural heritage, one of the most important aspects of human life, and this was under threat. Lord Belstead supported an enquiry and was supportive of the central place for Christianity in RE. Christianity, he reflected, needed to be taught with enthusiasm, rather than 'all the detachment appropriate to the study of the life cycle of a fish'.[12]

Lord Donaldson, for the Government, refused both an enquiry and a circular. He said that RE was a combination of parts; it retained a place for the Bible and the Christian faith deriving from the 1944 Act, but also embraced the child-related methods of the 1960s and the religious quest of the post-1971 period. Colleges of education included Christian studies as a major part of the course. In relation to the teacher, Lord Donaldson saw nothing wrong with personal commitment influencing their teaching of Christianity. The inclusion of contributions from other religions in his view could work to the advantage of Christian learning since such study could emphasise its significance. Christian faith, he said, offered all children 'the best hope of a secure and enlightened future based on Christian values on which to build an integrated and multi-racial society'.[13] A similar view was expressed by the Secretary of State for Education, Shirley Williams, speaking on 25 October 1977 at St Mary le Bow Church in London. She said that the Government had no intention of changing the law on RE. There was no public support for dropping the subject in schools. More than 70% of parents wanted their children to have religious instruction and to be brought up in the tenets of their nominal faith. Like Lord Donaldson, she said that some teaching about other religions should be included.

The Government appeared to support the idea of RE being based on the positive teaching of Christianity, but they were reluctant to insist on it. Perhaps they were unwilling to get involved in a battle with the profession and contented themselves with the thought that there was nothing in law to prevent the Christian faith being taught positively. This being so, the opportunity was there for the churches to take a leading role in providing Christian teachers and encouraging them to teach the faith enthusiastically.

Debate in the General Synod
of the Church of England

On the 5 July 1977, the General Synod received a major report on education. One motion debated was that proposed by the Bishop of Coventry, John Gibbs: 'That this Synod, recognising that county schools cannot be expected to take responsibility for Christian nurture among their pupils, calls upon each diocese to take steps to provide for such nurture, on a lifelong basis, from within its own resources.'[14] Bishop Gibbs wanted to alert the church to the fact that county schools could not be relied upon to do the work of nurturing the young in the Christian faith and that therefore Dioceses should put greater effort into it. His speech indicated a significant and recent shift in the role of RE in county schools: 'we have moved very rapidly from a cohesive, coherent society, which only a few years ago we could describe with some truth and with real content that it was a Christian society, to a quite new situation in which we have an open, pluralist society. . . . [T]he county schools can no longer be the reliable agents of Christian nurture. That is merely a statement of fact.'[15]

This aspect of his speech provoked a strong response amongst Synod members. The Rev. J. St H. Mullett reacted strongly to the negative statement that county schools could no longer nurture pupils within the Christian faith. On the contrary he believed that 'all of us should do all we possibly can to get the Christian commitment to Christian education in every State school in the country'.[16] The Bishop of London, Dr G.A. Ellison, insisted that nurture in the sense of 'totality of care in the business of becoming better Christians' had never been expected from a school. But he was concerned because 'the motion invites the Synod to go on record as expressing its belief that we cannot in future expect the bringing up, training and fostering care given to our children in State schools any longer to have a Christian content. We cannot expect that Christian principles and Christian philosophy will inspire and guide the teachers in their work. Presumably that training must now be entirely secular.'[17] Ellison went on to ask what the effect of such a motion would be on those looking to the Church to take a lead. The motion, he said,

> is in clear contradiction of the requirements of the law . . . and represents a radical departure from the accepted philosophy of centuries. The whole of our national life, its law, its institutions, its educational system, have been erected upon the fundamental acceptance of Christian principles . . . some adjustment to . . . religious convictions of others [is required], but this does not require the abandonment of Christian responsibility. . . . .I believe that this motion is a capitulation to the secularists, who have been pressing for precisely such an admission on our part as in contained

in this motion. Once the battle has been won in our schools they will press on for the secularisation of the whole of our society. I suppose the next thing we shall be asked to assent to is the removal of the Sovereign's title of Defender of the Faith, since she rules over people of many faiths and none. And then we shall have to look forward to the swearing in of the next Sovereign in Westminster Hall in place of the Christian rite in Westminster Abbey.[18]

Canon P.H. Boulton expressed a similar concern, shared by the educational team in the Southwell Diocese and the RE county adviser in his authority. He felt that education and nurture could not be so neatly distinguished. Since any educational endeavour impacted upon the lives of children by giving guidance and direction to children to take certain paths rather than others, to withdraw any specifically Christian guidance was simply to abdicate responsibility and to open the way for others to take up the task. He believed that the majority of Christian parents expected the state to continue to 'draw upon the resources of the Christian tradition to enrich the lives of their children. To carry this motion would be damaging to these expectations.'[19]

The MP, W.R. van Straubenzee, felt that a large number of parents, despite not having a Christian commitment, wanted their children 'inculcated with religious instruction and the values which go with it'.[20] He referred to the debate in the Commons in March 1976 which had not come about by chance. It had come about because of 'the Christian Members of all denominations quite deliberately seeking to put out certain marksmen on our frontiers, having reckoned that there had been enough occasions when it had been our opponents who had taken the initiative and it was time that we ought to do the same'.[21] This being so, it would be exceedingly unfortunate for the Synod to send out, even if unintentionally, opposite signals: 'How very disheartening it would be if triumphantly those taking a different view from us were able to quote this particular motion to us.'[22]

A head teacher said he was struck with horror when he read the motion. He was concerned to stop the defeatism about RE in so many county schools. The motion if passed would allow 'someone who wants to be slipshod in county schools to be so, and it will be a danger to those who wish to carry on as best they can'.[23]

However, not everyone was in agreement. The Bishop of Guildford, D.A Brown, was concerned that if county schools were to be expected to engage in Christian nurture it would send a message of non-acceptance to the Muslim community and others: 'Will they say that the Christian groups in this country are standing firm by the law and using it in such a way as to deny to their children the right to live, to be heard in the schools, and to be treated as individuals with respect and responsibility, with the school affirming their nurture?'[24] Mrs J.M. Mayland argued that schools were no longer adopting a Christian philosophy, and teachers who possessed no Christian commitment themselves could not be expected to engage in the Christian nurture of pupils.

An amendment was put forward by the Bishop of London which addressed the Government: 'That this Synod, recognising that it is the intention of the 1944 Education Act that religious education should mean Christian education, urges the Secretary of State for Education and Science to ensure that the daily act of worship and the periods of religious instruction in schools are conducted in such a manner as to fulfil the purpose of the Act, and calls upon each diocese to take steps to help teachers to this end and to encourage parents to insist upon their rights.'

However the Synod passed a different motion. It recognised the 'partnership that exists between Local Education Authorities and the Church in joint responsibility for Christian nurture among pupils of maintained and voluntary schools' and called 'upon each diocese to take steps for such nurture, on a lifelong basis, from within its own resources.'[25]

This motion steered away from abandoning a role for Christian nurture in the county school, while accepting the point that the churches must do more to nurture their young. The Church of England did not give negative messages about county schools withdrawing from Christian nurture but it failed to send any message at all to the Government.

ARE unwilling to take a stand

In the latter part of 1977 it was clear that ARE was having second thoughts. Ken Mullis was joint editor with Lefroy Owen. Mullis felt that despite it being a 'very dangerous and crucial time for RE' the association could not take a view on the matter, but must rather act as an open forum for the diverse views of its membership.[26] Mullis wrote: 'What kind of RE should we teach? As a professional association of RE teachers we can have no official position on such an issue. We must reflect the views of our members, and those views are varied.'[27] Yet the editorial revealed how strongly Mullis felt about the dangers of a relativistic, value-free approach: 'To be "value free" is not only impossible; to attempt it is positively dishonest. Our responsibility is to commend some values over against others in our education of children.'[28] The same responsibility might be said to be incumbent on an association of RE. John Hull was not afraid to take such a stance when he took over the editorship of *Learning for Living* in 1971, as had Harold Loukes before him. Between 1976 and 1977 ARE appeared to be coming to a view concerning the need to recover the Christian orientation of RE. They had communicated this view to the RE Council after consultation and discussion with members. Mullis' editorial, however, drew back, citing the need for a professional association to act as a forum, not a pressure group. Why the change of tack? In the same edition Mullis printed an article by Roger Howarth arguing strongly for world religions in RE and one by Donald Butler, the secretary of Shap. Perhaps the world religions lobby was afraid that ARE might take a stand and had put pressure on Mullis. In a later editorial, Mullis would speak of the difficulties facing the Christian teacher who would in the future find himself unable to teach within the framework of Christian truth.

The Association of Christian Teachers (ACT)

ACT was formed in 1971 by the amalgamation of three bodies involved in education in the 1960s.[29] The hope was to make a major evangelical Christian contribution to education and in particular to RE. Philip May, ACT's first chairman, hoped that ACT would encourage teachers through local groups and conferences to see 'that Christian principles could and should permeate all their practice as teachers'.[30] David Blair, the first National Secretary, spoke of 'projecting an evangelical Christian point of view in education'.[31] Brian Monks, chairman between 1975 and 1981, expressed the hope at the time that ACT might have 'a significant voice in national policy'.[32] In the 1960s Peter Dawson and Kenneth Howkins had written refutations of Ronald Goldman's work. May and Raymond Johnston had shown that parents and teachers wanted existing provisions for religious education and worship to be continued. Johnston contributed a chapter to *Comparative Religion in Education* in 1970 appealing for the retention of Christianity to be taught as truth and of supreme worth. Peter Cousins and Michael Eastman published a book arguing that RE should advocate Christian faith. The creation of ACT in 1971 offered evangelicals an opportunity to build on precedents set and challenge the way RE was being led.

Activities
ACT published a termly journal and reviewed RE textbooks. RE conferences were held every year both in the north and in London. An RE sub-committee was formed. A magazine, *Spectrum*, was set up to provide Christian insights into education generally. ACT held joint conferences with ARE; it was represented both on the 'confessional' and 'professional' wings of the REC. A conference centre, Stapleford House, was purchased and up and running by 1980. *Aims in RE* was published in 1976 as the first of a short series on RE and *Religious Education: A considered view* was submitted to the RE Council in 1975. Other leaflets of general educational concern were distributed.

Plans for an RE consultation
At the November 1972 meeting of the RE sub-committee, George Oliver said that ACT needed to provide an evangelical appraisal of RE. By January 1974 it appears that no progress had been made and Oliver, trying to get on

with the matter, proposed that a small group from the sub-committee work on a statement of ACT policy on RE. The group met in June of that year and prepared a detailed strategy, involving three carefully planned stages geared to producing such a statement. But the furthest it got was the sending of letters to selected people asking for comment on WP36.

The statement *Religious Education: A considered view*

ACT did, however, produce a statement on RE in response to a proposed Private Member's Bill in late 1975 to change the law on RE in line with the recommendations of the BHA. It argued that RE should 'foster a certain kind of understanding which will enable children to make intelligent and personal commitments. It does not try to produce in children a commitment to prescribed beliefs . . . no attempt should be made to manipulate young minds into conformity with any creed or ideology. An awareness of religious interpretations of life will be encouraged. . . . The relevance of religious beliefs . . . will be pointed out without pretending that most people consciously hold these beliefs or act on them . . . it makes sense to base an RE syllabus . . . on an understanding of Christianity, which is the religion of which most evidence lies to hand.'[33] It was a brave attempt but it lacked the clear advocacy of Christian faith found in the Durham Report. Perhaps no-one was entirely happy with it. In January 1978 Arthur Rowe wanted a conference to work on a new statement of ACT's position on RE. Unable to get a conference off the ground the necessary groundwork was never done. William Kay, who joined the RE sub-committee in January 1977, felt that members were unsure of their ground philosophically and unable to take on giants such as Paul Hirst.

Aims in RE[34]

A booklet on RE, edited by Norman Richards, argued that in return for keeping RE, Christian teachers must agree with the current objections to evangelism, indoctrination and an exclusive preoccupation with Christianity. Joy James wrote of the dangers of playing into the hands of those who would remove RE by defining RE in dogmatic Christian terms. At primary level there could be a degree of advocacy, but to base the whole approach to RE on such a commitment would be indoctrinatory: 'this is the situation in which we operate'. [35] Eric Bramhall, by contrast, argued for advocacy at all levels. He quoted from the philosopher R.S. Peters: 'The teacher, like Socrates, senses that really to understand what is good is, ipso facto, to be committed to its pursuit. . . . education . . . is the process of initiating others into activities, modes of conduct and thought which have standards written into them.'[36] In relation to RE this meant that 'the task is . . . to give such an understanding of religious belief, and particularly of the Christian faith . . . as may lead to an appreciation of the Christian view of the world, and society, and of the significance of Christian commitment'.[37] On the last page of Bramhall's contribution a dramatic change of direction took place. Such a view of RE was said to be 'confessional' and the paper ended with an appeal for initiation into 'religion' not Christianity: 'to concentrate on Christianity alone could hardly be seen as justifiable for an RE which aims to initiate into the religious mode of awareness'.[38] Howkins suggested that the hand of the editor might be responsible.[39] This was in fact the case; Richards had changed Bramhall's wording.[40]

Views came to reflect those of the mainstream

By the mid-1970s, some ACT members were unhappy about overtly Christian approaches to RE such as those of the OCU. Cousins argued that the price of not having to teach Islam or Marxism as true was that 'no Christian teacher or Hindu teacher may teach Christianity as if *it* were true'.[41] Other evangelicals largely concurred. A book called *RE in the Primary School* by Bert Hearn took a largely conciliatory approach to Ninian Smart, Ronald Goldman and others.

Conclusion
ACT was successful in many respects. Perhaps its greatest contribution was to establish a respected position for evangelicals in education where to be theologically conservative had been tantamount to committing professional suicide. However, it came at a price. The price was alignment with the 'new RE' and the loss of a critical voice. Those who stood out suffered at the hands of their editors. Cousins beat the retreat. It seemed a huge task to mount a case for the philosophical respectability of teaching RE from a Christian point of view. There was a need to distinguish between advocacy and indoctrination and to see that the former was entirely acceptable and indeed essential for anything worthy to be called education. ACT failed to make this distinction.

An analysis of agreed syllabuses
between 1976 and 1988

HMI published a curriculum document in December 1977 stating: 'Religious Education in county schools is most appropriately seen as an introduction to man's quest and some of its contemporary expressions in belief and practice, rather than a process of induction into a particular religious tradition.'[42] The syllabus conferences seemed to agree. The syllabuses of the period show that the battle for the hearts and minds of the profession was now largely won.[43] *Quest* did turn out to be a 'throwback'; an example that no other LEA followed. Indeed, despite its success, it did not receive a single mention in any of the syllabuses of this period.[44] Like

The Fourth R before it, it failed to set a trend.

These syllabuses largely pursued an 'open-ended' approach, with no one view taught as true. Bexley (1981) abjured the idea of making the pupil religious. Hampshire (1978) considered it 'no part of the responsibility of a county school to promote any particular religious standpoint', a phrase which, in modified form, would be repeated in many later syllabuses. Rotherham (1989)[45] warned against claiming any form of 'cultural superiority' for Christian faith. Occasionally a syllabus reflected on the fact that a different approach from that hitherto pursued was being adopted. Hampshire asked its teachers to approach the document without preconceived ideas about what constituted Religious Education. Croydon (1980) admitted that many people would be surprised at the form the syllabus took. However, for the most part, syllabuses were confident about their recommendations and showed little defensiveness.

The syllabuses reflected a degree of unanimity about aims. The three most common aims were:
  1. to understand religion
  2. to find personal meaning through open-ended search
  3. to understand religions.

Three syllabuses included learning to respect other religions, and two listed knowledge of Christianity as an aim. Many accepted Smart's six dimensions of religion, and often a thematic approach was recommended to help make sense of the religions. No syllabus recognised that they were offering a particular standpoint themselves; one which directly challenged the self-understanding of many of the religions studied. However, it was often acknowledged that it was difficult to define the word 'religion' and various attempts were offered in an attempt to give the syllabus coherence. At the same time the view was taken that it was important to give some awareness of the variety of religious belief in order to give pupils the widest possible field in which to search. The difficulty of narrowing down the field to something manageable was keenly felt and generally solved (one might say avoided) by delegating the task to the teacher or to 'ongoing curriculum development'.

The end result was a series of very thin syllabuses in which aims and objectives were set out, together with statements about general approach and reference to an accompanying handbook offering suggestions on how to implement the syllabus. Often lacking was any attempt within the syllabus to link content of teaching with aims and objectives. Manchester (1985) and Avon (1976) did not specify any particular content at all. When content was specified, it was not always linked with a particular age group or stage of development. So Berkshire (1982) set out the following areas of knowledge as examples for use with secondary children under the heading 'concepts and beliefs': 'the main beliefs in the Bible, Torah, Qur'an, Guru Granth, Bhagavad Gita; creation, incarnation, eternal life, the inspiration of scripture, sin, judgement, forgiveness, grace; the creeds of the churches; karma, nirvana; the five pillars of Islam; the four noble truths of Buddhism.'[46] Nothing was said about which should be taught at which stage. Refuge could be taken in the fact that a list was presented as containing examples only, but such lack of direction would not give confidence to the teacher to feel that he or she was likely to fulfil the aims of the subject. It did not seem to matter very much what was taught.

Sometimes syllabuses were quite open about the vagueness of their proposals. Lincoln (1980) stated: '"Aims" refers to the overall purpose and general direction, and "objectives" refers to the promotion by teachers of activities the outcome of which is, in principle at least, discernible.'[47] The reason given for lack of detailed content within this syllabus was the 'rapidity of social and educational change today as well as the wide differences between local needs'.[48] Humberside (1981) stated that it was 'inappropriate and undesirable to write one prescriptive syllabus for every school in Humberside'.[49] But this was what a syllabus conference was set up to do. Following the approach first taken by WP 36, Humberside stated that the objectives were 'merely a list of the elements needed to give balance in any school's syllabus'.[50] Manchester gave a list of experiences, concepts, skills and attitudes which required the teacher to supply the teaching material. Durham (1983) followed a similar approach, indicating concepts, said to derive from the 'basic themes of religions', which avoided almost entirely any reference to a particular religion or doctrine. So for pupils aged 11-16 : 'The concept of worship can be developed through the exploration of such ideas as festivals, rites and ceremonies, the sacred meal and sacrifice, for ritual is outward behaviour which reflects an inner intention to be in contact with deity.'[51] Other syllabuses betrayed the view that what really mattered was something other than the learning of religion and the religions. So Rotherham (1989) stated: 'the quality of the pupils' experience, understanding, mastery of skills and development of personal qualities in religious education is more important than the assimilation of religious knowledge, important though this is'.[52] Lincoln stressed the importance of reflecting upon experience and one can see here a movement towards the development of personal qualities, which would characterise how, for example, the Westhill Project would later understand the task of religious education.[53]

In effect these conferences abdicated their responsibility to write a syllabus. Surrey and Croydon were exceptions. These conferences gave precise instructions about content, particularly in relation to Christianity. Pupils aged 11-16 were to be helped to a 'deeper understanding of God; his creativity, fatherhood, and continued activity in the world.' Surrey was clearly based on Christianity and stipulated the birth stories, Harvest, Christmas and Easter, baptisms and weddings at infant level. At middle school level, the background of Jesus was prescribed, the composition, language and use of the Bible. At secondary level the Trinity was mentioned, the Church in the wider world, and further study of the Bible. This shows that it was possible for a strong conference to stand out against the trend. This is still the case today.

Conclusion

A significant opportunity was created in the mid-1970s for a restatement of RE as the teaching of Christian faith. Both in Parliament and the Church of England concerns were expressed about the way RE had abandoned its traditional task. There was a strong case intellectually for the new RE to be decisively rejected. However, two professional associations failed to line up behind those who had argued for the teaching (and therefore the advocacy) of Christian faith in the 1970s. The Church of England failed to take up the challenge and few syllabus conferences heeded the call. Instead conferences reconstituted the task and the language of RE in diverse ways. As a result fissures began to develop in the good ship religious education. It became unclear about its central purpose. If the purpose was to teach religion, then one had to face the fact that religion was not something with sufficient substance to be taught; it in fact refused definition. If, on the other hand, one decided that the purpose was to understand religions then one had to decide which religions, and which aspects of those religions would be introduced, and this was a very long business to engage in. It required more knowledge than most members on conferences were likely to have. No wonder they abdicated the job to the teachers. But awkward questions about which religions, and/or which aspects of which religions were to form the personal development of pupils could not be avoided in the classroom.

Under the previous regime Christian faith was taught because it was held to be true and as a means of developing personal qualities. But now pupils were to forge their own personal development from a bewildering array of options. Declaring that the teacher was not to tell the children what to believe seemed liberal and exciting, but it carried the risk that children might develop in undesirable ways, and it was likely to be unsustainable. The temptation to use religions or aspects of religions as means for development of suitable qualities would be great. It created a conflict between the need to respect a religion and the need to give acceptable guidance to pupils. It is unlikely, for example, that teachers in England and Wales would want children to adopt certain quietist attitudes found in Buddhism or aspects of the caste system in Hinduism.

So, where once there was unity of purpose, now there was an uncertainty which resulted in a clutch of aims, aims which had a disconcerting tendency to conflict with each other. These syllabuses struggled to specify aims and content which derived from them. Has it, in fact, become impossible to mount a coherent theory of religious education? Before considering this important question, the next chapter explores the efforts made in the 1988 Education Reform Act (ERA) to reclaim the ground and base RE on the truth of Christianity.

Chapter 9[1]
The 1988 Education Reform Act

In 1988 a major education bill became law. The Education Reform Act (ERA) ushered in the National Curriculum, thus instituting a major reform of education. The clauses concerning RE and worship, however, were intended to strengthen, not reform, the tradition of religious education in this country and were built on the 1944 Education Act. The passing of the bill became the arena where the battle for control of RE was fought out yet again. The resistance that faltered in the late 1970s, to be followed by the creation of slim, non-prescriptive syllabuses with little or no emphasis on Christianity in the 1980s, was revived in 1988 in the form of major efforts in Parliament to restate the case for proper teaching of the faith.

The background to the 1988 ERA Act

In early 1988, Kenneth Baker, Secretary of State for Education, introduced his bill to the Commons. His research into the situation in RE over the previous 18 months revealed that RE had fallen into neglect. Baker decided that what was needed was to strengthen the existing law, rather than amend it. His view of RE was that it should open up the spiritual dimension and that it was difficult for an agnostic or atheist to 'instruct children in religious education as an atheist does not believe in any kind of theistic philosophy'.[2]

A group of MPs and peers, headed by Baroness Cox, determined to introduce an amendment which would require that, for most pupils, the teaching given would be based on Christianity. They were concerned about the way RE no longer gave precedence to Christianity but rather taught several religions in relativistic fashion, producing a 'mishmash' – a way of teaching which used themes such as worship, founders and festival and did not give a grounding in any one religion. In February Anthony Coombs proposed an amendment in the Commons inserting the word 'Christian' to the phrase 'collective worship'.[3] He withdrew the amendment after a lively debate. Later that month, Baroness Cox asked what steps the Government was taking to ensure that state schools provided a Christian act of worship and Christian teaching. In a long speech she showed that she was fully aware of developments in RE. She accepted the case for some teaching of world religions: 'such teaching can increase understanding and respect, which are essential values in a pluralist society. But that is very different from presenting young people with a position of extreme relativism in which all belief systems are presented in a value-free hotch-potch.'[4] Baroness Blatch asked of the bishops, 'where have they been over these past years as this subject in our schools has been very much in demise?'[5] She spoke of having to fight like a tiger to retain Christian teaching as the major part of the agreed syllabus when she was a member of the Cambridgeshire ASC.

The bill came, unamended, to the Lords in April 1988. Graham Leonard, then Bishop of London, felt that it was wrong that the bill presented to the Lords merely referred to the sections concerning compulsory religious instruction in the 1944 Act, saying that they should be complied with. Leonard determined that the provisions for RE should be written on the face of the bill lest RE and collective worship be thought unimportant. At the same time, Cox's group had determined to get the word 'Christian' inserted into the bill both in relation to collective worship and RE. In the Lords on 3 May, Cox put forward an amendment requiring RE to be predominantly Christian. The Bishop of London, who disliked the word predominate, agreed to find a form of words that would satisfy the concerns of the peers and be acceptable on a broad front. Between 3 May and 18 June he consulted widely within the profession and concerned parties. He obtained agreement on a form of words, hammered out in the offices of the National Society, of which Leonard was Chairman: 'an agreed syllabus shall reflect the fact that the religious traditions in Great Britain are in the main Christian, whilst taking account of the teachings and practices of the other principal religious traditions represented in Great Britain'. This wording eventually became Section 8, 3 of the Act.

The meaning of Section 8, 3

Section 8, 3 was explained by the Bishop of London in this way:

> It does not mean that there will be a percentage of Christian teaching spread throughout the country with a proportion of other faiths. It means what it says which is that in the main, looking at the country as a whole with its present multi-cultural composition, the bulk of it will be Christian. The norm will be Christian if one likes to put it that way. But there will be exceptions because of local areas and what is proper to them in the educational setting. That is what we mean by "mainly" – not "mainly" in the sense of two-thirds rice and one third tapioca or something like that.[6]

When pressed in the House on what this meant he replied: 'It is the purpose of that package [the amendments now in Law] that Christian children should receive teaching in the Christian faith. Secondly, it is the purpose that children of other faiths should be taught their own faiths.'[7]

Further on in the debate the Bishop put it like this: 'If one looks at the country as a whole, one will see that there will be areas in which it is 100 per cent [Christian traditions] and areas in which it will be less, and so on.'[8]

This was backed up in other parts of the legislation, much of which was taken over from the 1944 legislation. The syllabus conferences were to be made up of representatives from religions present in the area and in proportion to their numbers. Where there were no Muslims (or Methodists for that matter) in an area, there could be no representation on the syllabus conference. To give maximum flexibility explicit provision was made for a conference to agree more than one syllabus.[9] No co-options could be made on to the conference, although there was nothing to prevent working parties consulting with those not on the conference.

The provisions for collective worship went to great lengths to provide for worship that is appropriate for the children receiving it. The syllabus conference was structured to provide a religious education tailored to the pupils receiving it. As Kenneth Baker said: 'Nor would we presume to require that religious education should be the same in county schools in Devon as in schools in Bradford'.[10]

Some peers recognised that the wording of the amendment was potentially ambiguous and might not prove sufficiently strong to withstand 'mishmash'. Several amendments were tabled which offered less ambiguous wording, but these were withdrawn on the understanding that they were unnecessary. Both Baroness Hooper for the Government, and the Bishop of London, (supported by Lord Elton) insisted that their proposals:

· meant an end to mishmash
· would require Christian education for Christian children
· would give proper rights to parents of non-Christian children.

On this basis the bill went to the Commons where an attempt was made by Jack Straw, opposition spokesman on education, to require the Secretary of State to bring in the changes education authority by education authority, rather than (apply them) simultaneously across the country. He did not like the law as it stood and was concerned that teachers did not want it either. It would seem that he expected the Government to insist on the meaning given in Parliament and was trying to mitigate its effects. However the law was passed intact on 18 July, 1988.

The press reported the outcome accurately.[11] *The Independent* for example reported that

[the] package of measures proposed a new basis for religious education in schools, expressing the centrality of Christianity but acknowledging and providing for the valid concerns of other religions. Agreed syllabuses should in the main be Christian but

there was room for flexibility in areas where the vast majority of pupils were from another faith. So a school predominantly Muslim could draw on the traditions of that faith.[12]

Within the profession there was considerable alarm. In July 1988, just as the clauses were going through the Commons, John Hull reacted angrily, speaking of the 'imposition of Christian supremacy through legislation'.[13] The 'Christianising amendments'[14] threatened to undo all the good that had been accruing in the last twenty or twenty five years; in particular the 'unique British experience of multi-faith dialogue in the classroom'.[15]

Vera Conway was a part-time teacher at an infant school in south London who taught stories from the Bible to children on the basis that they were true. After advice from the local authority (ILEA) it had been decided to give her duties outside the classroom so that pupils would not be 'indoctrinated'. Following the 1988 ERA, Conway was told by her head teacher that now that the Baker Bill had been passed and a positive image of Christianity was to be presented to children, she could return to classroom teaching.[16]

What would be crucial would be the way the government implemented the new provisions.

DES Circular 3/89

Circular 3/89 (issued in January 1989) is a model of clarity and prescription, setting out both the essential continuity with the 1944 Education Act and what had changed – in particular that now RE was part of the 'basic curriculum', its importance was enhanced.

The circular set out four specific changes in relation to agreed syllabuses. The first was the requirement of Section 8, 3, set out without comment: 'all *new* syllabuses . . . must "reflect the fact that the religious traditions in Great Britain are in the main Christian whilst taking account of the teachings and practices of the other principal religions represented in Great Britain".'[17]

The second was that while study of denominational formularies and catechisms was now allowed 'teaching by means of' such statements continued to be prohibited.[18]

The third laid upon the LEA the duty of only giving effect to a new syllabus if 'it appears to the authority to comply with the requirement of Section 8, 3 as to the nature of Religious Education.'[19]

The fourth amended the wording concerning the composition of syllabus conferences to make it clear that representatives of non-Christian religions could be appointed to Committee A (the other churches' committee) in accordance with their presence in an area.

The circular refrained entirely from explaining Section 8, 3 while, at the same time, requiring the LEA to decide whether a syllabus presented to them was in conformity with it. Yet it had been clearly explained by its promoters in Parliament. By contrast the circular went to considerable lengths to explain the parallel phrase concerning the legal requirements for collective worship, which states that the collective worship organized by a county school was to be 'wholly or mainly of a broadly Christian character'.[20]

And yet no-one could accuse the DES of neglecting to stress the importance of Section 8, 3. Of all the legal provisions to do with RE, this clause alone was considered sufficiently weighty to require a local education authority to reject the work of a syllabus conference in its entirety if, in their opinion, it was contravened. But the weight thus given to the clause was reduced to zero by the department's failure to spell out the meaning given in Parliament. The clause was in effect neutered, but in such a way that no-one could accuse the DES of neglecting it.

Why did the DES fail to give guidance on Section 8, 3? I have been unable to get replies to this question. Kenneth Baker advised contacting one of the senior officials who was responsible for it at the time.[21] Mr Nick Stuart was a senior civil servant in the DES at this point and involved in negotiations at all stages. So was Miss Jenny Bacon. Miss Bacon's office promised a reply but none has been forthcoming. Mr Stuart wrote twice, saying that he would do what he could to find out. He was unable however to locate the files dealing with the Circular and was unsure whether they were lost or had been destroyed. He apologized that he could not remember anything about the matter: 'it is a long time ago and I frankly cannot remember what considerations we took into account in preparing Circular 3/89.'[22]

Other researchers have tried unsuccessfully to find answers about policy decisions from civil servants and government departments.[23]

With no explanation forthcoming, one may only speculate as to why the DES failed to explain Section 8, 3. The minutes of a meeting of the executive committee of the REC in September 1988 report that the DES had decided not to interpret the Act but to leave it to the courts. Nothing is said about why this decision had been taken, nor is there any comment upon this unusual course of action. It is correct that the courts decide the meaning of the law in cases where a judgement is required. But it is the role of a circular to explain and carry forward the intentions of Government. This critical piece of new legislation cried out for explanation.

The DES refusal to answer queries

Understandably RE Advisers and syllabus conferences sought advice from the DES on the meaning of Section 8, 3. In the minutes of the REC executive meeting held on 19 September 1988 it is recorded that an officer of the ILEA stated: 'ILEA had been unable to obtain answers from the DES on a variety of fundamental questions.'

One RE adviser wrote to the DES for help on issues such as what percentage of time should be given to Christianity in view of the requirement to 'reflect the fact that the religious traditions were in the main Christian'. He found the DES reluctant to give guidance and commented that other LEAs had had similar experiences. As a result LEAs 'were not seeing things too clearly'.[24] A research project published in May 1989 documented confusion and uncertainty in LEA advisers' understanding of the Act.[25] Advisers felt that some form of emphasis on Christian faith was required. In relation to 'taking account of' there was a division of opinion between those who thought this meant that attention to other religions was to be secondary to reflecting the Christian traditions, and those who understood that now the teaching of other faiths was to be accorded as much time and attention as the teaching of Christianity. Overall one can see the Advisers struggling to make sense of the new requirements, containing as they did such phrases as 'means for me', 'indicates hopefully' or 'must mean'. Interestingly, one of the few areas of certainty amongst some advisers was the need to recognise the religions practised in their area.[26] But with the DES refusing to give guidance, exactly what the law required became an open question.

Interpretations given by the RE profession

The decision not to insist on the meaning given to Section 8, 3 in Parliament presented an opportunity to create and promote an alternative interpretation. By November 1988 John Hull had written *The Act Unpacked* – a word-for-word exegesis of Section 8, 3 which ignored the explanations given less than six months earlier in Parliament – just as draft Circular 3/89 had done. Hull stated that 'in the main' meant mainly and referred to a percentage of time to be given to the Christian traditions (the tapioca and rice mixture specifically stated to be incorrect) and that 'taking account of' meant that the other principal religions must be taught in every syllabus:

> for the first time, therefore, the basic curriculum of children and young people in our schools will not be meeting the legal standards unless they are taught the teaching of the principal non-Christian religions in Great Britain.[27]

This meaning was never raised in either House and ran counter to the main thrust of all the debates. Parliament intended to legislate for RE to be given to those of other faiths alongside those being taught by means of the Christian traditions. Clearly a small section on Judaism, for example, in a syllabus which majored on Christianity could never deliver that.

Hull's new interpretation was seized on enthusiastically by others: while the syllabus may reflect the important place of Christianity in Great Britain, it should also recognize the importance presence of other faiths. It will not be sufficient to engage in a study of Islam in Bradford and not in Truro, for the wording of the Act refers to 'Great Britain'.[28]

In spring 1989 Hull proposed names and numbers of principal religions now required by law:

the new Act requires the local Agreed Syllabus to take account not so much of the religious traditions present in the locality but those represented in Great Britain. On any reckoning, Judaism, Islam, Hinduism, the Sikh faith and Buddhism are major religious traditions which are represented in Great Britain . . . no Agreed Syllabus will meet the requirements of this section of the Act unless it takes account of their teaching and practices.[29]

Hull ignored other aspects of the legislation which restricted the syllabus conference to representation from religious communities present in an area. This provision is a major problem for Hull's interpretation, since, if the law required the principal religions to be taught, it would surely have provided for the conference to have experts or adherents appointed as members.

The REC produced a handbook to help SACREs and syllabus conferences in their work which effectively misrepresented this aspect of the law. This handbook stated:

It is important therefore that all these aspects of the context of religious education are reflected, as far as possible, in the composition of the Agreed Syllabus Conference. The first committee must include representatives of 'non-Anglican' Christian churches (Roman Catholic, as well as major Free Church traditions) as well as people from the other principal religious traditions.[30]

Yet the law specifically prohibited the appointment of representatives of religions or denominations of religions which were not present in an area.

While all this was going on, the DES remained silent.

Other interpretations

In 1989 Edwin Cox and Josephine Cairns, colleagues at the London Institute of Education, published a very different account of the Act.[31] They regretted the fact that conferences were unable to appoint members of religions not present in the area and did not mention a new requirement to teach all religions. The Act, they argued, viewed the purpose of RE as initiation into a religious tradition, generally Christianity. The retention of the conscience clauses underlined this, and may have suggested that it was expected that teachers would teach on the basis of their own understanding and possession of faith.

Two lawyers argued similarly. A. Bradney believed that the Act strengthened Christian teaching and worship in schools, now protected by statute. The law had 'ostentatiously abandoned any idea of neutrality in matters of religion'.[32] However, he warned that implementation might not be forthcoming; some unions had expressed disquiet along with some teachers. J.C.D. Harte viewed such disquiet partly as reaction to the new law which contradicted prevailing orthodoxy in school RE. He made a telling point when he wrote of those within the profession who had 'devised pluralist or sociological approaches to religion which they feel are threatened'.[33] Like Bradney he wondered if the opportunity to reassert the Christian heritage in the life and teaching of the schools would be taken.

The original meaning expressed in Parliament was set out in a pamphlet published by the Campaign for Real Education (CRE) in 1990.[34] It stated that the 1988 Act was intended to reinforce the role of schools in giving children the opportunity to grow up within a religious faith and tradition, which is usually Christian in this country. The pamphlet stressed that the Act gave full freedom to parents of other faiths to have their children worship and receive a religious education in conformity with parental religious and philosophical convictions.

Interestingly John Hull offered a variant on his own interpretation at this time. He was responding to those who argued that the intention of the legislators in relation to the RE clauses was very different from what had actually come to pass. Hull agreed that a careful reading of Hansard, the record of parliamentary debates, did indeed reveal that the legislators thought they were changing RE. He robustly countered that either the government was incompetent or their intentions had been mysteriously confounded by a benevolent deity. This rather underestimated his own influence. He argued that 'the teaching of Christianity was to be mediated through such realities as tradition, significance and area'.[35] He stressed the flexibility of the law: the wording was 'only a very general guideline'.[36] Local characteristics in the area must be taken into account. He wrote: 'Nothing is said about the criteria which would lead to a religion being "principal" nor how many adherents such a religion would have to have before it could be regarded as being "represented in Great Britain". Nothing is said about how many of these principal religions there might be; we are not told that the syllabuses must take account of *all* of them nor that they should be dealt with systematically one by one. This is all available for local deliberation.'[37] This represents a significant shift towards the interpretation outlined in Hansard and reads very differently from his earlier position.

Defending the new interpretation

These interpretations served to stir memories of the parliamentary debates, and questions continued to be asked about why it seemed as if nothing had changed in RE. It was therefore necessary for those within the RE profession who disliked the law to defend their interpretation. The National Society,[38] had played a pivotal role in the drafting of the amendments and indeed in negotiating with Kenneth Baker and the DES in the period leading up to and during the passing of the ERA. In 1989 the society published a booklet answering queries and misunderstandings about the new Act.[39]

It was argued that the law was changed to highlight the important place of RE in the education system of the country. It said, correctly, that schools did not have to approach pupils as committed Christian believers, but omitted to mention the right of non-Christian pupils to have religious education in their own faith. The answer to the question whether all pupils in a school should receive the same programme of RE was a firm 'yes', despite the fact that the law clearly allowed for more than one syllabus to be employed in a school.[40] The booklet argued that parents should not need to make use of withdrawal and might even be found to be intolerant in so doing. Provision had to be made for those parents who 'persist in withdrawing'.

Following John Hull's earlier view the booklet stated: 'In every school all pupils . . . will be expected to acquire some knowledge of Christianity and some knowledge of "the other principal religions", i.e. Judaism, Islam, Hinduism, Sikhism and possibly Buddhism'.[41]

The officers of the Society, despite their link with the Bishop of London (who was Chair of the Board of Education and of the National Society), were not entirely in tune with their leader. Colin Alves, General Secretary of the General Synod Board of Education, had worked closely with the Bishop of London during the period of consultation and as the bill went through the Lords. Yet, in a lengthy article describing the debates in the Lords, Alves failed to mention the explanation given in the House by the Bishop of London.[42] He wrote:

> What the Act has in fact achieved is the establishment of religious education (including the provision of school worship) as an essentially educational activity, an entirely appropriate part of the basic curriculum for every school, incorporating within the *one* curriculum for *all* pupils a proper exploration of *all* faiths. If it happens thereby to contribute to nurture in one particular faith, well and good, but that cannot, must not, be its prime purpose.[43]
> [italics in the original]

Alves was right to state that this is what the Act had achieved by 1991. However the intention of the Act was, as I have outlined, quite different.

And the former Bishop of London was at pains to point this out when shown Alves' article.[44]

Several articles were written in the three years between 1988 and 1991 to support the interpretation favoured by John Hull and the National Society.[45] But soon it became unnecessary to insist on this view since it was to be endorsed by the DES.

The DES gives a view following the Ealing Case

In March 1991 the DES finally gave a view on the interpretation of Section 8, 3 when a letter was sent to all Chief Education Officers to clarify the law. A parent had complained that the Ealing agreed syllabus did not comply with the requirement to 'reflect the fact that the religious traditions of Great Britain are in the main Christian'. The Department took legal advice which was relayed to all Chief Education Officers. The Department followed Counsel's opinion in its entirety. It took the view that a syllabus must give sufficient particulars for it to be clear that the teaching given would comply with the provision. In most cases most attention would be given to the Christian traditions. However, a syllabus must not be based on Christianity alone, or 'exclude from its teaching any of the principal religions represented in Great Britain'. In addition the department, using the exact words of Counsel, stated that a syllabus 'must not be designed to convert pupils, or to urge a particular religion or religious belief on pupils'.

But certain facts were missed by Counsel. He had been given a copy of *The Act Unpacked* which he deemed to be 'factually accurate'.[46] He asked within the RE profession as to the standing of John Hull and was told that there was 'none better'.[47] On the basis of this recommendation he appears to have accepted at face value all that Hull argued. He failed to see that the work was written with one end in view: to give a rendering of the law which would counter that given to it in Parliament. Indeed Counsel appeared to have no knowledge of the explanations given in Parliament. Like Hull, Counsel gave no weight to important aspects of the legislation:

·   the restriction on membership on the syllabus conference to those religions and denominations present in the area
·   the positive provisions for withdrawal in the legislation, arguing instead that a need to avoid withdrawals (nowhere stated in statute) meant that religious education must not urge any particular belief upon pupils
·   the provision for a plurality of syllabuses to take account of different beliefs.

In taking a view, Counsel relied partly on the prohibition of teaching by means of denominational formularies. But this was to leave out of account the fact that some teaching was to be given 'by means of' something else, implying that this teaching carried a degree of authority.

How could Counsel not have known of the explanation given in Parliament? Until 1993 it was customary for judges not to make use of Hansard in interpreting statute. Counsel therefore may have deliberately not looked up Hansard. However, there were witnesses, such as Cox and Cairns or the CRE, who could have alerted him to a different view. The opinion of Counsel has been enormously influential, yet it has never been tested in court, where its inadequacies might have been revealed. It is certain that if a case came to court now, appeal would be made to Hansard. This is because of a precedent set in 1993 by Pepper vs Hart, a case which has had considerable effect upon legal judgments ever since. The issue concerned the payment of tax by teachers whose children were receiving subsidised education at the private school where they were employed. The matter hinged on the admissibility or otherwise of the explanations of the law to be found in Hansard. The Law Lords judged that where an ambiguous wording was given a clear explanation by a promoter of the Bill in Hansard, that explanation should be accepted as the true meaning. What this means is that there is a precedent in law for accepting the explanation of Section 8, 3 given in Parliament as the true meaning.

Circular 1/94 and the SCAA model syllabuses

Baroness Blatch was Minister of State at the DES between 1992 and 1994, working under John Patten. A colleague of Baroness Cox, she was in a unique position to insist on the meaning given in Parliament in 1988. In June 1992 questions were asked in Parliament about why it was that the intention of the 1988 RE clauses had not been fulfilled. Baroness Cox spoke of many improvements in RE, but warned of 'a number of systematic attempts by representatives of the RE establishment to interpret the Act in favour of the thematic multi-faith approach which the amendments were designed to discourage'.[48] In answer to Baroness Cox, Blatch reiterated the explanation of the law set out in 1988. She also indicated that a new circular would be issued to replace 3/89.

However, Baroness Blatch experienced conflict with civil servants when working on the new circular at the DES. It seems that, armed with Counsel's opinion, civil servants now felt confident that the law required all the principal religions to be taught. Blatch was told repeatedly that this is what the law stated and her wish to give advice about teaching Christianity with conviction were resisted at every turn. She would write a section and have it returned to her altered. She would try again and the same thing would happen. Convinced by the civil servants, eventually she began to argue the case herself. In April 1993 she said: 'All agreed syllabuses must include the study of the other principal religions represented in this country as well as Christianity.'[49]

The Department began to receive complaints from LEAs who were concerned that they did not have the money to provide the necessary expertise to produce teaching on all the religions now stated (several years after the event) to be required by law. In response the Government funded working parties from the six religions, under the supervision of the Schools Curriculum and Assessment Authority (SCAA), to produce model syllabuses. This further entrenched the view that every syllabus had to provide for the teaching of six religions.

The DfEE's[50] misquoting of the law on RE

When the model syllabuses were published, the department quoted the words about not urging a particular religion or religious belief, first used by Counsel in the Ealing case, as if these words were contained in Section 26 of the 1944 Education Act.[51] Fred Naylor[52] pointed this out to the Department and after a lengthy correspondence and much determination on the part of Naylor, the mistake was corrected and a letter sent to all SACREs in England informing them of the mistake. It was stated, however, that it was still the view of the Department that syllabuses must not urge a particular religion or religious belief upon pupils and, given in support, was the same section 26 of the 1944 Act. This section prohibited teaching by means of denominational formularies. It seemed that the Department at this point felt confident that while this section of the law did not specifically prohibit such 'urging', it could nonetheless be used in support of the view that urging a particular religion or religious belief was against the law.

Fred Naylor was certain that this was wrong and a case came up in 1997 which proved him to be right. A parent from the Isle of Wight had complained to the Department for Education and Employment (DfEE) that the syllabus was urging 'New Age' beliefs upon his child. The DfEE wrote to Mr. Naylor saying that the complaint had to be rejected since the law did not prohibit the urging of beliefs upon pupils: '*no* religious beliefs urged on pupils would fall foul of Section 376 (2) of the 1996 Act.'[53] The same letter stated that it was the view of the Department that although not a statutory requirement, the nature of RE was such that it should not urge a religious belief upon pupils.

To this day, the Department for Education and Skills (DfES) stands by its view of the nature of RE and has refused to alter the advice contained in official documents. Paragraph 32 of Circular 1/94 states: 'Syllabuses must not be designed to convert pupils, or to urge a particular religion or religious belief upon pupils.' Section 26 of the 1944 Act (now Section 376 (2) of the 1996 Act) is still quoted in support of this statement. Yet the Department has stated categorically that this section of the law does not prohibit a syllabus that urges religious beliefs upon pupils. If the law allows something, is it right for the department to forbid it? The DfES should make it clear to all SACREs that the advice they are giving is not a legal requirement and is not supported by law. The reference to Section 26 should be rescinded since, on the Department's own admission, it does not prohibit the urging of a religious belief upon pupils.

Conclusion

RE operates in a very confused situation. It is an extraordinary thing that the very opposite of what was intended by Parliament has in fact not only come to pass, but has gained strength from the legislation. Those who might have been expected to oppose such an outcome have found themselves capitulating to it. How many teachers today know of the real intention of the law? They need to hear the view of Graham Leonard:

> But you can teach Christianity as true; it was the considered and widely held view, understood and accepted by both believers and unbelievers, that the provisions [of the 1988 ERA] allowed for and were intended to create, a situation where Christianity could be taught in the classroom as true.[54]

Chapter 10
'You Teach Us Wrong, Miss'

A critique of 'learning from religion' and the work of Michael Grimmitt, the Errickers and John Hull

This chapter and the following chapters bring the story up to the present and offer a critique of RE as practised in schools today. Concern expressed in Parliament prior to and following the 1988 ERA about what was happening in RE resulted in more attention being paid to the subject by Government bodies set up to regulate the curriculum. I begin this chapter by considering the effect of these bodies, in particular the way they advanced a particular theory of RE. QCA (Qualifications and Curriculum Authority) is the Government sponsored body responsible for curriculum development. It succeeded the National Curriculum Council and SCAA. Following the 1988 ERA and attempts to raise the profile of RE, the Government agreed to include RE within its overall remit for education and to allocate resources to it centrally by appointing an RE officer in charge of a team. This means that a move towards centralisation of RE has been set in motion, despite the statutory position whereby RE is locally determined. The SCAA model syllabuses, mentioned in the last chapter, are an example of this. In 1998, as part of a review of the National Curriculum, money was found for the RE team to carry out a review of RE. Non-statutory guidance was published following this review in 2000. The review concentrated on developing a rationale for RE, producing a scale of national expectations for RE and giving guidance on what has come to be known as 'learning from religion'. Its work is important because it was based on widespread consultation within the profession and on close analysis of agreed syllabuses. It gives a picture of what is happening in RE in England and Wales and what is considered professionally acceptable.

QCA and the Aims of Religious Education

QCA's aims for RE are set out on the inside front cover of the review of the RE curriculum[1] under the heading *The Importance of Religious Education*. They are:

- To gain knowledge and understanding of Christianity and the other principal religious traditions in Great Britain
- To respect different religions and ethical life stances
- To consider questions of meaning and purpose in life
- To make informed judgements on religious, moral and social issues.
- To develop a sense of identity and belonging as befits citizens of a plural society
- To evaluate their own beliefs, values and practices and communicate them to others

The following caveat, echoing the opinion of Counsel, is issued: 'RE does not seek to urge religious beliefs on pupils nor compromise the integrity of their own beliefs by promoting one religion over another. RE is not the same as collective worship, which has its own place within school life.'

The aims are similar to those found in the syllabuses of the 1980s. RE promotes understanding of the religions of the world with Christianity as the one named religion; it is about pupils developing their own personal meaning and respect for the beliefs of others in a plural society. No one view is to be preferred; hence the caveat which sits rather oddly at the end of the list of positive aims. The one omission from the aims set out in the syllabuses of the 1980s is the learning of 'religion'. However, one of the two attainment targets for RE, first set out in the SCAA model syllabuses in 1994, is 'learning from religion'. It seems odd that one of the two attainment targets (ATs) concerns a concept (religion) not mentioned at all in the aims of the subject. And it is clearly viewed as important, since much of the review document is devoted to explaining and exemplifying what it means in the light of findings that teachers had difficulty with this target.[2]

I now consider what is meant by AT2, 'learning from religion'.

Learning from religion

Confusion over terminology

The model syllabuses in draft form used the terms 'learning about religions and learning from religions'.[3] When the final version was published in July 1994, the latter target had changed to 'learning from religion'. This distinction was not observed by all agreed syllabuses in 1999 however, as a QCA consultant remarked: 'It is interesting to note that some syllabuses appear to miss the significance of the different use of "religion" and "religions". Many use the singular or the plural twice, apparently indiscriminately.'[4] However, even QCA is not beyond confusion over the matter. When I visited the QCA website on 9 December 2000, a page last updated on 4 October 2000 used the phrase 'learning from religions'.

This suggests that behind the use of apparently simple language there lies a problem with how RE understands itself. The basic language of RE masks an ambiguity which constantly runs the risk of misunderstanding, or exploitation. It looks as though the word 'religion' is being used in a different sense from the word 'religions'. It may be reasonably easy to say what we mean by religions[5] but what is this thing called 'religion' that pupils are to learn from?

QCA's definition of 'learning from religion'

In the 1999 review of annual SACRE reports QCA stated: 'The GCSE short course has moved awarding bodies towards greater attention to religion as a meaning-making activity, that is, learning from religion.'[6] Here, religion is defined as the activity of creating meaning. Learning from religion is said to be about response, evaluation and application of questions to do with identity and experience (making sense of who we are), meaning and purpose (making sense of life), and values and commitments (making sense of right and wrong). The teacher tells the pupils about the various answers provided by the religions (learning about religions) and then encourages the pupil to 'respond' (learning from religion). There are no right or wrong answers; indeed what is praised is the creative use of the data of religions so as to construct something new. What matters is not what meaning pupils find, but that they find a meaning, any meaning. Doubtless teachers will steer pupils away from certain meanings; but if teachers do so, they step outside of their brief. Learning from religion is 'concerned with active response of pupils . . . about valuing pupils' own ideas and concerns . . . raising questions from religious teaching that speak to pupils' personal experience . . . about enabling pupils to draw their own conclusions'. It is not 'about promoting a religious lifestyle . . . about providing pat answers . . . dogmatic . . . about providing set conclusions'.[7]

If 'learning from religion' is an activity then the phrase 'learning from religion' is misleading. There is no learning (in the sense of learning that can be assessed) going on. QCA sets out criteria for assessment and gives examples of what it would mean to meet these criteria. But both criteria and examples lack definition. At level 5 pupils are to 'make an informed response to a question such as "Does charity begin at home?"' But what is 'an informed response'? QCA does not tell us. It is not surprising that QCA states that 'not all aspects of learning from religion are assessable or measurable'.[8] Refuge may be taken in self-assessment: 'Self-assessment is particularly useful in some aspects of learning from religion.'[9]

Furthermore, if learning from religion is the creation of personal meaning steps must be taken to prevent the authoritative teaching of a particular religion or religions, since what is intended is not that pupils learn the lessons a religion teaches, but that they use the religions to create a meaning for themselves, whatever suits them. This, of course, trivialises the religions and puts a question mark over the degree of respect that is being given to them. This cannot be acknowledged however, and the use of the phrase 'learning from religion' masks what is really going on.

QCA's theory of religion

The theory of religion adopted by QCA is that there are shared human experiences and that religions are the product of human reflection upon such experiences: 'Pupils should be able to make clear links between common human experiences and what religious people believe and do. Rituals, festivals, rites of passage, beliefs about God and the world – all these connect with common human experiences of awe, celebration, passage of time, a quest for meaning, purpose and value. Learning from religion requires pupils to see how such experiences are understood and interpreted in varying ways by members of different faiths and by those without religious beliefs.'[10]

Such a theory of religion denies a role for revelation. Religions are stated to be a human construct and religion is the activity of creating religions out of reflection upon experience. The consequence of this is that no one religion may be used in any absolute sense to judge another, since all have derived from human experience. All that is possible is that an individual might judge one religion to be more adequate to her experience than another religion or view of life. This explains the importance of pupils bringing their experience alongside the teachings of a religion in their RE lessons. Pupils are encouraged to examine their experience and see how far it connects with, or resonates with a particular religion. QCA reflects the view that no religion amongst those practised today holds the answers. This may not be stated, however. The end result will be a profound hostility to all religions, as I shall show shortly.

I now consider the practical examples given both in the review document and in QCA schemes of work published in 2000.

Examples of 'learning from religion'

The extraction method

This involves presenting an aspect of a religion, extracting an idea from it, often an idea that is not central, and teaching that point rather than the central religious message. For example in Year 1, the stories of the Exodus, the burning bush and the giving of the Ten Commandments are told. Children are asked to identify Moses' qualities of leadership and make connections between how they have experienced leaders and the way Moses carried out his task. The lesson seems to be that Moses was a good leader: an incongruous lesson since arguably the point of the story, at least in the early stages to which children are introduced, is what a bad leader Moses was (he needed his brother to assist him and could not even speak clearly). He became a good leader when he learned to trust in God. However, this is not the lesson that is highlighted for the children.

The distraction method

This is where some religious teaching is given but attention immediately distracted onto a connected but different idea. In one illustration children are to be taught about the five pillars of Islam, and then asked to relate them to their own lives as follows:

Learning about Islam	Learning from Islam
All the time Muslims believe . . .	All the time, I believe . . .
Five times a day, Muslims . . .	Every day, I intend to . . .
Every week Muslims give . . .	If I chose to be generous, I would . . .
Once a year, for self discipline, Muslims . . .	My ambition for the next year is. . .
Once in a lifetime, Muslims hope to go . . .	In my lifetime, I hope to . . .

Attention is immediately taken off Muslims and the possibility of children taking their faith seriously, and put onto matters which have little relation to the Muslim equivalent. What relation for example has naked ambition to the self-discipline required of a Muslim? And giving to others, a sacred duty in Islam, becomes a matter of individual choice for the pupil. All these injunctions, which in Muslim thinking are related to worship of God, are used as aids to help the pupil make their own lifestyle choices. This is surely trivialisation of the worst sort.

The disjointed method

This is where there is a disjunction between the religious material and the lesson to be learned from it. In Year 5 a theme on Muslim beliefs is given where the role of angels in the story of Muhammad is explained. After comparison with the internet, text messages, etc., children are introduced to the idea that angels are messengers in Islam. This is then used to teach that 'there are mysteries in life'. But to Muslims, angels are not mysteries, and neither is the revelation to Muhammad. Angels clear up mysteries rather than raise them. Angels are a mystery only for the secularised western mind.

What is being taught by these methods?

1. Secularised Christianity

Pupils learn that they should forgive others, that there are mysteries in life, that they should have hope for the future and respect what religious people hold dear. These are the lessons that are hammered home, and reveal what QCA feels comfortable with handing on as true. Pupils should give to others, respect the old, love their neighbour, create special memories (like the Jews did at Pesach), use money and time well, have some values (not specified which), recognise some questions have no answers, look for guidance in life (not specified where or what), work for justice and contribute to community life.

What is clear is that the hand of the 'Christian mother' exerts a pressure still. Here are Judaeo-Christian traditions but in a secularised form. Mostly these values are disguised as 'human experiences', but there are moments when the message of Christianity is allowed to speak for itself. In sections on Christian prayer, for example, there is a piece which leads to pupils writing their own prayer.

2. Importance of the 'self'

From their very first lessons in RE, pupils are taught to reflect on their own identity. Year 1 pupils are invited to reflect on what is important to them, what they feel about giving to others, what is of value in their lives. Second year pupils are to think about special memories in their lives. Third year pupils must begin to be conscious of their own feelings and values. In Year 5 they think about who is special to them, who influences them and why. Year 6 pupils are to clarify their own attitudes and values by using a quotation from the apostle Paul. Pupils are taught via RE that they must find for themselves what is of importance and to be valued. They themselves are the source of what is to be held important and valuable. Children are encouraged to think that their experience is *sui generis*, and even self-generated.

Conclusion

RE as found in QCA documentation on AT2 is characterised by an amalgam of contradictory currents that render the whole project incoherent and incapable of taking pupils in any useful direction. They are:

1. The view that it is possible to teach respect for religions which claim to have been brought about by an act of God, while at the same time teaching that religions are human constructs deriving from reflection upon experience.
2. The view that pupils should create their own meaning at the same time telling them they must accept certain basic values, such as respect for others, forgiving others and hope for the future.
3. The requirement to study religions only to find that they must create their own.

'Learning from religion' has become a tool which prevents children from learning the lessons a religion has to teach. We may not teach, we are told, as if one religion were true or the religion to be believed above all others.

At the same time certain lessons are hammered home: those that do not trouble liberal westernised minds. The problem is that all this is taught in the context of particular religions, whose own doctrines are subject to the hidden censorial hand. The religions must be mined for the truth which may be found acceptable to the western mind, whereas much of central importance to the religion itself may safely be disregarded. This treatment is detrimental to all the religions studied.

However, individual religions still form the base of the teaching at all ages. So it is not surprising that measures will have to be put in hand, if only subconsciously, to present individual religions in ways which do not give the impression that that they are thought to be true. More powerful, however, are the subtle measures employed throughout these examples to distance children from taking seriously what the religions actually teach.

But this is not all. The element of self-absorption, of self-generated values, of being in control by choosing and creating meaning for oneself, all point to a form of self-deification. It is not only ironic that this should be the result of RE, it actively subverts faith in God and replaces it with rebellion against God. At the same time pupils are required to engage in a secularised and heretical form of religious activity which owes much to Christian culture – a fact of which QCA seems quite unaware.

A critique of the work of Michael Grimmitt

The phrase 'learning from religion' derives from the work of Michael Grimmitt. In 1987 he published *Religious Education and Human Development,* a complete theory of RE. It is from this book that the whole notion of learning from religion has developed.

The human givens
Grimmitt's scheme posits certain 'human givens' of interdependence, freedom and responsibility. These broaden out into seven core values:
- order, purpose and meaning
- ethical endeavour
- the value of human beings
- a just society
- the individual right to self-fulfilment
- commitment to interpersonal relationships, family and community
- human spirituality and the desirability of spiritual development

The human givens and core values are 'in some sense implicit within the human condition'.[11] Religions and other belief-systems give form and substance to the core values and aid what he calls 'humanisation'. To learn from religion is to use religions as tools to become aware of, and then to develop for themselves, what pupils believe: 'learning from religion about themselves.'[12] By studying religions pupils will discern ultimate questions and signals of transcendence in their own experience, discerning and interpreting the core values for themselves, leading to greater self-awareness and personal knowledge. What matters is not the truth of a particular religion, but how far it opens up the core values to pupils and enables them to respond and engage in self-awareness, thereby creating meaning for themselves. RE enables pupils to take control over their beliefs, not passively accepting what their family or culture has taught them. One might want to agree that personal appropriation is a necessary part of religious commitment, particularly within Christian faith. But personal appropriation is not the same as reconstructing the religion in question. Few religions would agree that they have arisen out of human reflection alone. Even fewer would accept that they must be put at the disposal of the young for them to discard or refashion at will, as best accords with pupils' own preferences.

The later Grimmitt

Grimmitt now advocates a radical form of a philosophy called Constructivism.[13] This states that there is no one reality to which humans must respond and come to terms with; rather human beings construct their own version of reality according to their individual experience of 'it'. Knowledge can only be assessed by how useful (viable) it is to the learner, not by how far it accords with an objective reality. Furthermore, language itself is fluid and dynamic and cannot convey 'pre-packaged' meanings to pupils. Children must 'construct' what a belief or practice means 'for them'. Religions, in Grimmitt's view, are powermongers imposing a particular meaning (their meaning) on others. Constructivism highlights acts of domination: 'constructivism . . . enables religious knowledge and understanding to be problematized and its language and meanings related to power and privilege to be deconstructed.'[14] RE therefore must engage in deconstructing what others want pupils to believe about their religion, in order to free up the creative possibilities inherent within each child. The RE teacher's task is to free the students from taking on board the interpretation authorised by a religion, and to encourage them to make their own meaning for themselves. The linking of power and privilege to religious knowledge enables Grimmitt to suggest that pupils be encouraged to '*deconstruct* and *reconstruct* traditional and formal religious interpretations and meanings in the light of their own experience and alternative perspectives'.[15] Pupils should reflect on the 'intrinsic sexism and racism'[16] of religion, thus preventing RE from 'furthering the hegemony of cultural and social reproduction involving the perpetuation of injustice, inequality and oppression'.[17]

Grimmitt gives a transcript of a lesson on the god Shiva. The Hindu ideas behind an image of the god Shiva are explained, and in the conversation that follows, attention is given to accurately answering pupils' questions and, in some cases, suggesting ideas. This might seem odd, given the premise that no one meaning is the 'right' one. It is, in fact, difficult to see how this lesson differs from the common practice of using an artefact to teach a religious idea and perhaps compare it with ideas from another religion.[18] It is clear that, despite what Grimmitt says about not conveying pre-packaged meanings, this is exactly what happens, and, indeed, what makes the lesson successful.

Criticism

The difficulty with the earlier scheme is that of finding categories that can be identified across religions. Grimmitt acknowledges that those he does identify (providence, the sacred, law, soul, discipleship, priesthood, revelation and worship) fit only the western religions, and even here there are difficulties. Is law for example a substantive category in *Christian* faith? Grimmitt argues that categories give rise to concepts and gives the example of the concept 'sin' deriving from the category of 'soul'. But the link seems tenuous and one might want to argue rather that sin is better seen as a category. However, it would not be so easy to see it as category in Islam. The problem for Grimmitt is to explain the undoubted disparity between the religions and other belief-systems of the world while retaining the belief that all derive in some sense from the same core values and human givens. Furthermore it is difficult to maintain that the core values are implicit in the human condition even in 'some' sense. Individual self-fulfilment has a distinctly modern feel, and some values are dated; why human and not animal spirituality? Notions of order, purpose and meaning are questioned by postmodernism. It is difficult not to see here a late 20th century summary of western liberal humanism, shorn of belief in God.

The later Grimmitt must reject the human givens. Such an idea, it would seem, must be problematised along with other 'constructions'. This is a quite extraordinary metamorphosis of RE. One might want to ask how exactly pupils are to reconstruct meaning? What could this possibly mean? That Christ as the Son of God should become the daughter of Gaia? That the idea of submission to Allah should be reconstructed as . . . well, what? The RE lesson is here used not only to deconstruct the sacred language and text of a religion, but to suggest that religions were created as a result of manipulative people whose lust for power led them to oppress others. What would this do to children with a faith? This shows a profound hostility to the religions as we know them.

Why meaning-making?

Meaning-making is a product of our Christian background. It is Christianity that seeks meaning in history, events and the universe; for the Hindu, meaning is construed altogether differently. The Hindu sees meaning as determined and foreordained according to the working out of karma; it is not to be *found* in the activity of a God in history. Reading the signs of God's presence is a Christian activity; the God who surprises us and goes before us is the Christian God who enters our world both as mystery and as revelation. Making sense of the world is both a command and a possibility in Christian thinking simply because God has gone before us and ordered the world in ways that can be understood if we will use our minds to do so. Meaning is to be found in things, people and supremely in history. Indeed, Nicholas Boyle writes that the Judaeo-Christian tradition seeks to find meaning in history because of the incarnation in time of the Incarnate Word.[19] In Michael Grimmitt we can see someone schooled in the Christian tradition where conversion and owning a faith for oneself is central. There is a sense in which every Christian has to make the faith his or her own, and cannot rely on passively accepting it from parents or authority figures.

However, meaning-making, and making faith one's own through personal response and exploration have their place only so far as they are encompassed within the faith tradition itself and are informed by the tradition of that faith. When they are taken out of this context they become heretical and damaging to the possibility of children coming to faith and coming to a proper knowledge of how the world is. We are not at liberty to create meaning as it happens to appeal to us, nor are we at liberty to present other religions as products of the same process. To imagine that other religions endorse meaning-making, in the sense in which Grimmitt uses the term, is a mistake and represents a covert and heretical Christianisation of the traditions of others.

It is an approach that has much in common with the Errickers.

Clive and Jane Erricker

Clive and Jane Erricker, of the Children and Worldviews Project,[20] attempt to ground RE in the experience of the individual child: 'The impetus for the Project derived from the conviction that education and religious education was too content led and paid insufficient attention to the capabilities and experiences of young children and young people.'[21] Few would want to disagree that education must take account of the child, her needs and horizons. However, underlying the Errickers' view is a radical relativism that insists on children themselves being the creators of their own futures, whether understood as their personality, goals or lifestyle. Anathematised therefore is any idea of imparting qualities, or stating goals which will focus the learning. Following Grimmitt they take the view that knowledge itself cannot be passed on, but rather must be constructed by each individual. 'No contrary to relativism' is their mantra.[22] It is not surprising therefore that the Errickers ask 'for a radical re-assessment of the pedagogical principles we employ to achieve a different educational purpose'.[23] The new educational purpose for RE is summed up as: 'the process of world construction for practical and moral purposes'.[24]

What of religion and the religions in the Errickers' scheme? They reject the notion of religion as an essence, which, they claim, is a construct placed upon the religions. They argue with Grimmitt that religions are wielded by the powerful as a means of control. Religions must be deconstructed and pupils freed to construct their own. The choice for educators is whether they treat the several religions as grand narratives and teach them as such, or whether 'we understand them as constructions with political purposes, in the context of which they make truth claims'.[25] In the Errickers' view the grand narratives 'silence' the smaller narratives, those of the pupils. Teachers must 'facilitate children's narratives in the context of the school community rather than imposing narratives upon them, to which they are expected to cònsent'.[26] Any attempt to teach the grand narratives will militate against the affirmation and development of the pupils' own narratives. This might be thought to create a problem for RE. Whereas Grimmitt does envisage the teacher introducing the 'grand narratives' of the religions, the Errickers appear to give them no place at all.

The role of the teacher is to provide a stimulus, a poem for example, and then stand back. Pupils talk about the poem and how they reacted to it. As they narrate, they are said to be constructing their own worldview. Teachers must learn to relinquish control: 'We are also asking them [the teachers] to yield their position of power and authority within the classroom. We are suggesting that children can be allowed to know as much or even more than the teacher, can publicly claim the position of the repository of that knowledge and have it acknowledged by the former holder of that exalted rank – the teacher.'[27] The Errickers also want to remove the educational apparatus of outcomes and precise goals that may hinder the process of free narration. The setting of desirable outcomes can be oppressive: 'These desired outcomes act as a protective device in terms of what can or cannot be heard or voiced, and they assume a lack of sufficiency in children'.[28] They specifically reject even the most basic outcome such as well-being or happiness.

Classroom examples

A child narrates a conversation she has with her dead grandmother. Her grandmother is in heaven, she is happy there and has lots of friends. Heaven is higher than space. Not everyone believes this, but when God talks to him or her, they will know that it is true. You can ride a white pony in heaven and have marshmallows to eat. Grandma works in a cleaner's and washes all the clouds in heaven. The child must be affirmed and encouraged to keep on talking and sharing her ideas with no interference. As she does this, she develops certain skills. These include self-criticism and criticism of others, but not by any publicly accepted criteria. It is stated that both take place 'according to one's own [i.e. the child's] recognised principles'.[29] The Project shows no interest in sorting out these ideas and suggests that the child has created the ideas herself. Their truth or otherwise is immaterial.[30]

A boy's account of his lifestyle includes a predilection to violence, along with a desire to be good, and a belief in God and the Bible.[31] He is a gang member (aged eight) and has committed acts of violence. During the interview he plays with a pair of scissors as if using a weapon. The analysis of the interview states that the boy, Kelvin, works within a basically violent 'genre' into which everything he learns is fitted. This causes problems for him at school since school requires him to live non-aggressively. Nothing is said about helping the boy to reject his violent genre, or about the fact that there is in his experience a sense of goodness and God that could be encouraged. It seems that he must be abandoned to his own self-construction for the sake of the theory. Yet it is acknowledged that this boy is continually in trouble in school. Exclusion (and worse) lies ahead if he is not helped to turn away from his present understanding of the world.

Criticism

There is a profound hostility to religions in the work of the Errickers. Religions, as the purveyors of knowledge that comes with the divine imprimatur, may be the worst oppressors of all, since they may come ready primed to avoid questioners. Religions, and those who teach them, are to be feared and exorcised from religious education as far as possible. Unless, that is, teachers consent to abdicate their position as teachers, and religions as religions. Any form of authority is suspect and children need above all to be freed from its chains. Nothing, not even a 'desirable outcome', must stand in the way of children determining their own futures.

Like all relativists the Errickers are not as wedded to relativism as they claim. They commend care for others, sensitivity and community. They write of 'subjects with faith and subjects of faith, subjects with values and subjects who are valued. Such an understanding suffices as the basis of spiritual and moral education, because it is the basis of community.'[32] So there is something objective out there after all, there is a community that may lay claim to teaching children about spirituality and morality. That being so, it is incumbent on us to introduce pupils to those values which promote harmony and goodness.

The strength of their position is that it takes the lives of the pupils and their struggle to make sense of life with great seriousness. In this, one may discern the emphasis within Christian tradition on personal faith. They are the archenemies of stereotype and static dogmatic formularies. But their rejection of received knowledge renders their approach vacuous. Yet again the 'unlimited voyages of spiritual discovery' beckon to the unwary. Their work reflects the passion of Old Testament prophets, exposing the failings of the corrupt priestly orthodoxy that is oppressing the children. Yet the profession is not being called back, or urged on, towards anything in particular. And, most ironically of all, the postscript recalls the authors to their relativist credentials and instructs the reader to put her own construction on the book.

It is important to see that the logical end-point of 'learning from religion' is a thorough-going relativism and hostility to traditional religions. But, it may be replied, surely this is not the only end-point.

John Hull

John Hull advocates learning from religion but is less extreme. He argues that RE must not become 'learning religion' where the religion controls what is learned and the methodology employed. Religions must be studied from a distance in such a way that some educational benefit is derived. In 'Gift to the Child', the project that Hull directed at Birmingham University, religions offer gifts to children that aid in the process of humanization. They do this by 'making a contribution to the pupils' moral and spiritual development'.[33] Primary school children are shown artefacts from religions and encouraged to learn something for themselves from the religion. Hull puts it like this: 'For example, Ganesha, the elephant-headed deity celebrated in southern Asia, might offer a stimulation to the curiosity of the children, challenge their values, deepen their distinctive sense of identity, and impart empathy for others. When this happens, the children may be said to have learned from religion.'[34] Clearly this approach is subject to the critique of 'learning from religion' presented earlier. Religions are used to teach something else. One might teach the same lesson without reference to Ganesha.

Unlike Grimmitt and the Errickers, Hull does not see religions as oppressors. His view is that religions are great treasures, the world's capital for good. He writes: 'The world religions must be recognised as the principal foci of disciplined and coherent moral and spiritual life . . . . they remain along with a humanised art, literature and science, the main resources that we have for the rehabilitation of human life.'[35] However, Hull has also written about the need to 'deconstruct' certain types of theologies, and it is clear that he is working with a particular view of what constitutes the genuine spiritual features of the religions.[36] Any notion to be found in a particular religion that encourages competitiveness between religions is unsound. Rather, religions should see themselves as partners in a global search for spirituality, freedom, love and the living of an ethical life as a challenge to a world that is ruled by the money god.[37] This assumes a large measure of agreement between the world religions and, while acknowledging differences, declares such differences secondary. Hull here advises that RE should teach the values held in common across the world religions. This quest has never proved successful. Indeed the values that are presented by Hull (spirituality, freedom, love etc.) bear all the hallmarks of the Christian radical that John Hull himself is. Not all Christians, Muslims and others are prepared to see certain beliefs (those that mark them out as different) reduced to the level of the second order, and those that Hull selects (because they fit in with his radicalism) promoted to first order.

Hull's view of RE is a restating of essentialism, the view that religions are expressions of a basic essence that may be said to underlie them all. Essentialism, however, as indeed the Errickers argue, is a construct, and in this country is likely to be a Christian construct. At the same time, Hull too shows a hostility to religions. He denies to religions their own self-understanding and domesticates them within his own theologically liberal standpoint. It seems that it is all right for liberal Christians to think they are right, but if conservatives do the same, they are likely to be summarily dismissed.

In the next chapter I consider other important theorists in RE who offer significantly different approaches to those discussed here.

Chapter 11
'Why teach them, if you don't know which religion is true?'[1]

A critique of QCA's 'learning about religions' and the work of Robert Jackson, Brenda Watson, Andrew Wright and Trevor Cooling.

In this chapter I consider QCA's advice on 'learning about religions' and then go on to consider the work of experts who offer theoretical support for this approach.

A critique of QCA Attainment Target 1: 'learning about religions'

Attainment Target 1 (AT1) is concerned with learning about religions. Concern has been expressed by OFSTED that pupil learning in RE often lags behind that in other subjects, particularly at Keystage 3 (ages 11-14) and the schemes of work have been produced with the aim of remedying this. Each religion is treated in a systematic way, from the point of view of adherents. QCA envisages that pupils will learn about both Christianity and other religions throughout the keystages. In Year 1 pupils learn about Noah, the friends of Jesus, Jewish beliefs and practices and some Christian beliefs and practices. In Year 3 the Hindu festival of Divali is studied and then the Bible for Christians. In Year 4 Hindu worship is introduced, followed by Easter. In Year 5 they learn about Muhammad, and do more work on the Bible. Year 7 begins with a unit on where to look for God, justice within Christianity, the Buddha, and ends with a topic on the environment. QCA's review states that pupils will explore 'issues within and across faiths'[2] but the schemes of work contain few examples where this happens.[3] Despite the claim that progression is built into the schemes of work, it is difficult to trace a coherent thread through it all, and the schemes resemble the diverse list of topics suggested by WP36.

QCA expects pupils to 'make reasoned and informed judgments on religious, moral and social issues'.[4] The important question is how children are to do this. Doubtless it is intended that the teacher facilitates such a process. But QCA offers little help, and the fact that no particular religious belief must be urged on pupils may make teachers nervous lest any guidance they give be taken to imply that a particular religious belief is true.

What this means is that religions are presented as conflicting claims to truth, which, it appears, cannot be rationally settled. The fact is that such an approach is founded on (and therefore teaches) relativism. And relativism leads to indifference. There is some evidence that this is what is happening.

A recent study of more than 2,500 secondary pupils in 22 co-educational comprehensive schools in England provided evidence for the dangers of teaching pupils more than four religions. It showed that pupils who learn more than four religions confuse religious terminology. In some cases, children who had only studied Christianity in school knew more about other religions than those who had studied four or more religions in school. Also of interest is the fact that studying the non-Christian religions appeared to have no positive effect on the attitudes of pupils studying them. However, where pupils were aware of the fact that they had studied Christianity this had a significantly positive effect upon their attitude to this faith. Where pupils studied religions both systematically and thematically, attitudes towards religions were shown to be less positive than where either the systematic or thematic method was used.[5]

I now consider the work of important experts which offers a theoretical underpinning for the sort of approach outlined here by QCA.

Robert Jackson[6]

Robert Jackson's work has concentrated on the important question of how one should go about learning about religions. Jackson asks; 'What *is* a religion? How should the religions be portrayed? What authorities should be appealed to in deciding how the religions should be pictured or represented?'[7] As one of the few to take these questions seriously his work is of great importance. He issues a powerful critique of certain assumptions which have underpinned the work of most religious educators. These assumptions relate to the possibility of giving an account of a religion that is faithful to its own self-understanding. Such assumptions are evident in SCAA's invitation to religious communities to write model syllabuses. The religious communities would set out what they wanted to be taught of their own religions and teachers could then be confident that they were giving a view of the religions from the point of view of its adherents. Jackson has questioned whether this is the right method to gain a proper understanding of the plurality of ways in which individual religions are lived out. Furthermore, while it has been commonplace to query the notion of 'religion' Jackson has queried whether we may usefully speak of individual 'religions'.

What is 'religion' and is there any such thing as 'a religion'?

Jackson shows how the word 'religion' came to mean a system of beliefs in the eighteenth century.[8] The idea was that 'natural' religion could be derived from reason alone and that the beliefs derived in this way were universally valid. Beliefs were contrasted with rituals and superstitions which were under the control of, and had been invented by, priests and suchlike. British Orientalists went to India in the eighteenth century and began to interpret Hindu belief and practice in the light of an understanding of religion that defined it by beliefs and tended to dismiss 'corrupt' practices. Rather than patiently sit at the feet of Hindus who would have given a range of responses, these scholars used their own categories to make sense of the other. This process may be described as 'colonising' the religious tradition (a term Jackson prefers to religion). Hence ideas familiar and acceptable to the West were used to interpret Hinduism, so that aspects similar to monotheism were highlighted, and 'polytheistic' tendencies understated or interpreted in the light of the former. So there developed a westernised romantic view of Hinduism.

Jackson has shown how this operates in RE.[9] QCA falls into the trap in one of its schemes of work on Hinduism, where there are numerous references to God and worship. Yet the Hindu has no concept of a personal deity and does not worship, rather he does *puja*, which is a form of service which varies according to the recipient. So parents receive one form of puja, the divas another, and the cow another. The western mind wants to domesticate such practice; to make it into something it feels comfortable with. 'God in many forms', a phrase which appears in the QCA schemes of work, is another example. This can work in reverse: the native wants to please the sahib so he presents his religion in forms that make it pleasing to the imperial master. The native has learned the idea of a personal God from the sahib and works it into his own religion.

It is not just the idea of an essence (religion) which is problematic. To declare that 'Hinduism' is 'a religion' is to state that it is one of a class (religion). We have to recognise something in 'Hinduism' which defines it as a religion. Our concept of what a religion is derives from an a priori which we bring to the study. In the West this can only mean that we use the categories of Christianity. So, it could be argued, when we think we are studying 'Hinduism', we are really studying a Christian construct. What we see as 'religion', others might see as washing statues, an example of oppression, or an interesting form of cultural expression. Jackson's view is confirmed by Ananda Dulal Sarkar: 'The white Britishers even today have an imperial view of Hinduism. They do not want to know what it is really all about. It has to be what they are comfortable with. That is to say that the subject must fit into the Christian frame. You Hindus have a God. God is a genus. There is this Hindu God, Buddhist God, etc. The immigrants who came here oblige because it gives them comfort to know that they are monotheists after all and not idol-worshippers.'[10]

But the problem goes deeper. Jackson's work amongst faith communities led him and his team to become aware of different views of what constitutes a particular religious tradition amongst those brought up within a religion. Jackson and his team spent many hours listening to believers, in particular, children, and were struck by how differently the same religion could be lived and expressed. Even in one city the way a particular faith is understood could be significantly different even amongst adherents.[11] For this reason Jackson is wary of even insider overviews and has been critical of the SCAA models.

Jackson's project deliberately selects first-hand accounts from children, membership groups and 'well constructed overviews' of the wider tradition, along with transcripts and other first-hand material when writing textbooks. Eclecticism is part of the theory. Sarkar's view is that one must give no comparison with Christian categories, Sanskrit terms must be used at all times and the religion would be best taught to mature students over many years.[12] What all this suggests is that it is not a straightforward matter to teach even one religion, never mind the six normally prescribed for study in schools.

Edification

Jackson wants pupils to be able to reflect on what they are learning so as to further what he calls 'personal learning', or edification. Edification is achieved by pupils being encouraged to move from learning aspects of a tradition back to considering their own personal views. Accounts from the religion being studied are interspersed with points for reflection, which ask pupils to make connections with their own views. Part of the edification process involves critical engagement with religious truth-claims, but no examples are given of how this may be done. Indeed Jackson admits that, in relation to the Project textbooks, sensitivity to individuals represented within the text precluded any attempt to engage with truth claims. His approach would therefore seem to fall foul, by default, of the charge of relativism.

Interestingly, it seems that it is pupils from a strong faith tradition who, in Jackson's experience, seem best disposed to engage in critical reflection. Perhaps this is because subconsciously they are making use of insights and criteria stemming from their own tradition. This might suggest that the way forward is for pupils to study largely by means of their own religious traditions (in line with the intention of the 1988 ERA) but this is not a way that Jackson recommends. He says little about which religions, in what order and how many, but he is certain that the way forward is not to return to teaching based on the truth of Christianity, or any other religious tradition.

Teachers may reject Jackson's views as extreme. It is not difficult to see an inconsistency in denying that expert overviews of the tradition should be accepted, at the same time as requiring teachers to construct overviews for classroom use. One might argue that the use of the phrase 'religious tradition' is used in the same way as the word 'religion', and therefore relies on the very reification of religion that Jackson wants to reject. Nonetheless, it must be accepted that Jackson has shown that it is a complex and involved matter to gain authentic understanding of the religions that we find in our midst. And this is unsettling for teachers.

What of the charge of relativism? Jackson himself admits that his approach does not deal with how to resolve conflicting truth claims, and that his theory is only a partial account of RE.

The matter of developing a critical approach to religions is surely important. Without such a critical approach no critique of anything is possible. The theologian John Milbank wrote: 'If it were accepted that all cultures (religions) have equal access to the (religious) truth, then all critique, including critique of sexist and racist constructs, would become impossible.'[13]

I now consider the work of Brenda Watson who sets out specifically to encourage critical engagement with religious traditions.

Brenda Watson

Watson has highlighted how RE as currently practised inculcates relativism. She writes: 'If a conscious effort is not directed to thinking about truth claims, the RE we give actually reinforces the fact/belief divide: it means that beliefs are just relative to what someone from a particular background or culture or experience or lifestyle happens to think.'[14] Her most recent work has been devoted to developing what she calls 'evaluative' RE. She argues that relativism is avoided by addressing truth-claims directly in the classroom. She says: 'It is for [schools] to help pupils and students to cope with controversy and to think through it, working towards truth. They have to come to realise truth for themselves – no-one else can give them the real convictions by which to live – but we, when we teach them, can help them to appreciate that truth is the objectivity towards which all of us work even though we may make mistakes and be dismayed by the misunderstandings under which we operate.'[15] Watson has developed a way of evaluating religious claims which enables pupils to grapple concretely with the issue of truth. She suggests seven Levels of Discernment which include questions concerning accuracy, context and integrity.[16] On the basis of the Levels of Discernment various criteria can then be applied in order to reflect on how true a belief might be. She identifies ten such criteria. The criteria are not rules of thumb to be applied rigidly, but considerations to stimulate thinking and reflection. As such they can work effectively and cumulatively, they need to balance each other.

Her approach to the teaching of religions is characterized by what she calls 'critical affirmation'. One looks first for insights and truths which may be found and affirmed, before considering aspects which might count against a particular religion. This is essentially the attitude of the peacemaker and is an attractive part of her approach. Importantly, however, it does not assume non-commitment on the part of the teacher, but perhaps presupposes it. Her eirenic approach allows her to encourage pupils to ask the question 'Is this true?', rather than simply being introduced to what 'Muslims believe', an approach which may, by silencing questions of truth, promote relativism and indifference.[17]

The merit of her scheme is that she offers real help to teachers whereas often this is lacking, both in QCA guidance, and the agreed syllabuses. But does this general approach avoid relativism? It holds out the hope of finding the truth and a sophisticated method of getting there, but does not declare in advance what that truth might be. It seems to be a case of travelling hopefully. It could be argued that it is not necessary to state in advance what the answer to a problem is, and that to do so might prevent the excitement of discovery. But at some point the pupil will want to know that they have got the sum right, or at least see where they have gone wrong. And for this to happen it is necessary that the teacher knows what the truth is, even if she keeps quiet about it at the start. Indeed it is knowing the true answer that means that the teacher can instruct the pupil in the way to find it for themselves. If the relevant criteria of discernment are valid they must, one assumes, be able to point in one direction or another when it comes to justifying a given religious belief. Watson wants to leave this question 'open', however, and this puts into question her belief that she has found a way of avoiding relativism in the classroom. Either her criteria do show which religion or religions are true (and to what extent) or they leave the matter open. If the answer is the latter, then it is difficult to see that she has found an adequate answer to the problem of relativism.

Watson takes the view that the current educational climate is so antipathetic to the idea of Christianity forming the base of RE that only some such system as hers, which does not assume the truth of Christianity, will be accepted. However, I will argue in my final chapters that this antipathy rests on a misconception[18] of what it means to teach Christianity and that rejection of such a form of teaching is not inevitable.

A further issue is how far such a method of teaching, with its continual problematising of every religious belief that is introduced, is suitable for young children. I agree that we often underestimate their abilities, but it would seem that some form of initial ground-laying is necessary for the young before bringing in the necessary reflection and critical awareness at a later date. And to lay the ground means that much will be taken on trust in the early stages. Without some such trust is it not likely that children will grow up lacking confidence in any religion? It certainly would seem wise to bring children up as far as possible to have confidence in their own religious tradition. This is the opinion of Andrew Wright whose views I now consider.

Andrew Wright

Wright offers a devastating critique of the way in which RE has domesticated the religions by either assuming essentialism, or working on the basis of an innate religiosity which must be nurtured by pupils following their own inclinations: 'At heart, contemporary spiritual education has embarked on a process of inducting pupils into the rules of the post-modern game, encouraging them to construct their own realities, on the basis of unrestrained freedom, desire, will and preference.'[19] This means that any idea of *teaching* has been abandoned and children are left bereft of the ability to judge: 'The act of relegating spirituality to the private sphere thus fails to offer criteria and interpretative frameworks through which such spirituality can be evaluated, assessed and developed positively.'[20] It also means that the claims of religions are secondary to the process of the child developing his or her own religious beliefs: 'The adoption of a progressively child-centred agenda means that the task of stimulating inner spiritual awareness has priority over the academic study of the external representations of religious culture.'[21]

Wright sets out his view of RE in the following way:

1. RE must avoid the pitfalls of presenting religions in unified fashion. Rather pupils must be presented with the plurality of religions and worldviews. He writes of a qualitative pluralism which 'reflects the genuine diversity of religious and secular perspectives on religion, and accepts the ambiguous, controversial, and conflicting nature of theological truth claims'.[22]

2. RE must allow for the horizon of the pupil. Children have 'an already developing religious worldview'[23] which will have been gained from adults and peers. Children must be given the freedom to 'recognise and articulate their emergent religious beliefs and attitudes without constraint or manipulation'.[24]

3. The fact of ideological bias or power structures must be acknowledged by both teacher and pupil. However, he rejects the model that envisages the child choosing without guidance or restraint. He describes such a model as 'immersion into an ideological worldview, in which personal preference is offered as the basic criteria of truth'.[25] Wright claims to offer a way through

which pupils can 'identify and explore both their own ideology and the various ideologies presented by religious and secular traditions'.[26]

4. The horizons of the child must engage with those of the religions. He puts it like this: 'the cultivation of intelligent conversation between the two horizons, in which the religious horizons of the child encounter a range of religious perspectives and options, and uses this encounter as a means of further clarifying, enriching and developing the child's religious beliefs'.[27]

5. The result of such an encounter will be both convergence and dissonance. This should lead to further reflection and engagement: 'What is important for the educator is not what is believed by the child, but the manner in which they come to own their particular belief systems.'[28]

6. The fundamental aim of his approach is stated to be 'pupils' ability to take part in an informed, critical, sensitive and ideologically aware conversation about the nature of ultimate reality, and of their relationships to this reality'.[29]

The question is whether Wright has succeeded in providing a way of avoiding the model of 'personal preference'. There is a large measure of 'Teach Yourself' methodology here. It seems as though the pupil, rather than the teacher, is in charge. The task of the teacher is to supply conflicting evidence, and to be on hand to make sure that pupils do not resist the impact of it. In an earlier work Wright wrote: 'If we can get away from the idea that to teach is to advocate and see the teacher as a fellow pilgrim in the search for meaning and truth . . . that the 'true' answer remains an open question is simply not a problem . . . in our society there is no one, generally accepted, religious "truth".'[30] It is clear that the teacher is not conceived as in any way nurturing children in a particular tradition of faith, nor even as teaching a particular faith. It seems that it would be important for the teacher not to prejudice the outcome of the child's decisions. The question arises as to what all this conveys to the pupil. It is likely that pupils will pick up the idea that it is a matter of indifference what views they come to hold, and that no one religion can be shown to be truer than another.

However, Wright has made a plea elsewhere for schools to nurture pupils into a particular religious tradition, with the agreement of parents and governors. A school, he argues, will and must nurture pupils in some form or other, and it is best for this to be stated, clearly understood, and planned for: 'Education will inevitably nurture children into a particular world view. The question is not whether this will happen, but how: consequently a primary task of spiritual education is to ensure that the spiritual tradition in which children are nurtured is appropriate, and the process of nurture is effective.'[31] Here Wright rejects the view that there is an education free of ideological framework. He also wishes to distance himself from the view of Rousseau that culture is polluted, and that the child must endeavour to escape from its effects.

A further strand in Wright's work is engagement with Trinitarian orthodoxy. Wright shows that Trinitarian spirituality has the resources for a positive engagement with society and does not lead to obsession with inner searching. Indeed it is surely his own inhabiting of this tradition which leads him to be so critical of the latter. Here what he has to say is rich, exciting and fit to set the feet a-dancing. Yet on his own view, at the very point when RE opens up to critical engagement, Trinitarian faith must be abandoned and put on a par with every other view (including essentialism). What was good for him in determining his own beliefs, must be set alongside other views and given no special place.

It may be that he thinks in terms of nurture at primary level, followed by open-ended learning at secondary. This involves inconsistency. It could also be damaging. To nurture children in one tradition, only to abandon that tradition when pupils come to secondary level, might possibly be the worst of all worlds, since it will send the message that a particular religious tradition was OK 'while they were young' but now must be seen for what it is, unsustainable in rational argument and merely one option amongst many. Children are wrenched from their traditions, and to the extent that they are given no alternative criteria of judgment, may end up choosing subjectively or via some nostalgic return to their roots, which will only fuel the view that religions have no rational basis.

The question arises therefore, as to why Wright does not solve the inconsistency by affirming the Christian traditions as the base to religious education, at least for those pupils whose parents deem it suitable? His work is characterised both by a passion for Christian orthodoxy and a passion for critical reflection and exploration. Why cannot both be combined in a productive way? It is possible to induct children into a tradition critically and in full awareness of conflicting views of reality. I will argue later that only something like this will enable children to engage productively with alternative views.

Wright embraces both ambiguity and wholehearted nurture into a particular tradition. At times it is the search that matters; at other times the treasures of Trinitarian orthodoxy. Do we have in all this the classic Christian divide between faith and reason and an unrealised eschatology which looks forward and yearns for what is yet to be revealed? Perhaps the Christian search for the *deus absconditus* lies behind the excitement that Wright conveys for the search and the unexplored. The embrace of ambiguity and preparedness to lay loose to tradition does not sit happily beside some religions in particular. Is it the case that laid upon his vision for RE is the strongly held, but self-critical, Christian faith of its author? It is significant that some critics see a form of Christian confessionalism and others a tendency to liberal views. Both may be seen to derive from the Christian tradition. However once critical exploration is unharnessed from the tradition, the tradition itself is endangered. An eschatology which is not rooted in tradition will lose sight altogether of the nature of the eschaton. Wisdom is to be sought 'wherever she may be found', but Proverbs also instructs us that 'the fear of the Lord is the beginning of wisdom'.

Trevor Cooling

Cooling too envisages that pupils have their own view of the world and of religion, which is to be challenged by encounter with the views of others. The primary purpose of encountering the Christian story is that the pupil should reflect on her own understanding of the world in the light of the view expressed by the biblical writer. A certain openness to change (conversion?) is implied by requiring children to reflect on Christian teaching and 'reprocess' it following such reflection. Pupils are encouraged to express what they learn 'in a way that makes sense to them by engaging with it both cognitively and affectively'.[32]

Cooling bases his teaching of Christianity on a method deriving from Jerome Bruner called 'concept-cracking'. It is based on the view that children can learn just about anything provided that it is presented in terms that make sense to them. It is 'beliefs-based' since Christianity is founded on beliefs which shape the different ways that Christians live. A religious concept is carefully 'unpacked' into its constituent parts and then attention paid to explaining these parts in ways that make sense to children. It is an approach that has been very successful and the textbooks produced by the Stapleford Centre where Cooling and his wife worked until the beginning of 2003 are widely used.

Cooling argues that personal development outcomes 'should result from the development of a systematic understanding of Christianity'.[33] Thus he envisages Christian faith helping to form pupils' character, a kind of nurture, even if somewhat minimal. Like Wright he has written powerfully about the domestication of the truth claims of religions, paying attention in particular to a theological liberalism which in his view reduces vibrant, Biblical forms of Christianity to a lowest common denominator type of Christianity.[34] The danger with the nurture model of the 1960s was that the Gospel was domesticated and watered down, both by the theological liberalism that was dominant, and secularising tendencies. Religions must be presented in their integrity and for the challenges that they present.

Clearly his approach assumes the validity and worth of the Christian traditions. He adopts a missionary model. That is, he thinks that children should be enabled to hear the Gospel in school, and be challenged by it.

The model is modified by distancing devices which make it clear that no pressure is being put on children to adopt any of the religions put before them. But I am not sure that it is suited to young children, particularly at primary level. Indeed Wright seems to think as much when he recommends that children be inducted into a particular tradition at this level. The nurture model has its drawbacks in RE, but it is arguably closer to the needs of children, qua children. Can it be right for young children to be faced with missionary Islam one week, followed by missionary Hinduism the next week and so on? And how can consistent character development take place when conflicting views of life are being offered week by week?

Cooling is not comfortable with taking Christianity as the basis of nurture in community schools and his adoption of the missionary model seems to be motivated as much by concern for fairness within a society containing many religions, as his evangelical background. Fairness for him means that if one allows one religion to present itself in its integrity and for the challenge that it presents, then one must allow the same right to others. In a pluralist society no one religious tradition can legitimately (that is fairly) form the basis of religious education in the common school, since to do so would be to privilege one set of citizens over another set.

He is aware that this leaves the school in a position of some difficulty when it comes to the overall view of education within which it is working. Like Wright, he stresses that there is no such thing as 'neutral' education. He suggests that some values in religions and other views of life overlap, and may form the basis of the community school. Although the values that may be identified are grounded and justified in different ways, they serve as a common focus. Translated to RE, this would mean that values common to all religions are taught with authority, so as to avoid relativism. However this is not a policy recommended by Cooling. In practice children will be taught from within the Christian view of reality, then within the Muslim view, and so on, without any one position being given authority. But this brings us back to the problem of relativism.

There is a question about how far his approach to RE is coherent. Children learn by means of the very different concepts of several religions. No unified, coherent view of RE structures the learning. Cooling has written about the importance of 'identifying the key concepts that are central to religious education'[35] but only identifies the key concepts of Christianity. Cooling does set out a theory of RE in some detail.[36] But he has not identified the key concepts which might structure the learning across the religions, thereby giving coherence to the subject.

Conclusion

All theorists discussed in this chapter have expressed important concerns about RE and certain tendencies that have been exhibited in recent years. All are concerned that RE should treat religious traditions with great seriousness rather than reducing them to something else, whether that be secularism or essentialism. All are concerned to teach in a way that avoids a relativism which endangers all religions. At the same time all seem reluctant to base RE on one particular religion, while accepting at the same time that no education, least of all religious education, can be neutral. They wish to place 'openness' centre stage. This means that their approach is premised on agnosticism. But agnosticism, if taken seriously, would render RE unable to move in any direction at all. Hence in practice certain beliefs and assumptions are brought in, often those with which the western mind is comfortable, and a special role for Christianity maintained.

The conclusion of this and the previous chapter is that RE is in need of a new direction, one which will restore coherence to the learning without expressing hostility to the religions studied.

CHAPTER 12
'Teach the Faith, Miss'[1]

I begin by setting out the view of education I want to adopt and then go on to develop a theory of RE based on it.

The view of education

Education is the task of introducing pupils to what is considered true and of value in a particular society. Learning takes place within traditions which are circumscribed by their own particular boundaries and undergirded by particular assumptions. Such traditions will carry weight in society generally and be capable of inspiring the imagination and hearts of the young, although the young are not always appreciative at the time. A tradition will have a scholarly base at university level. It will have its own rules or grammar into which the learner must be inducted and in which much will be taken for granted, at least in the early stages of learning. This means that the tradition dictates the methods of learning, the basic concepts and procedures.

Donald Hudson[2] argues that all subjects teach both 'about' and 'in' their subjects. Information about maths or history is given, but at the same time teachers try to get their pupils to do maths and history by first learning and then using the principles of procedure determined by the subject. In the case of science a basic principle is natural causation according to rules which apply uniformly across the universe.[3] Pure science discovers the laws of nature and applied science seeks their application. The basic principles also determine what is to count as an explanation. A finding that does not 'fit' with laws already discovered may be labelled an 'anomaly'. It will only be called an explanation when a fit is discovered or previous knowledge declared to be inadequate.

'Pure religion', according to Hudson, is about discovering God's nature and will; applied religion about working out what it might mean to act in accordance with such knowledge. When he uses the word 'religion,' it would seem that Hudson means a particular religious tradition. To the charge that such a way of teaching religion is tantamount to evangelism, Hudson replies that this way of teaching is a way of helping pupils to *think for themselves* (my italics) in a religious way and that it does not require or necessarily result in pupils becoming believers. It may do, and it may be hoped for, but the result cannot be depended upon. Rather this form of teaching puts pupils in a position where they can make a meaningful choice. In order to be able to get to this point it is necessary to take much on trust. One must accept and work with the basic principles of the subject, even if one is only testing them out. It may be argued that not all children will be able to engage cognitively at the sort of level that is required. But it would seem important to at least make room for it.[4]

Inherent in learning is the possibility of revision in the light of contrary evidence. Evidence will be weighed differently by different people. However, the only way that such revision (or one might say development) can take place is when learners are thoroughly conversant with the subject-matter such that they have a real understanding of the issues that are unclear or controversial. Hence the only way to be critical (and to develop the traditions of a faith) is by being immersed in it first. Basil Mitchell argued: 'It is folly to suppose that one can learn to be critical and creative without first having been introduced to something of substance capable of seizing the imagination and stimulating criticism. The point is entirely general. The way to help people become genuinely creative and critical is not to try to bring them up without imparting to them any definite beliefs and values but to offer them a coherent framework – the best one is able to find – within which they can grow, or, if they choose, eventually reject with some understanding of what they are doing.'[5]

The Task of RE

I take the view therefore that the task of RE is one of careful introduction to a particular religion, best carried out by those who have both insight into and a degree of devotion to the faith. In that sense it is the same task as that undertaken by teachers of all subjects in our schools. As Astley argues, it would seem unassailable philosophically: 'I can see no obvious *philosophical* rebuttal of this argument that on examination does not turn out to be a case of special pleading. On logical grounds the argument is won.'[6] Astley goes on to argue that for moral and sociological reasons, only confessional Christian education in the church should proceed in this way, while non-church schools must limit themselves to engaging in second-order activity, i.e. learning about what religions say and do. But this raises the question of how such teaching can develop the ability of pupils to think for themselves and put them in a position to make an informed decision. I take this point up later.

I now consider what this would mean for teaching the Christian faith.

Central beliefs and practices

The central beliefs and practices of the Christian faith must be clearly set out: creation, fall and redemption, the incarnation, passion, resurrection and atonement, the Church and the future life. Mention should be made of its antecedents, history, effect upon societies and other faiths, the different ways it has been interpreted and enacted, its contribution to the present and the future, and, in the later stages of education, problem areas and answers to its critics. Also to be included are festivals, fasts, prayer, forms of worship, sources of authority, types of revelation, attitude to suffering, justice, war and peace, faith and reason, realist and non-realist views of God, science and religion and ethical issues of our time. Pupils need to know that some of our best minds are engaged in renewing the Christian tradition for our own time.

Creating a mood

Clifford Longley has written:

> What we would need to do is to provide and offer not facts and information, but exposure to a culture, a mood, a tradition, to plant a layer of memories. The teaching of the Bible will have an important place in that process; and I would strongly advise some comparative study of a modern version in parallel with the Authorized Version,[7] because of its value as poetry. The teaching of liturgy will also have such a place . . . something that will enable them to see the Christian religion in particular not as alien but as available.[8]

He suggested using music and literature from the Negro spiritual to the Mozart Requiem, speeches of Martin Luther King and trench poetry. One could think of much more, including the rich tradition of Christian art, sculpture, iconography, architecture and the crafts that go into the making of our churches and cathedrals, C.S. Lewis, Kierkegaard, John Donne and T.S. Eliot. Those who could do set theory could be expected to cope with Chesterton on Aquinas and even Aquinas himself. Some learning by heart is useful.

Something of the mood that one is looking for is expressed here by Marius Felderhof:

> If the Christian voice could once more speak in the world of education it would be a voice which beckons to vocation. It would entice the youth to love the transcendent, to love the world which forever issues from the creative power of transcendence, and to love their neighbour as themselves. It would invite ministry rather than mastery as the true prize of education.[9]

Relation to culture

Pupils should learn that much of our language, literature, music and art; in fact, the foundation of our thought, derives from Christian traditions, mediated to us through a Hellenistic and Jewish background. They should begin to ponder the nature of secularism and its relationship to Christian faith. Why is it that exhibitions like *Seeing Salvation* could draw so many thousands in the millennium year? Pupils need to know that our reaction to suffering, whereby we acknowledge the duty to relieve it, and are ready to share in the responsibility for it, is not common to humankind universally. Equally they need to engage with ethical issues of the day, and consider them in the light of what the faith may have to offer.

The teaching of commitment

Rowan Williams, Archbishop of Canterbury, argues that there must be a telling of the whole story and the whole story includes an encounter and the invitation to commitment. There is 'the need to preserve the possibility of this kind of encounter with the truth-telling Christ that stands at the source of the Church's identity'.[10] Children should know that 'the proclamation of Jesus invites into active commitment to a concrete community in which liberation from the dominance of violence and denial is the mainspring of life and hope'.[11] This does not legitimise excessive emotional or intellectual pressure upon the young to commit to the Christian faith But to help the young to make up their minds on the matter of religion means that we must explain that Christianity invites commitment and give some account of the benefits commitment brings.[12] Not to do so would be to withhold information about an important part of Christian faith. Not to teach children that commitment to Christ is a central part of being a Christian, would be like telling a person all about the properties of a headache pill, but forgetting to say that it must be swallowed for its effects to be realised.

Undenominational

The law forbids teaching by means of any particular denominational formulary or catechism. What this means is that central doctrines and practices will be taught with a degree of authority, where others will be taught as matters of opinion amongst Christians. In these cases (e.g. baptism and the other sacraments) a teacher may express her own view and give reasons for it, but say that Christians differ over the matter. *The Fourth R* recommended that within the teaching of a broad spectrum of Christian belief, the teacher could 'commend his own option'.[13] For children to make sense of plurality within Christian faith, (surely a necessary part of their learning) they will need exposure to the different beliefs, and this takes time. With one GCSE class recently I was able to engage the children in a meaningful debate concerning differences of opinion between Protestants and Catholics on issues of authority and interpretation of the Bible. But this was only possible because I had spent quite some time explaining the history of the Christian Church. It was also made easier because the children knew something of the Reformation from their history lessons. They were particularly intrigued by the fact that the phrase *hocus pocus* (deriving from 'hoc est corpus meum', this is my body), concerning the nature of the sacrament, was debated in Parliament at the time of Henry VIII. Pupils learned that all Christians locate authority somewhere, and that all place importance on the Bible, but that exactly where that authority is understood to lie, and how the Bible is to be interpreted, are disputed matters.

A role for 'openness'

An important part of teaching the *Christian* traditions is that such traditions allow for 'openness', and indeed thrive on it. But it is important to be clear what is meant by 'openness'. I am not talking about the sort of openness which fears to take a position, and claims to take no stand upon any prior assumptions. It is rather an openness to criticism and the existence of alternatives. *The Fourth R* put it like this:

> 'openness' . . . must mean 'not being doctrinaire, encouraging people to think for themselves, being ready to consider arguments against one's own position'. As such it is compatible with having and communicating a definite position which one is prepared to defend.[14]

At the later stages of education therefore, pupils will be encouraged to encounter difficulties and consider alternatives. Basil Mitchell writes: 'For any developed tradition to maintain itself in a healthy state, faith and criticism must reinforce one another. Hence, to be religiously educated is not a matter of being led to accept in an uncritical and unreflective way, a set of beliefs and values, which are themselves so neatly parcelled that they can properly be handed over in this way, but of being encouraged to share in a tradition which is continuously being rethought and reapplied.'[15] It is possible to go further and say that there is a place for not resolving all the problems.[16] There is a proper place for ambiguity. One may teach the faith on the basis that it is true while not claiming to know all the answers and accepting all the while that one may be wrong. And pupils are invited to make the exploration, not required to give assent to something that they do not as yet comprehend.

Who is RE for?

Is such a way of teaching RE suitable for the variety of pupils to be found in our classrooms? Is it possible to both provide a meaningful experience of committed Christian teaching for those pupils being brought up as Christians, and one which respects the integrity of those for whom the Christian faith is either contrary (in parts) to their own, or for whom no religion makes any sense? While there is provision in law for pupils to learn by means of their own traditions of faith, often such pupils will not be withdrawn. I believe that what I have argued for above is important here. One is teaching from the point of view that the faith is true, but not in a way that implies that the matter is beyond reasonable doubt, or that those who do not accept the faith are fools. A necessary 'openness' allows for the expression of difference, but does not 'lose the plot'. The sort of thing I am thinking of was expressed very well by a teacher quoted earlier: 'The believer has begun to work out the reason for his moral belief, and the agnostic and the atheist have been shown the Christian position and challenged to work out their own ideas.'[17] I now offer a few anecdotes from my own experience to illustrate my argument.

Some anecdotes from the classroom

Cherag believed that only Muslims were acceptable to Allah. However he enjoyed a series of lessons based on a video presentation of Christianity. He roared with laughter at the comic sketches and thoroughly enjoyed the lessons. Afterwards Cherag told me, with feeling, that he now felt that he understood something of the Christian faith and was glad he had had the opportunity to take part in the classes. Rafia is a Muslim girl whose class was asked to look up the business section of the Liverpool telephone directory to find out how many schools and other organisations were named after Christian saints. She reported: 'There are millions of them, Miss!' She gave a presentation on an artist's impression of the parable of the rich man and the beggar at the gate. The class wanted to concentrate on the fact of the unfairness of life. Rafia wanted to teach them that this did not matter as things were put right in the afterlife. She was very insistent on this and had obviously found something in the parable to identify with. She it was who saw in the troubling story of Abraham being asked to offer up his son as a sacrifice, that Abraham had done what was asked of him. Sarah, a Roman Catholic, presented a more down-to-earth view: 'What would have happened, Miss, if the angel of the LORD had been on a coffee break?'

Paul told me that he could not see the point of spending a whole year of his life on Jesus (only one lesson a week). He could not see what the fuss was all about. I suggested that he write down all his objections as clearly as he could. He enjoyed doing this and it marked a change in his attitude. I encouraged him to be patient. Perhaps he would see the point by the end of the lessons. Towards the end of the year we watched a video account of Jesus' trial. Pilate puts the question to Jesus: 'Are you the King of the Jews?' I stopped the video at this point and asked the class how they thought Jesus would reply. Various answers were suggested to the effect that Jesus would probably say that he was a King and that Pilate should believe in him. Paul gave the most accurate answer: 'No he won't. I bet he puts a question to Pilate'. The unbeliever (as he considered himself) had gained greater insight than those in the class who were more sympathetic.

I believe that it is possible to *teach* Christianity in a class that contains Rafia, Paul, Cherag and Sarah. The unbeliever raises the hard questions which might otherwise go begging, and the Muslim may see the point more quickly than those who identify with the Christian faith. She may develop a sense of fellow-feeling with the not-so-foreign Christian traditions. A class is a community of learners, where, although the content of the lesson is the same for all, the outcomes may be different.

The OCU Bible Project

Every year since 1991, the OCU has run a Bible competition for secondary pupils. A mailing is sent to secondary schools in Britain, inviting pupils to imagine that they are present at an event in the life of Jesus. Pupils are asked to write an account of the event or make up a dossier of evidence about the life of Jesus. Prizes are offered which are presented at a ceremony each year and merit certificates are sent out to be presented to pupils at schools. On average, 5000 essays are received each year, from about 400 schools. These schools are a mix of community comprehensives, maintained church schools and independent schools. The fact that pupils are invited to imagine they are present at the scene the Gospel narrates means that they are encouraged to take the narrative to be true. The competition has proved to be highly successful with schools returning entries year after year. Teachers report no problems with the way the tasks are set and pupils of all abilities clearly enjoy doing the work. Some Muslim children make the point that they do not believe Jesus to be the Son of God, but rather a prophet, but this has not prevented them from taking part and doing well.

The task of the teacher

What of the teacher in all this? Edward Hulmes writes of the need for 'quiet advocacy': 'It is the responsibility of teachers of music, history, art, religious education, science or any other subject for that matter, to present their subjects as powerfully and as imaginatively as possible so that students may be encouraged to see at least two things: first, that with sufficient time and application they may emulate, and even excel, their teachers; second that failure to reach high academic standards in a given field of studies need rob no subject of its intrinsic value, and no student of self-respect and human dignity.'[18] It is right that teachers should present the Christian faith as positively as possible and in the hope that it will convince and inspire. Christian teachers should be encouraged to be positive and enthusiastic about Christianity. Not all teachers however are possessed of Christian commitment. Can such teachers do the job? A degree of respect for the faith and of insight is necessary. It is difficult to see how a strongly held atheism could be compatible with respect for and insight into the faith. But a sensitive agnostic could accept the presupposition which underlies the legislation and the view I am putting forward, that Christianity represents a serious and important option which people in this country ought to be in a position to choose, or not to choose, with adequate knowledge.

The place of non-Christian religions

Children need to understand something of Islam, both militant and non-militant, the Hindu tradition, Buddhism, and the secularism that has developed in reaction to the western Judaeo-Christian traditions. Some might argue that such knowledge is part of a general education and I would agree. Indeed it seems unfair that RE should have to meet this requirement in the limited time given to it. All societies have developed as a result of the influence of particular religions. The British tradition of philosophy has been conducted within a framework of ideas deriving from our Judaic and Greek forebears as mediated by Christian thinking. Science, politics, law are all the way they are because of our immersion within Christianity. Pupils need to realise that enlightenment philosophers do not escape the Christian milieu against which, in some cases, they were reacting. Secularism challenges Christianity, but may be shown to have strong genetic links with the faith. It is helpful to know that the question of whether to go to war is understood quite differently. For the Hindu who is a member of the warrior caste it is a matter of fulfilling dharma; the Christian has the more difficult task of weighing up the arguments for and against war in the light of the 'just war' tradition. These differences matter and they need to be seen to matter. But these differences will only make sense when children have a thorough grasp of Christian ideas and influence within western culture with which to begin to compare alternative ways of understanding reality. This means that lessons must concentrate in the early stages on introduction to Christianity, and mostly as it has developed in the West.[19]

This is not to say that religions are introduced only, or merely, for comparison. They should be presented as serious options. The fact that religions offer contrary visions of reality means that we must at some point enter into dialogue with other religions in the classroom. Truth matters. Here what is required is not a climbdown on the part of the teacher or a lurch into agnosticism. What is required is a careful treatment of the evidence which is fair and impartial, and a willingness to argue the point with grace and honesty. This is best done at an age when children are able to handle controversy and when they have an insight into what Christianity is all about. I have found it useful at Year 9 to discuss the differing views of the nature of God in Islam and Christianity, and why Muslims find it impossible to believe that Jesus partakes of the divine nature. Again, this can only be done meaningfully when children have developed insight into the Christian understanding of the Trinity; not an easy undertaking! Indeed, I would argue that a committed teaching of Christianity will enhance the way children view Islam. The Muslim rejection of the Trinity is a principled one, and will be taught as such; it is prefigured in the Arian controversy, and it would be good to introduce this to pupils. In this case the doctrine of the Trinity may be understood more thoroughly by being brought into comparison with the perspective of another faith.

To teach on the basis that Christian faith is true does not imply that nothing in other religions is thought to be true or valuable. On the contrary, where a belief in Christianity is firmly held, it provides a basis for affirming that belief where it occurs in other religions. Much may be learned from the devotion with which believers in other religions follow their faith. One may embrace an element of openness to other religions while nonetheless affirming that there are sufficient reasons for continuing to hold that Christianity is true. To do otherwise is to put one's own beliefs in question. At some point, and this will differ from school to school, and teacher to teacher, a serious study of some other religions must begin. I think this is best left until secondary level. It is not realistic to attempt to *teach* several religions in progressive fashion as is often attempted today. Is this really taking any of them seriously? If one starts from a position of commitment to one religion, then other religions will be taken seriously, since they challenge that commitment. Not to begin from a position of commitment to one religion, but rather refusing to be committed, may undermine respect for them all. I have found it useful to show how the western religions differ radically from the eastern, and this helps children to get a handle on them more effectively than presenting one religion after another, as yet another separate belief system to get their heads round. Some schools now teach only Christianity at GCSE level. In Sefton LEA there are three community comprehensives that have decided to go down this path.

Making use of current theory and practice

Cooling's 'concept-cracking' has proved fruitful and clearly fits in well with my approach. Watson's important work on critical affirmation provides a positive approach to other religions which can sit happily beside the teaching of Christianity as true, and allows children to have aspects of their faith affirmed. Equally her insistence on truth-finding and the avoidance of relativism is a valuable part of the teacher's methodology. Andrew Wright has argued that primary children should be brought up as far as possible within their own tradition of faith, and his concern for the need to introduce children to diversity is met within my own approach. The only difference is that I think this can be done while still holding to the truth of Christianity. I consider the work of Robert Jackson on the domestication of the non-Christian religions to be vital and indeed my work has been influenced by this diagnosis. In practical terms I think his approach to plurality within a faith tradition could be most useful as a tool to illustrate the diversity within Christianity. Like him, I think there is a role for 'well-constructed overviews' of the tradition. I have not had space to consider the work of David Hay and John Hammond here.[20] They have illustrated how an 'experiential' methodology may be employed in RE. I have myself found this approach very productive in the classroom when linked firmly to Christian insights.[21]

How different is my approach?

This raises the question of how far my approach is in fact any different from current approaches. In practice many lessons would look exactly the same. But this is not necessarily a disadvantage! Clearly a main difference would be a greater concentration upon Christian teaching and practice, and I would hope that pupils would understand the faith at a greater depth than is possible under present constraints. I would expect pupils to have a greater awareness of what the faith has to offer, and the challenges to it that arise from secularism and other faiths. This means that there will be a role for apologetics. My approach would give greater weight to the role that the faith has played and continues to play within culture. Few agreed syllabuses seem to take this aspect seriously. It may be that in certain areas children would learn their RE in groups according to faiths. This is rare at present, although in some areas there are schools where children are taught only the Muslim topics of the agreed syllabus.[22] The children would know that the faith was being taught because it was believed to be true, not because it was one of many options, none of which was considered by their teachers credible enough to form the basis of their RE. A main difference would be that Christian teachers would no longer feel that they have to keep their faith 'battened down' below decks, as one bishop put it, unable to inform the day-to-day teaching.[23] I am told that in some areas, Christian teachers fear for their jobs, aware that it is impossible to disguise their own commitment.

In accordance with the law

I have shown earlier that the 1988 Education Reform Act was intended to bring about a situation where RE was taught on the basis of introduction to Christianity except where children were largely from other faiths. As I have argued earlier, the structures for agreeing a syllabus and the wording of certain parts of the legislation assume some such reading of the law. Had the civil servants insisted on the interpretation given in Parliament, the profession would have found it difficult to mount a contrary interpretation, and might well have decided to press for change in the legislation. Michael Grimmitt in fact now regrets that they did not do so.[24] Under this reading of the law, my proposals clearly are in conformity with the legislation. Even if one allows that the law means that a syllabus must take account of the teachings and practices of the other principal religions represented in Great Britain in the sense that the principal religions must be included in a syllabus (the interpretation developed by the profession) there is nothing to say that this may not be done by including them at some point at later secondary stage (as I myself advocate) or by comparing them with prior learning in Christianity (not necessarily in a negative sense).

In accordance with major reports

My position accords with all the major reports on the teaching of RE in the last century. Spens,[25] Crowther,[26] Newsom,[27] Plowden[28] and Durham[29] recommended that RE should:
  1. introduce pupils to a religious or spiritual dimension of life
  2. encourage a personal engagement with, perhaps even the practice of, a faith that has been found to work and is believed to be true
  3. generally be the Christian faith

None of these reports intended that children be set off on an open-ended exploration, the 'voyages of unlimited spiritual discovery' that first emerged in the late-1960s and which I have commented on in earlier chapters. Put another way, their approach assumed that there was something to learn and that children should be engaged in learning it. All these reports made the assumption that the Christian faith, which will normally provide the subject matter of the exploration, is worthy of learning and can be shown to be true.

Supported by philosophers, teachers and others

The work of Donald Hudson and Basil Mitchell has been mentioned. Mitchell was a member of the Durham Commission and has maintained an active interest in RE since. He has written several articles similar to the sort of RE I am proposing, and in 1994 published *Faith and Criticism* which contains a chapter setting out a vision for RE similar to that set out above. John Haldane and David Carr[30] have written similar defences of this vision of RE. Clifford Longley is a journalist who has written over the years about RE and in his Hockerill lecture of 1988 proposed a return to the teaching of Christianity for its own sake. David Martin has entered the fray and I have referred to his work in earlier chapters. Marius Felderhof is another.

In the 1960s and 1970s there were many teachers who were quite happy with the traditional view of RE. How many teachers today would support my position, I am unable to say. However, I have had some interest and support from serving teachers through my website, and it may be that were the climate of opinion to change, many more would be found to be in support.

Never refuted

It is a striking fact that the position advocated by *The Fourth R* has never been refuted. In fact it has never been properly addressed. I have shown in earlier chapters how its argument was either ignored (Ninian Smart) or misrepresented (Colin Alves). In fact Ninian Smart expressly said that there was a place for the 'committed approach' and in 1973 Brian Gates presented a case very similar to that presented by *The Fourth R* as a serious possibility.[31] Basil Mitchell has yet to see his arguments on RE addressed in print.[32] The critics have been content to criticise a stereotype of Christian education which is seen as closed and indoctrinatory. I have shown in earlier chapters how influential leaders within the profession came to reject teaching based on Christianity as true as 'uneducational'. This has been the position for a period of about 30 years. It has become unnecessary to do more than state that 'confessional' RE is unacceptable for the case to be won.

What then are the objections to my proposal?

CHAPTER 13
Answering Objections, Supporting Arguments and the Way Forward

Objections

I now consider the objections likely to be raised to the position outlined in the previous chapter.

It is unfair

This objection may be stated in two ways. The first states that it is unfair to base RE on one particular faith because parents of 'deselected' faiths would be denied the right (given to those of the 'selected' faith) to have their children educated within their own faith. Indeed, such a form of RE might well contravene European and international human rights legislation[1] which states that the right to have children educated according to their own beliefs should be granted to all parents. However, the view of RE here proposed does not deny the right to parents to have a religious education for their child that accords with their own convictions. Withdrawal guards against imposition, and the law, if understood in the way outlined in chapter 9, allows for alternative forms of RE. Indeed, I would want to charge those who resist my interpretation of the law with denying parents what the law allows.

The second way of stating this objection is that the state must not favour one particular religion in its public education.[2] There are, it is argued, significant minorities belonging to non-Christian religions and 'non-religious' stances, who are citizens of Great Britain. For the state to endorse one particular faith in an education offered to all its citizens is unfair, discriminatory, promotes exclusivity and may say to such families that their religion is inferior and their contribution unwanted. In a time of international tension, exacerbated by religious differences, the state must remain neutral as between religions and do nothing to raise religious tensions. The following words of John Hull sum up this view succinctly: 'The only sort of religious education acceptable to the state school is one given without favour and without discrimination in relation to the traditions studied.'[3]

My proposal does not necessarily endorse the view that the state is giving a privileged place to Christianity since it may be understood as responding to the wishes of parents by providing a religious education best suited to family background. However, I believe that there are good reasons for preserving a special role in education for Christianity in public education. And this is the case that I wish to defend.

The argument that it is wrong to grant a special role to Christianity in public education is a powerful dissolvent, not only of the place of Christianity in RE, but also of many of our existing institutions, way of life, and even our language. If the state may not give emphasis to the Christian traditions through its schools, what is to be made of the law against bigamy, the place of bishops in the Lords, the use of St Paul's and other cathedrals for special occasions, the many carol concerts that take place in public places, the fixing of holidays around Easter, and so on? Put like this, the argument that it is unfair to base RE on Christianity looks suspiciously like a political agenda to further marginalise the role of the Christian faith in society. The strange silence about the fact of unfairness to those religions not deemed principal might confirm this conclusion. It has become the norm to include six religions on agreed syllabuses but this is clearly unfair to the Bahais, Jains and Rastafarians to name but three.

What other consequences may follow? Tariq Modood,[4] not a Christian, has argued that maintaining a central role for Christianity within society (and in particular the Church of England), may be important to prevent erosion of other religious voices within society. He endorses a central place for Christian traditions, particularly when the establishment maintains respect for the contribution of other religions (as it does in his view). The argument is that it is better to have one religion centre stage, than for all to be on the periphery. Presenting all religions on a par reduces them all to matters of little significance. Howard Jacobson, a Jew, expressed it well when he argued against 'cute interdenominational sampling of everybody's amazing customs – Wow, Baruch, love your fringes! – but that's just ethnic ring-a-ring o' roses, after which we all fall down'.[5] One mother, declaring herself an agnostic, was upset that Christianity was no longer taken seriously: 'Pick 'n' mix RE . . . is denying children the idea that such myths matter. If you learn only small titbits about a handful of different religions, you lose the very essence of the idea of religion, which is that there are fundamental values; you lose any sense of religious awe; you have no concept of an overarching system of belief that holds a major religion together.'[6]

The push to deny a special place to Christianity in RE favours the secularist. This is the view of Modood. Indeed an atheist website states: 'by giving information about a multiplicity of religions, the religious education authorities are assisting in undermining belief in any one of them. For this reason I do not automatically advocate the removal of atheist schoolchildren from RE classes.'[7] Arguments demanding fairness in religious education have a way of becoming special pleading for secularism.

Uncertainty about religion forbids it

'You are surely not going to say that Christianity is the true religion?' may be the shocked response. This may be declaimed with a sense of 'self-ratifying superiority'.[8] No-one, it is implied, could possibly believe Christianity to be *true*. The speaker thereby declares her belief that no-one can possibly know, in the matter of religion, what is true or what is false. Such a statement may be used to brush aside the genuine claims to knowledge that are put forward by Christian thinkers. Yet often it is mere dogmatic assertion.[9] What may pass notice is that such assertion denies all religions the possibility of true knowledge. Clearly children taught in this way may learn to disregard the arguments of religious believers. This should be a matter for serious concern.

But there is another problem with this argument. If the whole area of religion is so bound up with ambiguity and uncertainty, how could one begin to decide which religions to introduce to children? If we are not in a position to know what is true and what is false, then we have no means of discriminating between religions at all. We could not really begin to construct a coherent syllabus. In fact we should not really start at all.

Let us grant that religion is a controversial area, along with many other areas of human concern. In all areas of controversy it is common to take the best view that can be found, and teach it as well as possible, in the light of conflicting theories, all the while being open to correction. Jeff Astley quotes the view of the philosopher Alasdair MacIntyre that we always and inevitably begin from some tradition of thought: 'There is no access to any subject matter that is not conceptualised in terms that already presuppose the truth of one set of claims rather than another.'[10] It is not possible to begin from nowhere. The charge of relativism is generally made at this point. MacIntyre, however, argues that we are not imprisoned within our own view of things. We hold our position on the basis of evidence and must accept the possibility of being converted to another viewpoint when contrary evidence warrants it. Belief is thus firmly based on evidence and therefore does not necessitate a relativist approach to knowledge. We must hold our beliefs in such a way that they are open to correction. What we must not do is to abandon our beliefs in the vain hope that there is a neutral place on which to stand. The choice comes down to taking a position in the matter of which religion is true, and teaching on this basis (while remaining open to criticism and giving freedom to pupils to explore and ask questions), or adopting (and therefore teaching) agnosticism.

The faith is no longer believed to be true

It might be argued that while this is so, it is no longer possible to teach Christianity as true since it is no longer widely believed to be true.[11] Jeff Astley wrote: 'In the context of many Western nations we simply have to say that a society that increasingly does not share the . . . fundamental principles of theism is unlikely to want its publicly funded schools and colleges to induct learners in the practices of religious thinking.'[12] But is it true that society in this country generally rejects Christian belief? A survey suggested that 75 % of the population of the UK identified themselves as belonging to one of the Christian denominations.[13] The 2001 Census included a question about religion for the first time.[14] It asked 'What is your religion?' The question was voluntary and 92% of respondents chose to answer it. 72% said that their religion was Christian, Islam was the next most common faith with nearly 3%. Other religious groups each accounted for less than 1% and together accounted for a further 3% of the UK population. About 16% of the population stated that they had no religion. While it is not possible to correlate belief precisely with religious affiliation, the fact that 72% of the population identify with Christian faith suggests that the faith retains intellectual credibility. It could be higher, since it is possible that some of those not answering the question hold Christian beliefs.

A great deal of public money goes into church schools (85% of their running costs). Church schools are full and increasingly popular. It may be that this is because such schools are well disciplined and get good results.[15] There is doubtless some truth in this. It may be that parents are prepared to 'put up' with Christian teaching and practice for the sake of a good education, but it indicates, at the very least, that they do not have serious objections to their children being taught the faith. One suspects that many parents, while not committed Christians themselves, would prefer that their children should be given the opportunity of making an informed choice for or against the Christian faith as being a serious possibility for thoughtful people, rather than be left with little or no guidance in these fundamental matters. There is for them no single alternative in the field which carries with it anything like the accumulated weight of Christianity.

It would lead to intolerance
It may be argued that it is necessary to learn about the various religions in our society in order to develop tolerance. Ignorance breeds fear and so schools must increase the understanding of different religions so that harmony in society may be achieved. To concentrate on the Christian traditions would reduce unacceptably the amount of time left for learning about other religions. A further argument is that to teach on the basis that one religion is true is divisive and would lead to children viewing other religious traditions (and therefore their adherents) as inferior. John Hull has coined the term 'religionism'[16] to describe those who see their own theology as normative.

Does tolerance and acceptance of others depend on understanding their religion? If it does, then we have a problem since it will never be possible to understand all the religions in the world that we are likely to come across in a lifetime. What is important is that a basis for tolerance is laid and that other religions, where taught, are given a fair hearing, their right to think differently is respected, and that teachers show by example that it is possible to learn from other religions. The fact that no-one worries about the many religions that are not taught in schools indicates that this argument is not decisive.

What do I mean by a 'basis for tolerance'? In Parliament there were many who advocated the teaching of Christianity as a way of increasing tolerance and promoting harmony. Kenneth Baker said this: 'We believe that there must be a bedrock in the basic teaching of Christianity in our schools, in both religious education and worship, because in that way our society is strengthened in a tolerant, humane and spiritual way.'[17] On the face of it, it is difficult to see how the ethical teaching of Jesus could be said to promote intolerance. The Bible is full of injunctions to 'do justly', to love one's neighbour, to remember the poor and the stranger within the gates. The relationship with other religions is variously conceived, but in general the Christian Church accepts that there is truth and value in other religions.[18] The 'brotherhood of man' is founded on the fatherhood of God and gives a firm foundation for human rights. The Pope has been a forthright champion of human rights in the last century. This is not to claim that only the Christian churches teach such matters, of course. But it is to claim that where Christianity is taught, such matters will be part of the teaching too. The Church of England published a report into the future of church schools in 2001. This report argued that church schools attempt to instil in children the call of Christ to serve all people: 'Our own vision of inclusiveness is based on Christ's commandment to love all people, and his own sharing fully in the life of humanity.'[19] They argued that the notions of distinctiveness and inclusiveness are not mutually exclusive. Children who learn through their RE to accord respect and freedom of conscience to all and to regard all human beings as of absolute worth, are, one may hope, going to be tolerant of others and keen to work for harmony and the rights of all.

Supporting Arguments

An important argument is the role that the faith has played, and still plays, in our culture.

One has only to look around one to recognise this role. The most conspicuous monuments in the British countryside are its parish churches and cathedrals. They are visited by many more than those who regularly worship in them, and are felt to be an essential part of what it means to be British. One can have only an impoverished appreciation of them if one does not know why they were built, what was and is their purpose, and what is the function of their furnishings, the altar, the font, the choir-stalls, the pulpit. Much is lost if one cannot recognise the Christian symbols and the Christian story as told in stained glass, paintings and carved capitals. Those who have been told nothing of such things are disinherited. The same could be said in relation to our tradition of music, art, sculpture and literature.

Furthermore, from time to time most of us, whether we are regular churchgoers or not, attend church for weddings, funerals, memorial services, carol concerts and services of thanksgiving for local or national occasions. Most indispensable are services held in a school or local church to pray for those who have suffered in a local tragedy, or a worldwide one such as occurred on 11 September 2001. The Church provides the language and the decent ceremonial which people feel the need of on such occasions. It is sad when people are unable to express their deep emotions because they are unfamiliar with the Lord's Prayer, the 23rd Psalm or once familiar hymns. On such occasions convinced atheists or agnostics have the option of remaining silent, but most non-churchgoers, I suspect, are uncertain of what they believe, and undergo a sort of 'suspension of disbelief', wishing for the time being to identify themselves with the collective worship, in Thomas Hardy's words, 'hoping it might be so'.

There is more. Much of our law, language and way of thinking derives from Christian faith. Feelings were aroused when an England football manager, Glenn Hoddle, suggested that the disabled were so because of some wrongdoing in a former life. This is standard teaching in much eastern religion, but a very large number of English people found it abhorrent. Why did they feel this? It is surely because of the conviction, deriving from the Judeo-Christian tradition, that each human being is of supreme value, that we have but one life, and that the disabled are not paying any penalty from a previous one. It was risky to be a Christian under the Roman Empire when the emperor worship was considered to be a duty of every citizen, and many Christians died as a result. But it has given us our tradition of the rights of conscience. The terrible events of the Roman arena with its gladiator fights and feeding the lions with human flesh, were brought to an end because of arguments put forward by Christian priests and theologians. Progress, and the idea of an open future, are not innate ideas that come built in to human thinking. To the animist everything is as it should be, and the spirits are in control. But to the Christian, charged with the stewardship of the earth and its creatures, progress and the ability to influence the future ourselves is both a possibility and a sacred task. Science is often thought to have arisen in the west because biblical ideas taught us that nature was not divine, but given to us by God to discover and make use of wisely. This was in contrast to the view that nature itself was sacred, and not to be interfered with, except under severe constraints. A.N. Wilson, not known for being a devout Christian, wrote: 'Christianity invented a way of looking at human nature and the inner life which is part and parcel of our very civilisation.'[20]

These arguments suggest that some of our most basic ideas and categories were conceived and have been nurtured within a Christian framework. But even our most basic values can disappear if they are no longer practised and taught. The environmental movement has performed a much needed task in calling the West back to a proper understanding of stewardship which had become distorted over the years. However, the danger is that the environmental movement may herald a return to animistic ideas of 'mother nature', and with this can come a refusal to interfere with, or exploit nature at all. If such thinking gained the upper hand, who is to say that science and the experiments needed to prove its theories will not struggle to survive? This may seem an unlikely scenario but in a society that once believed in the sanctity of the human unborn and now routinely takes their lives, one cannot be so sure. There are important matters at stake.

Rabbi Julian Jacobs, argues for the Church of England to remain the established church: 'The Bible's declaration that every human being is made in the image of God remains the most powerful defence of liberty.'[21] Professor John Haldane argues that our common life is premised on values derived from Christianity and that society has a positive duty to teach Christianity:

> The notions of freedom, moral equality and social responsibility which feed into Law and Government through concepts of Justice and Democracy, themselves derive both meaning and justification from Christian doctrines. In claiming that all men are created free children of a loving God, Christianity gives content and support to the idea that each person is a moral agent and thereby the bearer of responsibilities and entitlements, which in turn renders him (or her) apt for praise and blame. . . . Again, the notion of democracy is fed from two sources deep in this religious tradition: first, the dignity of man, as possessor of freedom and reason; and second, his propensity for evil, as inheritor of original sin. The former warrants pride and makes democratic government possible, while the latter prompts arrogance and conceit, thereby making it a necessary source of restraint. The conclusion of the present argument therefore, is that religion should be taught in state schools since it is the duty of government to provide education the aims of which derive from the common values of society.[22]

It may be argued that Christianity is taught in our schools and that I am tilting at the wind. There is some truth in this charge. Christianity is taught, or should be taught, in all our schools. But as much of this book has been concerned to show, the problem lies in the way it has become customary to teach the faith: as one of many options, with no conviction of its truth and in fearful awareness of the sin of 'urging a particular religion or religious belief' upon pupils. John Haldane was well aware of the current situation:

> The teaching of religion should be included in the curriculum of state schools and cannot be the uncritical presentation of information envisaged by the advocates of value-free, moral and religious studies. Not all views are of equal coherence, interest and worth, and education is necessarily selective and partisan. That it is exclusive and committed is not a deficiency of teaching, it partly defines the activity and gives point to it.[23]

The faith must be allowed to appeal to the emotions as much as the intellect, and children must be provided with opportunities to experience awe and practise such virtues as patience, charity and sacrifice. Some are happy to make use of the cultural argument in order to guarantee a role for RE, but do not go on to teach the fact to pupils. Agreed syllabuses are shy of teaching the central role of Christianity in our culture. Perhaps because of this, I was unable to find any RE textbook which addressed the matter, when preparing a unit on the topic for my classes. The only suitable book I could find, and it is an excellent one, was produced by Day One Publications to celebrate the millennium.[24]

But Christianity is important not just because it underlies some of our most basic convictions about who we are. It offers help in working out answers to some questions of fundamental and far-reaching significance. One of the great issues of our time is that of gender. The question is not so much how far the Church has oppressed women,[25] but what can the churches offer in assessing anew the role of woman and man in the order of things? What resources does the Christian tradition have to enable us to see the outlines of a new understanding which will serve to guide us today? We might want to note that the issue has arisen in a *Christian* society, and ask whether this is not therefore another example of new treasures arising out of the deposit of tradition. The women's movement recalls us to the basic equality of women and men made in the image of God, but also challenges us with what it means to be created male and female. Other issues confront us: the response to terrorism, national identity and the possibilities presented to us by cloning, to name but three. The ancient Augustinian principles of the 'just war' have been constantly revisited by the press in the light of the problem of terrorist groups across the world. These principles may need restating but they offer western society a means of thinking about how to respond to aggression.

If we do not teach Christianity what shall we teach?

As Peter said, 'To whom shall we go?'[26] What other philosophy or religion can replace Christianity? I have shown that the alternatives proposed both now and when RE first wobbled in the 1960s are deeply problematical.

Essentially they founder because they can name no replacement. Either children are encouraged to launch out on voyages of unstructured spiritual discovery, or they are taught some form of essentialism. The former may suit a postmodern age, but requires the children to invent their own religion. This may destroy any faith they possess, since it effectively denies that any of the existing religions, including their own, is good enough. The latter denies truth to any religion that claims it, and puts a question mark upon the religions that may be found amongst the children. The end result of this is that religions are seen as oppressors, since they impose a particular structure upon the lives of their adherents. To go along this path is to liberate children from the 'false' religions of their parents.

Most teachers of RE accept the impossibility of neutrality, yet many continue to create schemes that refuse to take a stance, on the basis that a syllabus must be 'open' and non-indoctrinatory. This may take the form of teaching 'what Muslims believe' alongside 'what Hindus believe' and so on. To many this is unsatisfactory, rather like attempting to teach history as 'one damned fact after another'. Such a form of instruction leaves little room for the teacher. Indeed on this way of providing RE the teacher is clearly a problem since human beings have a habit of believing something, and 'marking out the lesson', according to what they want to achieve and the insights they want to convey. The idea that one must teach RE on the basis of some assumptions about what is true and of worth (as is the case in other subject areas of the curriculum) continues to be problematic within the profession. And yet it is not difficult to show that there are assumptions taken for granted by even the most sophisticated theorists. This means that we cannot escape making a choice in the classroom. The choice must be justified, however, or we lose all grip on religious *education*. What other religion or philosophy has the coherence and influence that Christianity has in this country? A further consideration is, which religion or philosophy can work alongside other subjects on the curriculum, so that pupils are not faced with contradictory views of reality when they come to RE? Spiritual yearnings find many outlets, but no outlet would seem to offer the objectivity and intellectual structure that may be found in Christianity and which undergirds our national life. It is not unimportant that this is what has been legislated for in Parliament.

Why has this been so strongly resisted within the profession?
This book has told the story of how what has happened to RE over the last 40 years. The most significant change was the move away from the traditional view that took place in the 1960s, following the failure of the profession to stand up to the attacks upon the Christian hegemony made (not for the first time) by the humanists. Ever since then, the profession

has attempted to develop new forms of RE that do not presume the truth and worth of Christianity. The foundation of religious education is a strange one; it can be anything (almost) but it may not be the faithful presentation of Christian faith to the young, in the hope that it will form the basis of their spiritual development. To admit to such an aim would be to unravel forty years of thinking within the profession. Put simply, it has become an unquestionable dogma that RE is not about introducing the young to Christianity as true. So my first answer to why the position I am advocating continues to be resisted, is that it has not been considered. It is not that the case has not been made, but that the case has been either ignored or misrepresented.

What has happened is that people have come to associate all sorts of undesirable attitudes and outcomes with teaching the faith. At root this is an intellectual error borne of prejudice. It is possible to teach Christianity while remaining open to criticism and challenge, and without claiming that anyone who thinks differently is a fool and a knave. It is possible to take other religions seriously for the genuine worth and challenge that they present, while nonetheless taking the view that Christianity is true. Indeed I would argue that only some such position as this takes other religions seriously. When the profession was pressured into giving up teaching in this way in the 1960s and 1970s, the argument was that 'indoctrination' of any form was wrong. Nothing, the argument went, could be taught as true. Such an educational philosophy is self-contradictory and sterile. Furthermore, it neuters the insights of all and every religion. To reclaim the ground in a Christian sense, is to restore the possibility of truth to every claimant.

The way forward
It is right that children should have the freedom to respond, to make up their minds on the basis of understanding, to be tolerant, sensitive, willing to go on growing and learning, and not to get stuck in their religious thinking. What is wanted is a certain 'openness' to the world and God, to religious experience and to the 'sheer deep-down loveliness' of it all. Such concerns come naturally to those brought up in a Christian culture. I have shown in the previous two chapters how some of our theorists argue as they do because of an almost umbilical link to Christian ways of thinking; but they lack awareness of it. There is an acute embarrassment about taking a stand upon our Christian heritage and, it seems, a strongly felt need to distance RE from it. But the faith exerts its grip still, and it is generally from within Christian categories, that whatever is taught positively derives. What is needed is a recovery of confidence in the task of teaching the source of the values that, as I have argued, enthral us still.

The failure of the 1988 legislation to effect change in RE shows that what matters is persuading hearts and minds, and this takes time. The current climate is more favourable to a rethink of RE along the lines I have suggested than at any time in the last 30 years. The Church of England is building new church schools and church schools are popular. Within the RE profession itself, the arguments that led to non-confessionalism are being shown to be unsustainable.[27] Christian education is experiencing something of a comeback.[28] David Hargreaves, recently QCA Chief Executive, has argued that faith schools can provide a vibrant, confessional form of RE which contrasts favourably with the 'multi-faith pick 'n' mix tour of religions [which] easily trivialises each faith's claims to truth'.[29] There is every reason for community schools 'in the main' to offer RE based on Christianity.

A return to traditional ways of teaching literacy and numeracy has been widely welcomed. Now is the time to reconsider RE. SACREs and ASCs need to know that the law does not require all the principal religions to be taught, although there is every reason to begin to learn something of them. What the law (arguably) requires is a proper introduction to one faith, that most appropriate for the pupils concerned. A serious rethink of teacher training in RE needs to take place. I have found that students can be attracted to the sort of RE that I am proposing; but few will even get to hear of it under present regimes in colleges and universities. The advice that a syllabus may not 'urge a particular religion or religious belief upon pupils' must be withdrawn. The DfES has already acknowledged that the law does not forbid such 'urging'. It needs to go because it has been interpreted to mean that nothing of a religious nature may be taught as true and it may privilege secularism. It is in conflict with the widely held view (now enshrined in international law) that education should assist parents in bringing up their children according to their religious convictions. It may even be found to be undermining the foundations of our culture. Christianity can be taught in accordance with educational concerns about openness, fairness and critical reflection. To 'teach the faith' is to embrace a future in which RE can flourish, since it has a proper ground from which to explore, and to which to return.

ABBREVIATIONS

ACT	Association of Christian Teachers
ARE	Association for Religious Education
ASC	Agreed Syllabus Conference
AT	Attainment Target
BCC	British Council of Churches
BHA	British Humanist Association
BJES	British Journal of Educational Studies
BJRE	British Journal of Religious Education
CEM	Christian Education Movement
CRE	Campaign for Real Education
CSR	Comparative Study of Religion
DES	Department of Education and Science
DfEE	Department for Education and Employment
ERA	Education Reform Act
ICE	Institute of Christian Education
IJER	International Journal of Education and Religion
ILEA	Inner London Education Authority
JECB	Journal of Education and Christian Belief
JPE	Journal of Philosophy of Education
LEA	Local Education Authority
NCC	National Curriculum Council
OCU	Order of Christian Unity
PACE	Parental Alliance for Choice in Education
QCA	Qualification and Curriculum Authority
RE	Religious Education
REC	Religious Education Council
REP	Religious Education Press
SACRE	Standing Advisory Council on Religious Education
SCAA	Schools Curriculum and Assessment Authority
SCM	Student Christian Movement
SWP	Shap Working Party
TES	Times Educational Supplement
WP36	Working Paper 36

Notes

Chapter 1

1. *Learning for Living* was the major journal of what was then called Religious Instruction (RI). To avoid confusion I use the term Religious Education (RE). *Learning for Living* contained articles, news of conferences, book reviews, letters, events etc. It was the professional journal for teachers of RE in both church and county schools. It succeeded *Religion in Education*.
2. *Learning for Living*, vol. 1 no. 1, September 1961, p.5.
3. H. Loukes, *Teenage Religion*, SCM, London, 1961, pp.152-3.
4. Ibid, p.8.
5. Ibid.
6. *Learning for Living*, vol. 2 no. 1, September 1962, p.4.
7. *The Church of England Board of Education Evidence to the Central Advisory Council for Education*, The Church of England Board of Education, London, 1961, p.9.
8. Ibid, p.16.
9. Ibid, p.6.
10. Ibid, p.37.
11. *Learning for Living*, vol. 2 no. 1, September 1962, p.35.
12. *Learning for Living*, vol. 1 no. 5, May 1962, p.15.
13. *Learning for Living*, vol. 2 no. 1, September 1962, p.9.
14. *Learning for Living*, vol. 1 no. 2, November 1961, p.33.
15. Ibid, p.34.
16. *Learning for Living*, vol. 1 no.3, January 1962.
17. *Learning for Living*, vol. 2 no. 3, January 1963, p.5.
18. The Cowper Temple clause prohibited teaching that was distinctive of a particular denomination in county schools.
19. *Learning for Living*, vol. 5 no. 2, November 1965, p.4.
20. *Learning for Living*, vol. 2 no. 2, November 1962, p.4.
21. F.H. Hilliard, *The Teacher and Religion*, James Clarke and Co., 1963, p.28.
22. Ibid, p.47.
23. Ibid, pp.48-9.
24. *Learning for Living*, vol. 3 no. 1, September 1963, pp.11-12.
25. *Learning for Living*, vol. 1 no. 3, January 1962.
26. *Learning for Living*, vol. 2 no. 3, January 1963.
27. *Learning for Living*, vol. 3 no .2, November 1963, p.24.
28. In the early part of the 20th century there was vociferous opposition from humanists to the Bible being read in schools and up until 1944 school boards could choose whether or not to have religious instruction in schools at all.
29. *Learning for Living*, vol. 2 no. 2, November 1962, p.7.
30. *Learning for Living*, vol. 2 no. 4, March 1963, p.4.
31. H. Loukes, *New Ground in Christian Education*, SCM, London, 1965, p.165.
32. Ibid, p.28. The aims of teaching children RE were to ' inspire them with the vision of the glory of God in the face of Jesus Christ, and to send them into the world willing to

follow Him who was among us as one that serveth, because they know that in such service alone is perfect freedom'.

33. *Teenage Religion*, p.151.
34. Op. cit., p.151.
35. Op. cit., p.150-1.
36. Op. cit., p.160.
37. *Learning for Living*, vol 4 no 2, November 1964, p.19.
38. Material for this section was found in Miss Bliss's papers, lodged at the Church of England Records Office at Bermondsey, London.
39. *Learning for Living*, vol. 3 no. 3, January 1964.
40   Quoted in *The Gospel and Our Culture*, 33, Spring 2002, p.2. See C. Brown, *The Death of Christian Britain*, Routledge, 2001.
41. *Learning for Living*, vol. 3 no. 1, September 1963, p.5.
42. *Learning for Living*, vol. 4 no. 1, September 1964, p.18.
43. *Learning for Living*, vol. 3 no. 4, March 1964.
44. *Learning for Living*, vol. 5 no. 1, September 1965, 'An Open Letter to LEA Religious Advisory Committees', p.8.
45. Ibid, p.7.
46. The book does not give details of when the new survey work was carried out.
47. H. Loukes, *New Ground in Christian Education*, SCM, London, 1965, p.57.
48. *Learning for Living*, vol. 3 no. 2, November 1963, p.4.
49. *Learning for Living*, vol 5. no. 2, November 1965, p.8.
50. *Learning for Living* vol. 2 no. 2, November 1962, p.7. Francis Venables, retired Principal of Culham College, was the writer.
51. *Learning for Living*, vol 10. no. 2, November 1970.
52. Op. cit.
53. *Learning for Living*, vol. 5 no. 4, March 1966, p.16.
54. *Learning for Living*, vol. 6 no. 2, November 1966, p.17.
55. *Learning for Living*, vol. 9 no. 4, March 1970, p.8.
56. *Learning for Living*, vol. 7 no. 2, November 1967, p.6.
57. *Learning for Living*, vol. 9 no. 1, September 1969, p.14.
58. *BJES*, vol. 14 no. 1, November 1965, 'Morals, Religion and the Maintained School', p.15.
59. Ibid, pp.17-18.
60. Letter dated 22 June, 1999.
61. *Learning for Living*, vol. 5 no. 2, November 1965, 'Religious and Moral Education in County Schools', p.7.
62. E. Cox, *Changing Aims in Religious Education*, Routledge and Kegan Paul, London, 1966.
63. Ibid, pp.68-9.
64. Ibid, p.66.
65. Ibid, p.91.
66. *Learning for Living*, vol. 5 no. 1, September 1965, p.16.
67. *Learning for Living*, vol. 4 no. 4, March 1965, p.35.
68. *Learning for Living*, vol. 5 no. 4, March 1966, p.16.
69. CEM was formed in 1965 by the merger of ICE with the Schools Christian Movement in Schools (SCMS). It was the major professional association for RE at this period. It sponsored *Learning for Living* and provided regional secretaries who acted like present day advisers, putting on courses for teachers and giving advice and practical support to RE teachers. They also set up local support groups. In addition, residential conferences were put on regularly for teachers at New Year and Easter. It had an overseas mandate and organised workcamps for children from deprived areas.
70. *Learning for Living*, vol. 8 no. 4, March 1969, p.23.
71. *Learning for Living*, vol. 8 no. 3, January 1969, p.48.
72. *Learning for Living*, vol. 9 no. 2, November 1969, pp.22-4.
73. *Learning for Living*, vol. 10 no. 2, November 1970, p.11.

74. *Learning for Living,* vol. 8 no. 4, March 1969, p.16.
75. *Learning for Living,* vol. 9 no. 1, September 1969, p.32.
76. *Learning for Living,* vol. 10 no. 3, 1971, p.29.
77. *Learning for Living,* vol. 10 no. 5, May 1971, p.29.
78. *Learning for Living,* vol. 7 no. 3, January 1968, p.5.

Chapter 2

1. *Learning for Living*, vol. 5 no. 2, November 1965, 'Another Open Letter to LEA Advisory Committees', p. 19. It was signed by three university postholders, five college lecturers, one head master, one school chaplain and a former Schools Advisor.
2. *Learning for Living*, vol. 3 no 1, September 1963, p.25.
3. Ibid, p.21.
4. *Learning for Living*, vol. 4 no 5, May 1965, p.14. Hargreaves was Chief Executive at QCA in the 1990s.
5. J. McQuarrie, I. Ramsey, I.M. Crombie, F.W. Dillistone, R. Funk, A. Farrer et al.
6. *Learning for Living*, vol. 5 no 2, November 1965.
7. K. Howkins, *Religious Thinking and Religious Understanding*, Tyndale Press, September 1966.
8. *The Head Teachers Review*, June 1967, 'Readiness for Goldman', p. 120.
9. Ibid, p.120.
10. P. Dawson, *Learning for Living*, vol. 6 no 1, September 1966, p.29.
11. Ibid.
12. *Learning for Living,* vol. 5 no. 2, November 1965, p.13.
13. *BJES,* vol. 14, no. 2, May 1966, p.278.
14. *Learning for Living,* vol. 1 no. 3, January 1962, p.19.
15. *Learning for Living,* vol. 5 no. 3, January 1966, p.22.
16. *Learning for Living,* vol. 6 no. 2, November 1966, p.12.
17. *Learning for Living,* vol. 8 no. 5, May 1969, p.12.
18. Quoted by Ian Birnie in *Learning for Living,* vol. 4 no. 2, November 1964, p.17.
19. *BJES*, vol. 18 no. 1, February 1970.
20. *Learning for Living,* vol. 11 no. 4, March 1972.
21. Ibid, p.14.
22. See the Bliss papers lodged at the Church of England archive in Bermondsey.
23. Information given to me by Alexander Wedderspoon who, with Hilliard, had called the conference. Interview on January 25, 2001.
24. Ed. A. Wedderspoon, *Religious Education 1944-1984*, George Allen and Unwin, London, 1965, p.219.
25. See M.V.C. Jeffreys, *The Truth is not Neutral*, REP, Oxford, 1969.
26. *Learning for Living*, vol. 8 no. 2, November 1968, p.9.
27. *Learning for Living*, vol. 8 no. 5, May 1969, p.9.
28. Op. cit., p. 227.
29. Op. cit., p. 238.
30. Ibid.
31. M.V.C. Jeffreys, *The Truth is not Neutral*, p.66.
32. *Learning for Living*, vol. 8 no 5, May 1969, p.9.
33. *Learning for Living*, vol. 10 no. 5, May 1971, p.29.
34. *Learning for Living*, vol. 7 no. 1, September 1967, p.9.
35. *Learning for Living*, vol. 3 no. 1, September 1963, p.21.
36. *Learning for Living*, vol. 3 no. 3, January 1964, p.18.
37. See her chapter in *Religious Education, drift or decision?* Ed Philip Jebb, London, Darton, Longman and Todd, 1968.
38. Eds P. Cousins and M. Eastman, *The Bible and the Open Approach in Religious Education,* Tyndale Press, London, 1967.
39. Ibid, p.46.

40. A minority report was also submitted which took a different view.
41. These were a survey of young people aged 16-25 carried out the by the research department of Odhams Press in 1962, a survey of parents by the ICE in 1964 and a survey by the National Opinion Poll of views in five regions of the UK in 1965.
42. *Children and their Primary Schools*, The Plowden Report, London, 1967, para 572.
43. Ibid.
44. The Durham Commission, *The Fourth R, the Report of the Commission on Religious Education in Schools*, National Society and SPCK, London, 1970.
45. Op. cit., p.103, para 216.
46. Information given to me by A. Wedderspoon.
47. Ibid.
48. Ibid, p.72, para 142.
49. Ibid. pp. 62-3, para 121.
50. *Religion in Maintained Schools*, National Association of Schoolmasters, 1971, p.11.
51. Ibid.
52. Ibid.
53. See, for example, C. Dixon, *Journal of Christian Education*, vol 43 no 1, May 2000, 'There *is* an appetite for religious studies: Religious Education in the public domain', p.30.
54. See C. Alves, *Religion and the Secondary School*, SCM, London, 1968, p.186.
55. C. Alves, *The Christian in Education*, SCM, London, 1972, p.59.

Chapter 3

1. Dr W. Owen Cole in a personal email.
2. Ed, Jon Stone, *The Craft of Religious Studies*, 1998, ch. 2. 'Methods in My Life' by Ninian Smart, p.26.
3. Ibid, p.22.
4. Ibid.
5. Ibid, p.24.
6. *Learning for Living*, vol. 5 no. 4, March 1966, p.37.
7. *Learning for Living*, vol. 7 no. 1, September 1967, p.28.
8. Ibid, p.29.
9. Ibid, p.28.
10. *Learning for Living*, vol. 10 no 1, September 1970, p.13.
11. Ibid.
12. Ibid, p.14.
13. This was the idea of teachers in county and church schools working together on programmes of study.
14. Ibid.
15. Ibid, p.15.
16. Ibid.
17. Ibid.
18. Ibid.
19. Ibid, p.13.
20. *Religion*, vol. 18 no 1, January, 1988 'Religious Studies in the UK', p.8.
21. Ibid.
22. Schools Council Working Paper 36, *Religious Education in Secondary Schools*, Schools Council Publications, Evans Brothers Ltd, 1971.
23. Information given to me by Mary Hayward, an original member of the Project team.
24. Ibid, p.85.
25. Ibid, p.9.
26. Ibid, p.16.
27. Ibid, p.23.
28. Ibid, p.26.

29. See chapter xii, pp. 88-91.
30. Ibid, p.26.
31. This phrase derived from Husserl's philosophical approach known as phenomenology. However, Husserl used the phrase to indicate that human consciousness is always directed towards something.
32. Ibid, p.50.
33. Ibid, p.26.
34. Ibid, p.25.
35. Ibid, p.48.
36. Ibid.
37. N. Smart, *Sophia*, vol 36 no 1, 1997, 'Does the philosophy of religion rest on two mistakes?', p.4.
38. Ibid, p. 21.
39. Ibid, p.9-10.
40. Ibid, p.25.
41. Ibid, p.33.
42. Ibid, p.31.
43. Ibid, p.38.
44. Ibid, p.41.
45. Information given to me by Holley in a personal letter dated 29 March, 1999.
46. *Learning for Living*, vol. 10 no. 4, March 1971.
47. *Religion*, vol 27, 1997, 'Phenomenology, Religious Education and Piaget'.
48. Kay told me this in an email.
49. R.C. Zaehner, *Concordant Discord*, Clarendon, Oxford, 1970, p.11.
50. Ibid, p.19.
51. E. Hulmes, *Commitment and Neutrality in Religious Education*, Geoffrey Chapman, 1979. See in particular the illustration of a Rake's Progress from neutrality, through subjectivism to indifferentism, humanism, agnosticism and finally atheism on p.48.
52. *Religion*, vol. 18 no 1, January 1988, 'Religious Studies in the UK', p.6.
53. For a modern critique see L.P. Barnes, *JECB*, vol. 6 no. 1, 2002.
54. *Religion*, vol. 18 no 1, January 1988, 'Religious Studies in the UK', p.3.

Chapter 4

1. *Learning for Living*, vol. 10 no. 4, March 1971, p.2.
2. Ibid.
3. Ibid, p.4.
4. Ibid, p.3.
5. Ibid, p.4.
6. Ibid, p.5.
7. *Learning for Living*, vol. 10 no. 2, November 1970, p.13.
8. Ibid, p.14.
9. *Learning for Living* vol. 15 no 1, September 1975, p.29.
10. J.W.D. Smith, *Religious Education in A Secular Setting*, SCM, 1975.
11. *Learning for Living*, vol. 15 no. 4, Summer 1976.
12. Details are in the Church of England archive in Bermondsey, within the Bliss papers.
13. Saffron Walden College Prospectus, 1964-7, lodged at Borough Road Archive, p.9.
14. Prospectus for 1969-71.
15. Much of this material is in the Marratt archive lodged at the British and Foreign Schools' Society centre at the old Borough Road College, now Brunel University.
16. *Learning for Living*, vol. 10 no. 5, May 1971, p.4.
17. *Learning for Living* vol. 9 no. 4, March 1970, p.30.
18. *Learning for Living*, vol. 9 no. 5, May 1970, p.26.
19. *Learning for Living*, vol. 10 no. 1, September 1970, p.28.

20. Ibid, p.29.
21. This information was given to me by Earwaker in a telephone conversation in October 1998.
22. So 'badly written' that Cambridge University awarded Howkins the Diploma of Education when the book was presented in thesis form. Tyndale Press printed three editions of the book.
23. This information was given to me by Howkins.
24. This information was given to me by Wilkes in an interview on 4 November 1998.
25. A view expressed to me by Dawson on 14 October, 1999.
26. In a preface to the third edition of his book on Goldman.
27. In a telephone conversation on 5 December 1998. Peter Cousins taught at Gypsy Hill College.
28. I am grateful to Mrs Anthea Kay for this information.
29. Hinnells, now an internationally renowned expert on Zoroastrianism, set up the first Shap conference.
30. *AREA Bulletin* no 11, vol. 4 no 3, Winter 1972, p.54. AREA was the name given to the bulletin by the association.
31. Ibid, p.61.
32. Undated, but a reply was penned by Howard Marratt on 9 October, 1974. Both documents in the Marratt archive.
33. *Primary Mailing no. 4,* RE in a Multi-Faith Society', CEM, May 1972.
34. Ibid, p.67.
35. Ibid, p.70.
36. *AREA Bulletin* no 3, Autumn, 1969.
37. An undated leaflet published by ARE.
38. *AREA Bulletin* no 9, vol. 4 no. 1, Spring 1972, p.54.
39. See 'A Professional Approach to Religious Education', ARE Working Paper 3, 1972.
40. 'Outline Plans for a National RE Research and Development Centre', ARE Working Paper 2, 1971.

Chapter 5

1. M. Grimmitt, *What can I do in RE?* Mayhew McCrimmon, Essex, 1973.
2. In *Digest,* the review publication of the Association of Christian Teachers (ACT).
3. Op. cit., p.100.
4. *Learning for Living,* vol. 10 no. 4, March 1971, p.29.
5. *Learning for Living,* vol. 13 no. 2, November 1973, p.74.
6. Ibid, p.80.
7. Ibid.
8. Ibid.
9. Ibid, p.78.
10. Ibid.
11. *Learning for Living,* vol. 14 no. 5, May 1975.
12. *Learning for Living,* vol. 17 no. 1, Autumn 1977, p.41.
13. Ibid.
14. *Learning for Living,* vol. 14 no. 2, November 1974, p.79.
15. *Learning for Living,* vol. 12 no. 1, September 1972, p. 32.
16. Ibid, p.36.
17. *Learning for Living,* vol. 14 no. 4, May 1975, p.168.
18. *Learning for Living,* vol. 12 no. 5, May 1973, p.42.
19. Ibid.
20. *Learning for Living,* vol. 10 no. 3, January 1971, p.41.
21. *Learning for Living,* vol. 13 no. 2, November 1973, p.42.
22. *Learning for Living,* vol. 12 no. 1, September 1972, p.8.

23. Ibid.
24. Ibid.
25. Ibid, p.9.
26. Ibid, p.18.
27. *Learning for Living,* vol. 16 no. 4, Summer 1977.
28. *AREA Bulletin* no 9, vol. 4 no. 1, Spring 1972, pp.18-19.
29. The title is indicative of an underlying indifferentism.
30. *AREA Bulletin* no 10, vol. 4 no. 2, Summer 1972.
31. *Learning for Living,* vol. 16 no. 4, Summer, 1977.
32. M. Grimmitt, *What can I do in RE?* second edition, Mayhew-McCrimmon, London, 1982, p.31. Italics in original.
33. Schools Council Working Paper 44, *Religious Education in Primary Schools*, Evans Brothers, 1972, p.58.
34. Ibid, pp.58-9.
35. *AREA Bulletin*, vol. 6, 1974, p.13.
36. *Learning for Living*, vol. 15 no 1, Autumn 1975, p.24.
37. Ibid, p.34.
38. Ibid, p.38.
39. *Learning for Living*, vol. 16 no 2, Winter 1976, p.82.
40. *AREA Bulletin*, vol. 6, 1974.
41. *Learning for Living*, vol. 14 no. 3, January 1975, p.89.
42. *What Future for the Agreed Syllabus?* The RE Council of England and Wales, 1976.
43. *Learning for Living,* vol. 12 no. 2, November 1972, p.29.
44. *Learning for Living,* vol. 9 no. 5, May 1970, p.30.
45. *Learning for Living*, vol. 12 no. 2, November 1972, p.29.
46. *Learning for Living,* vol. 12 no. 5, May 1973, p.36.
47. *AREA Bulletin* nos 12 & 13, Spring and Summer 1973, vol. 5 nos 1 and 2, p.57.
48. Ibid, p.56.
49. Ibid, p.58.
50. *Learning for Living*, vol. 14 no. 5, May 1975, p.185.
51. Ibid.
52. Ibid, p.193.
53. *Learning for Living,* vol. 12 no. 2, November 1972, p.36.
54. *Learning for Living,* vol. 12 no. 5, May 1973, pp.37-8.
55. Ibid.
56. *Learning for Living,* vol. 16 no. 4, Summer, 1977, p.146.
57. C. Alves, *The Christian in Education*, SCM, London, 1972.
58. Ibid, p.70.
59. Ibid, p.71.
60. Ibid.
61. Ibid. pp.71-2.
62. *Learning for Living,* vol. 16 no. 4, Summer 1977, p.146.
63. Ibid.
64. Ibid.
65. Schools Council Religious Education Committee, *A Groundplan for the Study of Religion,* Schools Council, Spring 1977.
66. Ibid, p.17.
67. Ibid.
68. *Learning for Living,* vol. 16 no. 4, Summer 1977, p.177.
69. In a telephone conversation on 20th November, 2000.
70. He himself would fall foul of this approach when, in 1977 as Adviser for RE with Nottinghamshire, he helped to produced a syllabus containing largely Christian material.

Chapter 6

1. For the history of RE in this country prior to the 1960s, see F.H. Hilliard, *The Teacher and Religion*, James Clarke, London, 1961, chapter 1. For the period 1944-94 see T. Copley, *Teaching Religion*, University of Exeter Press, 1997.
2. By 1952 only 31 of 163 LEAs had set up a SACRE and there was a wide variation in activity found by ICE which reported on them in 1954.
3. The Act allowed for more than one syllabus to be adopted by a local authority in order to allow for this situation, a stipulation which still exists today.
4. *Learning for Living*, vol. 12 no. 5, May 1973, p.2.
5. Ibid, p.37.
6. *Learning for Living*, vol. 13 no. 4, March 1974, p.130.
7. Ed. Monica Taylor, *Progress and Problems in Moral Education*, Windsor, 1975, p.201.
8. *AREA Bulletin* no 8, Autumn 1971, p.3.
9. Ibid, p.4.
10. Ibid.
11. *Learning for Living*, vol. 11 no. 1, September 1971, p.13.
12. *AREA Bulletin* no 11, vol. 4 no 3, Winter 1972, p.69.
13. *Learning for Living*, vol. 11 no 1, September 1971.
14. *Learning for Living*, vol. 14 no 1, September 1974, p.10.
15. Occasional Paper no. 8, 'Structuring the RE Syllabus, some preliminary considerations', ARE, 1971.
16. ARE, *Evidence to the working party of the Religious Education Council on the Future of Agreed Syllabuses,* September 1975.
17. *What Future for the Agreed Syllabus – Now?* REC, 1977, p.28.
18. From a letter in the Marratt archive at Brunel University.
19. REC, in conjunction with the Christian Education Movement, *The Development of Religious Education: A report on the recruitment and training of RE teachers*, 1978, Arrow Press, Aldershot.
20. Ibid, para 9.15, p.23.
21. *Guide to Religious Education in a Multi-Faith Community*, p.4. The publication is undated.
22. Ibid.
23. Ibid, p.28.
24. Ibid, p.29.
25. *Learning for Living*, vol. 14 no. 2, November 1974. The article was written by Owen Cole.
26. I am indebted to Cecil Knight for much of this section. Knight gave me an interview on 20 September 2000 at the school where he was head teacher, Small Heath Secondary in Birmingham. He was drafting secretary to the ASC and a member of two committees of the conference.
27. The law then (as now) did not allow humanists to be members of the committee representing religions.
28. *Agreed Syllabus of Religious Instruction*, City of Birmingham Education Committee, 1975.
29. Ibid, p.4.
30. *Living Together*, A teachers' handbook of suggestions for religious education, City of Birmingham Education Committee, 1975, p.2.
31. Hull's book, *School Worship: An Obituary*, was published in the same year as the Handbook.
32. Op. cit., p.3.
33. Ibid, p.8.

Chapter 7

1. *Learning for Living*, vol. 15 no. 4, Summer 1976, p.129.
2. Ibid, p.130.
3. Ibid, p.129.
4. See *Learning for Living*, vol. 17 no. 2, Winter 1977.
5. Multi-Culture and Multifaith Societies: Some Examinable Assumptions, Farmington Institute for Christian Studies, 1978, para 7.2.2.
6. See *Learning for Living*, vol. 16 no. 2, Winter 1976.
7. Eds N. Smart and D. Holder, *New Movements in Religious Education,* Temple Smith, London, 1975.
8. *Learning for Living*, vol. 15 no. 2, Winter 1975, p.74.
9. *Learning for Living*, vol. 16 no. 1, Autumn 1976, p. 24.
10. *Learning for Living*, vol. 15 no. 3, Spring 1976, p.86.
11. *Learning for Living*, vol. 17 no. 2, Winter 1977, p.64.
12. *AREA Bulletin*, vol. 8 no. 21, 1976, p.10.
13. Ibid.
14. Ibid, p.16.
15. *Learning for Living,* vol. 17 no. 2, Winter 1977, p.59.
16. Ibid, p.60.
17. *Learning for Living*, vol. 17 no. 2, Winter 1977, p. 87.
18. *Learning for Living*, vol. 12 no. 5, May 73, p.12.
19. Op. cit., para 8.2.
20. *AREA Bulletin*, vol. 8 no 21, 1976, p.9.
21. Eds, C. B. Cox and C. Rhodes Boyson, *Black Paper*, 'The Threat to Religion', Maurice Temple Smith, London.
22. Ibid, pp.101-2.
23. *Learning for Living,* vol. 13 no. 4, March 1974, p.135.
24. Op. cit., para 7.2.4.
25. *AREA Bulletin*, vol. 11 no. 28, 1978, p.61.
26. Op cit, p.63.
27. Ibid.
28. In addition to this article in *Learning for Living*, Martin published several others in different journals in an attempt to do something about RE.
29. *Birmingham Post*, 17 March 1975.
30. B. Mitchell, *Heirs and Rebels*, Bloxham, 1982.
31. This information was given to me in an interview on 11 February, 2001.
32. *AREA Bulletin*, vol. 9 no. 24, 1976, p.11.
33. *What future for the Agreed Syllabus?* REC, 1975.
34. *Church of England Newspaper*, 23rd July, 1976.
35. R. Acland, *We teach them wrong*, Gollancz, 1963.
36. Op. cit., p.98.
37. Ibid, p.99.
38. Ibid.
39. Ibid, p.103.
40. Occasional Bulletin of ARE. This publication was a sermon delivered by Abba at a consultation on RE held at Whitelands College.
41. *AREA* Bulletin vol.10 no. 24, 1977, p.6.
42. Ibid, p.28.
43. *Quest*, Agreed Syllabus for Religious Education, Nottinghamshire County Council, 1977, p.59.
44. Written by a sub-committee of three under the guidance of the adviser, the Rev. D.E. Bennett.
45. Ibid, p. ix.
46. *Learning for Living*, vol. 17 no 4, Summer 1978, p.177.

47. Ibid.
48. In a telephone conversation on 20 November 2001.
49. In a telephone conversation on 13 November 2001.

Chapter 8

1. *Ways Whereby – Christian Education in State Schools Should be Saved,* OCU, 1973, p.23.
2. Hansard, H.C., 19 March, 1976, col. 1786.
3. Ibid, col. 1792.
4. Ibid, col. 1795.
5. This booklet, *Objective, Fair and Balanced, a new law for religion in education,* published in Autumn 1975, was a manifesto for change in RE. It set out a new bill, intended to replace the 1944 Act, which would provide education in several beliefs or 'stances for living', with Christianity given no special place.
6. Hansard, H.C., col. 1837.
7. Ibid, col. 1841.
8. Ibid, col. 1853.
9. Ibid, col. 1870.
10. *Hansard,* H.L, 16th February 1977, col. 841.
11. Ibid, col. 1679.
12. Hansard, H.L., col. 855.
13. Ibid, col. 872.
14. *Report of Proceedings,* General Synod of the Church of England, 5 July, 1977, p.448.
15. Ibid, p.449.
16. Ibid, p.456.
17. Ibid, p.457.
18. Ibid, pp.457-8.
19. Ibid, p.460.
20. Ibid, p.462.
21. Ibid.
22. Ibid.
23. Ibid, p. 463.
24. Ibid, p.466.
25. Ibid, p.474.
26. *AREA Bulletin* no 26, vol. 10, 1977, p.1.
27. Ibid.
28. Ibid, p.2.
29. These were the Teachers' Prayer Fellowship, the Christian Education Fellowship, a branch of the Graduates' Fellowship and the Inter Schools Christian Fellowship, a branch of Scripture Union.
30. *ACT NOW* Autumn 1996, p. 22.
31. Ibid, p. 21
32. Op. cit., p.22.
33. *Religious Education: a considered view, ACT,* undated.
34. Ed. N. Richards, *Aims in Religious Education,* ACT, 1976, RE Booklet Series No.1.
35. Ibid, p.9.
36. Ibid, p.25.
37. Here he was quoting from K. Howkins, *Religious Thinking and Religious Education,* Tyndale Press, 1966.
38. Ibid, p.28.
39. *RS Today,* vol. 2 no 3, Summer 1977, p.9. 'Perhaps the sudden change of direction on the last page indicates the hand of the editor.'
40. Bramhall told me this in a telephone conversation on 1 October 2000.
41. *Spectrum,* vol. 6 no. 3, May 1974, p.23.

42. Reference missing.
43. Avon 1976, Hampshire 1978, Dudley 1979, Lincolnshire 1980, Croydon 1980, Bexley 1981, Humberside 1981, Berkshire 1982, Durham 1983, Manchester 1985, Redbridge 1987, Surrey 1987, Rotherham 1989.
44. Syllabuses often acknowledged previous syllabuses which they had found helpful.
45. Included because the syllabus was written before 1988 ERA.
46. *Religious Heritage and Personal Quest*, Royal County of Berkshire, 1982, p.28.
47. *Religious Education in Lincolnshire*, Lincolnshire County Council, 1980, p.5.
48. Ibid, p.2.
49. *Agreed Syllabus of Religious Education*, Humberside Education Authority, 1981, p.1.
50. Ibid, p.14.
51. *Growing in Understanding*, Durham County, 1983, p.16.
52. *Building Together*, Rotherham Metropolitan Borough Council, 1989, p.12.
53. A project set up at Westhill College, Birmingham in the 1980s.

Chapter 9

1. Some material in this chapter appeared in *Faith In Education*, 2001, published by Civitas. I am grateful to Civitas for permission to use it here.
2. *Hansard*, H.C., 18 July 1988, col. 825.
3. *Hansard*, H.C., 9 February 1988, col. 1269.
4. *Hansard*, H. L., 28 Feb 1988, col.1456.
5. Ibid, col.1464.
6. *Hansard*, H.L., 21 June 1988, col. 717.
7. Ibid, col. 718.
8. Ibid, col. 721.
9. This provision was taken over from the 1944 Education Act.
10. *Hansard*, H.C, 23rd March 1988, col. 421.
11. I have consulted the following publications: *The Times, The Observer, The Church Times, The Independent, The Telegraph, The Sunday Telegraph, The Tablet* and *The Guardian*. All reported similarly to the example quoted. Later interpreters would claim that the press had misreported the debates in Parliament.
12. *The Independent,* 22 June 1988.
13. *British Journal of Religious Education (BJRE)*, vol. 11 no. 1, Autumn, 1988, p 2.
14. Ibid.
15. Ibid.
16. This information was given to me by Vera Conway.
17. DES, *The Education Reform Act 1988: Religious Education and Collective Worship*, Circular No 3/89, 20 January, 1989, para 26, p.35.
18. A modification of the 1870 Cowper Temple clause.
19. Op. cit., para 26, p.35.
20. Ibid, para 34, p.37
21. In a personal letter.
22. Personal letter to myself received in June 2000.
23. Terence Copley has written: 'From a research point of view, hard evidence is difficult to acquire and the writer has found it impossible to get detailed answers by letter or interview about how specific policy decisions and content have been arrived at and who has been dominant in the process.' *Spiritual Development in the State School*, University of Exeter Press, 2000, p.7.
24. Personal interview with Rev. Gerald Miller on 11 June 2000.
25. M. J. Taylor, *Religious Education Values and Worship: LEA Advisers' Perspectives on Implementation of the Education Reform Act 1988*, National Foundation for Educational Research and Religious Education Council, May 1989.
26. 'each agreed syllabus must recognise the other religions which are practised in its

area', op. cit., p.28.

27. J. Hull, *The Act Unpacked*, The University of Birmingham and CEM, 1989, p.14.

28. 'Teaching Religious Education', *Education Digest*, 18 November 1988, page i.

29. *BJRE*, vol. 11 no. 2, Spring 1989, p.61.

30. *Handbook for Agreed Syllabus Conferences, SACREs and Schools*, the report of a working party of the Religious Education Council of England and Wales, 1989, p.5.

31. E. Cox and J. Cairns, *Reforming Religious Education, the religious clauses of the ERA*, Kogan Page, London, 1989.

32. A. Bradney, *Education and the Law*, vol. 1, part 2, 1989, 'The Dewsbury Affair and RE', p.57.

33. J.D.C. Harte, *Ecclesiastical Law Journal*, Issue 5, 1989, 'The religious dimension of the Education Reform Act 1988', p.36.

34. *Acts of Worship and Religious Education*, Helpsheet no. 9, CRE, 1990.

35. *BJRE*, vol. 12 no. 1, Autumn, 1989, p.3.

36. Ibid, p.4

37. Ibid.

38. Offices are at Church House, Great Smith Street, London, SW1 2NZ.

39. The National Society, *Religious Education*, 1989.

40. See Circular 3/89, Annex E, p.61.

41. Ibid, p.5.

42. *BJRE,* vol. 13 no. 3, Summer 1991.

43. Ibid, p.174.

44. In a personal interview on 16 November, 1998.

45. See *Forum for the Discussion of new trends in education*, vol. 32 no. 2, Spring 1990.

46. The phrase used by the barrister in his opinion. This opinion is the property of the DfES.

47. I am grateful to John Hull for this information.

48. *Hansard*, H.L., 17 June 1992, col. 252.

49. *Hansard*, H.L., 27 April 1993, col. 244.

50. At this point the DES had become the Department for Education and Employment (DfEE).

51. 'The Education Act (1944) requires that an agreed syllabus 'must not be designed to convert pupils, or to urge a particular religion or religious belief on pupils' (Education Act 1944, Section 26 (2).' *Religious Education*, SCAA, Model Syllabuses: Model 1 Living Faiths Today, 1994.

52. Mr. Naylor is an educational consultant and honorary secretary of the Parental Alliance for Choice in Education (PACE).

53. Letter to Mr. Naylor, dated 25 March, 1997 from C. Drury of the Curriculum and Assessment Division of the DfEE (emphasis in the original). Section 376 (2) of the 1996 Act replaces Section 26 of the 1944 Act.

54. In an personal interview on November 18 1998.

Chapter 10

1. QCA, *Religious Education*, 2000.

2. A similar situation exists in Scotland where inspectors have reported that teachers have most difficulty with this aspect of the teaching. In Scotland the terminology is different (they use the phrase 'personal search') but the meaning is the same.

3. *Model Syllabuses for Religious Education Consultation Document, Model Attainment Targets*, SCAA, January 1994. para 2.1, p.1.

4. *Religious Education and Collective Worship, an analysis of 1999 SACRE reports*, QCA, 2000, p.27.

5. But we see the work of Robert Jackon discussed in the next chapter.

6. Ibid, p.31.

7.   QCA, *Religious Education*, 2000, p.18.
8.   Ibid, p.23.
9.   Ibid.
10. Ibid.
11. M. Grimmitt, *Religious Education and Human Development*, McCrimmons, Essex, 1987, p.121.
12. Ibid, p.141.
13. See ed. M. Grimmitt, *Pedagogies of Religious Education*, McCrimmons, Essex, 2000, ch. 11, pp. 207-26.
14. Ibid, p.224.
15. Ibid, p.225, italics in the original.
16. Ibid, p.224.
17. Ibid, p.225.
18. Artefacts are widely used in RE. An artefact is an object used by religious believers. A Bible, stand for a Qur'an, image of a god, can all be 'artefacts'.
19. N. Boyle, *Who are we now?* University of Notre Dame Press, London, 1998, see ch. 10.
20. A project set up in 1993, now funded by University College, Chichester and King Alfred's College, Winchester.
21. *Pedagogies of Religious Education,* ch. 10, 'The Children and Worldviews Project: A narrative pedagogy of Religious Education', p.188.
22. Ibid, p.194.
23. Ibid, p.193.
24. C. and J. Erricker, *Reconstructing Religious, Spiritual and Moral Education*, Routledge, 2000, p.62.
25. Grimmitt, p.194.
26. Errickers, 2000, p.68.
27. Grimmitt, 2000, p.202.
28. Errickers, 2000, p.69.
29. Grimmitt, 2000, p.200.
30. Ibid, p.198.
31. Ed. R. Best, *Education, Spirituality and the Whole Child*, Cassell, 1996, ch. 14, 'Where angels fear to tread: discovering children's spirituality', p.184-96, C. and J. Erricker.
32. Ibid, pp.76-7.
33. *Religious Education in Schools: Ideas and Experiences from around the World*, 2001, International Association for Religious Freedom, 2 Market Street, Oxford, OX1 3EF, ch. 1, p.5.
34. Ibid, p.6.
35. Ibid, p.8.
36. See J. Hull, *BJRE*, vol. 14 no. 2, 1992, 'The Transmission of Religious Prejudice', pp. 69-72 and a reply by P. Thompson, *BJRE,* vol. 16 no. 1, 1993, 'Religionism: a response to John Hull', pp.47-50. See also LP Barnes, *IJER*, 111-11, 2002, 'Religionism and Religious Intolerance', pp. 97-116.
37. See J. Hull in D.F. Ford and D.L. Stamps, *Essentials of Christian Community*, T and T Clark, Edinburgh, 1996, 'Christian Education in a Capitalist Society: Money and God'.

Chapter 11

1.   The question put to me by a 12-year-old pupil, Jonathan.
2.   *Religious Education*, non-statutory guidance on RE, 2000, inside front cover.
3.   In Year 9 the theme of suffering is looked at first within Christianity and then within Buddhism but no links or comparisons are made.
4.   Ibid.

5. W. Kay and D.L. Smith, *BJRE* vol. 22 no. 2, 2000, 'Religious Terms and Attitudes in the Classroom (Part 1)'. Part 2 to be found in *BJRE* vol. 22 no. 3, 2000.
6. Professor Robert Jackson of Warwick University is also editor of the *BJRE*. He has made a study of the history of religions and in particular ethnography, a branch of anthropology.
7. R. Jackson, *Religious Education: an interpretive approach,* Hodder and Stoughton, 1997, p.1.
8. Prior to this it meant something like piety as in a 'religious man'.
9. See R. Jackson, *Panorama*, vol. 8, no. 2, Winter 1996, 'The Construction of 'Hinduism' and its impact on Religious Education in England and Wales'.
10. In a personal letter to me dated 11 December 2000. Professor Sarkar has worked for many years to give a proper understanding of Hinduism to people of this country and was a member of the Liverpool ASC. His view is that the native Briton finds it virtually impossible to understand Hinduism.
11. Jackson's experience has been largely with Hindu children. It is interesting to speculate whether, had his experience been with Jewish or Muslim children, he would have found such plurality.
12. This was the view of Professor R.C. Zaehner, Spalding Professor at Oxford University and an acknowledged expert on eastern religions.
13. J. Milbank, in ed. G. D'Costa, *Christian Uniqueness Reconsidered*, 'The End of Dialogue', p.184.
14. *REsource*, vol. 24 no. 2, Spring 2002, 'Getting beyond relativism: a response to Penny Thompson's article "Can RE challenge relativism?"'
15. Ibid.
16. B.Watson, *The Effective Teaching of Religious Education*, Longman, 1993.
17. For an account of how this happens in RE see Watson's article mentioned above (*REsource*, Spring 2002).
18. A. Wright, *Spiritual Pedagogy*, Culham College, 1998, p.67.
19. Ed. R. Best, *Education, Spirituality and the Whole Child*, Cassell, London, 1996, p. 144.
20. Ibid, p.36.
21. Grimmitt, 2000, p.177.
22. Ibid, p.178.
23. Ibid.
24. Ibid, p.179.
25. Ibid.
26. Ibid.
27. Ibid, p.180
28. Ibid.
29. A. Wright, *RE in the Secondary School,* Fulton, 1993, p.73.
30. *Spiritual Pedagogy*, p.95.
31. Grimmitt, 2000, p.161.
32. Ibid, p.163.
33. See T. Cooling, *A Christian Vision for State Education*, SPCK, 1994.
34. Grimmitt, 2000, p.156.
35. Cooling, 1994.

Chapter 12

1. The advice of a former pupil of mine, Christopher.
2. See ed. J.G. Priestley, *Religion, Spirituality and Schools*, Exeter, University of Exeter School of Education, 1982, 'The Loneliness of the Religious Educator', *New Universities Quarterly*, Autumn 1980, 'Trusting to Reason', and eds Straughan and Wilson, *Philosophers on Education*, MacMillan, 1987, 'Two Questions about Religious Education'.

3.   Not in quantum mechanics, but even quantum mechanics constitutes a rule of the universe.

4.   See J. Astley, *The Philosophy of Christian Religious Education*, REP, 1994, p.74 and p.87. Astley argues that we ought to consider whether a person will be fulfilled by developing such critical acumen. I am indebted to Astley's book for much of this section.

5.   B. Mitchell in *Heirs and Rebels*, The Bloxham Project, 1982, ch.3, p.29.

6.   Op. cit., p.183.

7.   See my website (www.angelfire.com/pe/pennyt/) for an example of this in practice.

8.   C. Longley, *Hockerill Lecture,* 1988, 'Time for a Fresh Vision'.

9.   M.C. Felderhof, *Journal of Beliefs and Values*, vol. 16 no. 1, 1995, 'Is there a place for the religious voice in public education?' p.25.

10. R. Williams, *On Christian Theology*, Blackwell, 2000, p.81.

11. Ibid, p.82.

12. A thorough study of this topic is to be found in Elmer Thiessen's *Teaching for Commitment*, Gracewing, Leominster, 1993.

13. *The Fourth R*, para 116.

14. Ibid, para 158.

15. B. Mitchell, *Faith and Criticism*, Clarendon, Oxford, 1994, p.139.

16. See J.V. Taylor, *Hockerill Lecture*, 1983, 'The importance of not solving the problem', Hockerill Educational Foundation.

17. *Learning for Living*, vol. 3 no. 3, January 1964. The teacher was Don Hassall.

18. E. Hulmes, *Education and Cultural Diversity*, Longman, 1989, p.153.

19. It would be important of course to introduce the eastern branches of the faith at some point and also the vibrant expressions of Christian faith in the developing countries of Africa and elsewhere.

20. See ed. Hammond, Hay and others, *New Methods in RE Teaching: an experiential approach*, Oliver and Boyd, 1990.

21. See *RE Today*, vol. 12 no. 2, Spring, 1995, 'If God were . . . ', pp.30-1.

22. See OFSTED, *The Impact of new agreed syllabuses on the teaching and learning of religious education*, 1997, p.18.

23. Richard Harries, Bishop of Oxford, in a sermon given in July 2000 to a conference of Farmington Fellows. A reflection on this sermon may be found on my website.

24. 'the agreement of this clause [section 8,3] was a far from satisfactory outcome and, in my view, put back the cause of educational RE some thirty years – a state from which the subject will not recover unless the specific naming of Christianity is removed from Section 8 (3) of the Act.' Grimmitt, 2000, p.12.

25. Report of the Consultative Committee of the Board of Education on Secondary Education with special reference to Grammar Schools and Technical High Schools, HMSO, 1963, p.208.

26. *15 to 18*: a report of the Central Advisory Council for Education (England) HMSO, 1959.

27. *Half our Future*, a report of the Central Advisory Council for Education (England) HMSO, 1963.

28. *Children and their primary schools*: a report of the Central Advisory Council for Education (England) HMSO, 1967.

29. See chapter 2.

30. See *JPE*, vol. 28 no. 2, 1994, 'Knowledge and Truth in Religious Enquiry' and *JPE*, vol. 30 no. 2, 1996, 'Rival Conceptions of Spiritual Education'.

31. B. Gates, 'Varieties of Religious Education', *Religion*, vol. 3, Spring 1973.

32. Personal conversation.

Chapter 13

1. *The UN Declaration of the Rights of the Child* and the *Protocol to the European Convention on Human Rights* support parents in this way. The former exhorts this an ideal and the latter has laid down legal sanction.
2. See Trevor Cooling's *A Christian Vision for State Education*, SPCK, 1994.
3. *Learning for Living*, vol. 10 no. 4, March 1971, p.2.
4. See *Political Quarterly*, 65(1), Jan. 1994, 'Establishment, Multiculturalism and British Citizenship'.
5. *The Independent*, The Weekend Review, 3 March, 2001, p.5
6. Jackie Wullschlager, *The Spectator*, 2 December 2000, p.2.
7. www.eclipse.co.uk
8. The phrase is used by Maurice Cowling of those who make it their business to attack Christianity and assume that only fools would stand against them.
9. See J.H. Newman, *The Idea of a University*, Image Books, 1959, pp. 352-70. Newman called this attitude a 'form of infidelity of the day'.
10. J. Astley, *The Philosophy of Christian Religious Education*, REP, 1994, p. 279.
11. This point was expressly made by *The Fourth R*.
12. Op.cit, p.183.
13. This survey on how the population planned to celebrate Christmas 2001, reported in *The Church Times* on 21 December 2001, was an independent survey carried out by Opinion Research Business on behalf of the Church of England, Methodists and Baptists and the Tablet.
14. www.statistics.gov.uk/census/ Results were published on 13 February, 2003.
15. Though this is not always the case. For a good summary of the situation see the chapter by John Marks in *Faith in Education*, Civitas, 2001, pp. 5-36, 'Standards in Church of England, Roman Catholic and LEA schools in England'.
16. See p.186 n. 36 for references to discussion of religionism in the RE literature.
17. *Hansard*, H.C., 18th July, 1988, col. 841.
18. See 'Nostra Aetate' in *The Conciliar and Post Conciliar Documents of Vatican Council 2*, ed. Austin Flannery OP, Dominican Publications, Dublin, 1975, pp. 738-40.
19. *The Way Ahead: Church of England Schools in the New Millenium*, Church House Publishing, 2001, p.17, para 3.36.
20. Quoted in the article mentioned above in *The Spectator*.
21. *The Times*, 9 July, 1994.
22. J. Haldane, *BJES*, vol. 34, 1986, 'Religious Education in a Pluralist Society', p.176.
23. Op. cit., p.177.
24. Although it lacks awareness of the contribution of the Roman Catholic Church. See www.dayone.co.uk/ad.
25. For a spirited rebuff of this charge in relation to the Roman Catholic Church, see Joanna Bogle, *Does the Church oppress women?*, The Incorporated Catholic Truth Society, 1999.
26. John 6:68.
27. See P. Barnes, *JECB*, vol. 6, no. 1, 2002, 'Working Paper 36, Christian Confessionalism and Phenomenological Religious Education'.
28. See, for example, J. Astley, *IJER*, vol 111-11, 2002, 'Evangelism in Education: Impossibility, Travesty or Necessity?' pp. 179-94. Astley, following an article written in 1963, argues that evangelism is a necessary part of Christian education.
29. D. Hargreaves, *The Mosaic of Learning*, Demos, 1994, p.34.

Select Bibliography

Alves, C., *The Christian in Education*, London, 1972.

Astley, J., *The Philosophy of Christian Education*, Birmingham, Alabama, 1994.

Cooling, T., *A Christian Vision for State Education*, London, 1994.

Cox, E. and Cairns, J., *Reforming Religious Education, the religious clauses of the ERA*, London, 1989.

Cox, E., *Changing Aims in Religious Education*, London, 1966.

Grimmitt, M. Ed, *Pedagogies of Religious Education*, Essex, 2000.

Grimmitt, M., *Religious Education and Human Development*, Essex, 1987.

Grimmitt, M., *What can I do in RE?*, Essex, 1973.

Haldane, J., 'Religious Education in a Pluralist Society', in *BJES*, vol 34, 1986, pp 161-181.

Hilliard, F.H., *The Teacher and Religion*, London, 1963.

Howkins, K., *Religious Thinking and Religious Education*, London, 1966.

Hull, J., *The Act Unpacked,* Birmingham, 1989.

Hulmes, E., *Commitment and Neutrality in Religious Education*, London, 1979.

Jackson, R., *Religious Education: an interpretive approach,* London, 1997.

Jeffreys, M.V., *The Truth is not Neutral*, Oxford, 1969.

Learning for Living, *A Journal of Christian Education*, 1961-1978.

McIntyre, J., *Multi-Culture and Multifaith Societies: Some examinable assumptions,* Farmington Institute Occasional Paper 3, Oxford, 1978.

Mitchell, B., *Faith and Criticism*, Oxford, 1994.

QCA, *Religious Education, non-statutory guidance on RE*, 2000.

SCAA, *Model Syllabuses for Religious Education*, Consultation Document, Model Attainment Targets, London, 1994.

Schools Council Working Paper 36, *Religious Education in Secondary Schools,* 1971.

Smart, N. and D. Horder, Eds, *New Movements in Religious Education*, London, 1975.

The Durham Commission, *The Fourth R*, London, 1970.

Thiessen, E., *Teaching for Commitment,* Leominster, 1993.

Watson, B., *The Effective Teaching of Religious Education*, London, 1993.

Wedderspoon, A, Ed, *Religious Education: 1944-1984*, London, 1966.

Wright, A., *Spiritual Pedagogy*, Oxford, 1998.

Index